SOCIALITY, ETHICS, AND SOCIAL CHANGE

A Critical Appraisal of Reinhold Niebuhr's Ethics in the Light of Rosemary Radford Ruether's Works

Judith Vaughan

UNIVERSITY
PRESS OF
AMERICA

LANHAM • NEW YORK • LONDON

Copyright © 1983 by

University Press of America,™ Inc.

4720 Boston Way
Lanham, MD 20706

3 Henrietta Street
London, WC2E 8LU England

Library of Congress Cataloging in Publication Data

Vaughan, Judith.
    Sociality, ethics, and social change.

    Bibliography: p.
    1. Niebuhr, Reinhold, 1892–1971. 2.
Ruether, Rosemary Radford. 3. Social ethics--
History--20th century. 4. Social change--
History--20th century.
I. Title.
BX4827.N5V38   1983   241   83-1293
ISBN 0-8191-3100-8
ISBN 0-8191-3101-6 (pbk.)

ACKNOWLEDGMENTS

This work has been a shared project of persons-in-relation. Many people have contributed their experiences, support and skills to its writing. To these people mentioned here, and to many others as well, I am grateful.

I thank, first of all, the people in Woodlawn on the South Side of Chicago, especially the members of St. Clara/St. Cyril's church; and the Chicago Religious Task Force on Central America/El Salvador in solidarity with the insurgent people of El Salvador.

I thank Professors Robin Lovin, Anne Carr and Lee Cormie for their advice and assistance; and Dr. Rosemary Ruether for her suggestions and encouragement.

I also thank the people with whom I have lived during my years in Chicago, and from whom I have learned much: members of Nativity of our Lord community, especially Pat Manning and Tilly VonPlinsky; members of the Woodlawn community, especially Dean Brackley and Jack Barron; and Marjorie Tuite.

I am grateful to the members of the Ethics and Society Field at the University of Chicago Divinity School, especially Dean Brackley, David Harris, Ismael Garcia, Matthew Kamitsuka-Foster, Al Pitcher, Bob Stark, George Taylor and Kodzo Tita-Pongo for their friendship, insights and challenges. Special thanks are also due to Lynn Harris, Evangeline Kamitsuka-Foster, Terry Kelly, Tom Nairn, Christoph Stauder, and Ellen Stauder.

In a spirit of solidarity, I especially thank Catherine Brousseau, Brenda McCarthy, Karen McLoughlin, Rhonda Meister, Marlene Perrotte, Yolanda Tarango, and the Cluster Catholic Women's Group; Mario Barron, Margaret Collins, and Maureen Filter--co-members of the Sisters of St. Joseph of Carondelet Congregational Team for Justice Issues; and the Los Angeles House of Ruth community, including Judy Molosky, Georgeann O'Brien, Claire Williams, and Helene Wilson.

Finally, I express my appreciation to my family for their constant love, and to the Sisters of St. Joseph of Carondelet of the Western Province for their moral and material support during my time of study at the University of Chicago.

iii

TABLE OF CONTENTS

CHAPTER I

THE STARTING POINT

People throughout the world are engaged in the struggle against conditions that brutalize human life. Women and men are seeking deep-seated changes to address radical inequalities that exist between rich and poor persons, and between rich and poor nations. Latin America, the Philippines, Poland, South Africa, South Korea, the United States: conditions in these and other areas offer concrete illustrations which give credence to the claim that we are living in a revolutionary situation.[1]

Those who are committed to the struggle for justice are confronted with many different approaches to social change. As ethicist Denis Goulet points out, there is "no single ethical strategy for dealing with revolutionary situations."[2] In my own experience, the Catholic Worker movement, the United Farm Workers, and the Religious Task Force on Central America exemplify this diversity of approaches to social change. All three of these movements are committed to the alleviation of suffering and the elimination of injustice, but their basic philosophies and programs of action, including strategies for social change, are marked by fundamental differences.[3]

The fact that there are differing approaches creates a moral dilemma for those who are seeking social change. The ethical question arises: What criterion does a person use to evaluate these conflicting approaches and judge one to be more adequate than another? This question is the starting point for this work. The purpose of this study is to suggest a way to evaluate critically approaches to social change and the ethical systems of which they are a part.

In this study I am concerned with the fundamental assumptions which serve as the basis for ethical systems, including approaches to social change. More specifically, my focus is on the anthropological presuppositions--an essential component of the comprehensive network of basic assumptions which form a person's world-view[4]--which give rise to ethical systems and approaches to social change.

The study is based on two assumptions. The first assumption is that a person's world-view, and in

1

particular his or her view of the human condition, has important and often decisive consequences for ethics. Anthropologist Clifford Geertz emphasizes that "the overwhelming majority of mankind[5] are continually drawing normative conclusions from factual premises."[6] Denis Goulet agrees with Geertz's assertion and applies it specifically to the ethics of social change. According to Goulet, each person

> must draw a line beyond which he will
> not compromise. The locus of that
> line depends ultimately on his con-
> ception of the human person and of
> society, and on the moral quality of
> his goals.[7]

Although the fundamental assumptions which support a person's ethics often remain implicit, it is possible to make these assumptions explicit and then subject them to critical analysis and judgment.

The second assumption of this study is that an acceptable ethical system, including its approach to social change, must be based on adequate anthropological presuppositions.

In my examination of anthropological presuppositions and how they affect ethics, I am especially concerned with presuppositions about sociality, or the social dimension of being human. Three types of evidence indicate the significance of sociality for an understanding of the human person.

First, a survey of political philosophy and social theory reveals that an interpretation of sociality has had a place of prominence in the anthropology of many thinkers through the centuries.[8] Responding to the societal conditions of a particular historical period, social philosophers and theorists struggle to develop an understanding of sociality, often placing their interpretations in juxtaposition to the notion of individuality. Historically, the integration of the social and individual dimensions of the human condition has been one of the major tasks for anyone trying to develop a coherent anthropology.

Second, recent social, economic and political developments indicate the significance of sociality. Competition over natural resources, the increase of world hunger even while food production rises, the

2

consequences of one country's military expenditures on
other countries, the results of environmental abuse on
the one life support system, the development of atomic
power and the possibility of global warfare and species-
annihilation--these realities call attention to the
interdependence and mutual responsibility of human
beings, and challenge further exploration of what it
means to say that human beings are social.

Third, a commitment to structural transformation
suggests the importance of sociality among anthropological presuppositions. Since systemic injustice
integrally involves social relationships--whether these
be expressed in terms of master/slave, oppressor/
oppressed, upper-class/lower-class, have/have-nots--it
is appropriate to concentrate on the social dimension
of human existence in a study related to social change.

The task of this work is three-fold: (1) to
establish a notion of sociality as an adequate one on
which to base an ethical system and an approach to
social change; (2) to use this notion of sociality as a
criterion of adequacy for evaluating interpretations of
sociality basic to two different ethics; and (3) to
appraise critically two ethical systems, including
their approaches to social change, that are based on
contrasting notions of sociality. The theological
anthropology and social ethics of Reinhold Niebuhr and
Rosemary Radford Ruether are used to accomplish this
task. Throughout this study I argue that Rosemary
Ruether's ethics, which include her approach to social
change, are superior to Reinhold Niebuhr's because
Ruether's work is based on an adequate interpretation
of sociality and Niebuhr's work is not. Thus
Ruether's ethics are to be preferred. By focusing on
the notion of sociality, I provide a criterion at the
fundamental level of anthropological presuppositions
for those who must choose from among the various
ethical systems and approaches to social change in
their struggle for justice.

The notion of sociality which is used as the
criterion of adequacy is drawn from radical social
thought, and in particular from the conflict tradition
in the social sciences and from feminist writings. In
the next part of this chapter, I justify my use of
radical social thought to develop an interpretation of
sociality, which then serves as the criterion of adequacy for evaluating the positions of Reinhold Niebuhr
and Rosemary Ruether. The chapter concludes with a
brief overview of the remainder of the book.

3

Establishing the Criterion
of Adequacy

The Use of the Social Sciences and
the Conflict Tradition

The perennial concern of the social sciences has been the social dimension of being human. Referring specifically to sociology, Dawe writes that it "is rooted in and articulative of the human social experience."[9] Sociology is, by definition, the science of social relationships. It is for this reason, then, that it is appropriate to turn to the social sciences, and particularly sociology, for an understanding of sociality.[10]

The social sciences do not comprise, however, a homogeneous and unified body of thought. From the initial development of the discipline, a number of "schools" or traditions have been identifiable, each with its own model of the social world, methodology for studying this world, and background assumptions for supporting and sustaining its theories. Thus, in turning to the social sciences, it is necessary to select a particular orientation from among the various schools or traditions.

Although it is difficult to simplify such a complex reality, it is possible to discuss sociological development in terms of two major orientations: system theory and conflict theory.[11] These two dominant schools have been described in different ways by a number of social scientists: social system and social action (Dawe); conventional and radical (Forsythe); priestly and prophetic (Friedrichs); academic/non-Marxist and Marxist (Gouldner); and functionalist and voluntarist (Winter).[12]

System analysis, and its theoretical development of structural-functionalism,[13] dominated the paradigmatic life of sociology in the post-World War II period.[14] However, conflict theory has always been an alternative, and Friedrichs suggests that in the last several decades this tradition "has claimed an allegiance at least the equal of the system stance."[15]

In this study I use writings located within the broad conflict tradition of the social sciences to develop the notion of sociality which serves as the

criterion of adequacy. I have selected the conflict
tradition for two reasons. First, certain assumptions
that characterize the conflict tradition are integral
to the concerns of a work on social change.
Second, these assumptions in the conflict tradition
correspond to my own presuppositions which are the
basis for this study[16]--presuppositions that are
expressed in feminist writings.[17] As sociologist Lee
Cormie explains:

> Social theories are . . . obviously
> and intimately related to the social
> theorist's own social world and self-
> understanding. . . . Social theories,
> whatever else they are, are also
> attempts by concrete individuals to
> make sense of their own experiences,
> beliefs, feelings, hopes. Each
> social scientific perspective is,
> then, both a logic and a morality, and
> is adhered to in part because it
> resonates with the theorist's own
> experiences and vision of the world.[18]

In the next section I support my reasons for
selecting the conflict tradition by describing four
themes that are found in both feminist writings and the
conflict tradition. A consideration of these themes
also suggests the relevancy of the conflict tradition
to the ethics of social change.

Feminism and the Conflict Tradition

Although feminist writings are far from being a
unified body of thought, there are general themes that
emerge in a survey of the literature. Four themes
found in feminist writings are similar to the methodological assumptions that support the conflict tradition. These include: (1) an interpretation of reality
as conflictual, (2) an expression of value-commitment,
(3) an orientation towards social change, and (4) an
emphasis on praxis. In order to illustrate the congruency between a feminist perspective and the conflict
tradition, these themes are described as they serve as
methodological assumptions for the conflict tradition.

The Interpretation of Reality

Similar to the interpretation of reality expressed
in feminist writings, the view of reality found in the

conflict tradition is one of contradictions, conflict, alienation and oppression.[19] Thus conflict-generating forces are considered the central clues for understanding social phenomena.

In the conflict tradition, attention is focused on the existing social relationships, structures, and other cultural components which produce tensions and conflicts,[20] and to the counter-elements which arise in situations of conflict as a response to the status quo.[21] The conflict tradition also allows for an extensive analysis of the process of change which occurs through conflict between antagonistic groups, whether this change be indigenous or exogenous, spontaneous or guided, evolutionary within a given system or designed to overthrow the status quo.[22]

Expression of Value-Commitment

A second theme in feminist writings is an explicit expression of underlying value-commitments. Feminist writings do not claim ethical neutrality. In the same way, work done by those who follow a conflict orientation is consciously and explicitly value-committed.

Value-commitment, in the conflict tradition, "is expressed largely in the choice of themes of research and in the working hypotheses that guide inquiry in the field."[23] It also affects the interpretation of facts and the recommendations which often are made at the conclusion of a project.[24] Proponents of the conflict tradition argue that the research of every social scientist is, in fact, value-committed and investigative results are used either in support of or against the present system.[25] Thus those in the conflict tradition strive to be conscious of their ethical judgments and biases and make them known.[26]

Orientation Toward Social Change

From a feminist perspective, social reality, with its alienating and oppressive social relationships and structures, is not inevitable and inescapable. It can be changed. Feminists, acting in solidarity with other oppressed groups, work to bring about this change.

Similarly, the conflict tradition is "concerned with the positive formulation of new societies . . . in which [people] might live better."[27] Social analysis "does not simply offer a picture of the way a social

6

order works; . . . [it] is itself a catalytic agent of change."[28]

Traditionally, the majority of those who accept the conflict model choose to align themselves with those who are suffering from the dominant system and are seeking to change it. They attempt to view society from the position of oppressed groups.[29] As Fals-Borda maintains, research "must be conducted 'with the people' . . . in allegiance to the cause of the masses and against the interests of their exploiters."[30] As part of the research method, scientists ask: what are its concrete applications for bringing about a more just society.[31]

Emphasis on Praxis

The fourth theme found in feminist writings is an emphasis on praxis. Feminists stress that it is in and through revolutionary activity for social transformation that awareness of present injustices deepens and insights about new, alternative forms of social relations and social structures develop. This theme also acts as a methodological assumption for the conflict tradition.

Conflict methodology "requires social scientists to become actors in the process they study in accord with the political decisions they have taken."[32] Within the conflict tradition there is "a pervasive and critical sensitivity to the dialectical complementarity between word and deed"[33] which leads to the conviction that "there is . . . no valid theory without praxis."[34] Specific forms of commitment, modes of struggle and choices of political action may vary, but in some way, conflict social scientists "opt for personal and social liberation tasks."[35]

In this section, four congruencies between themes in feminist writings and assumptions of the conflict tradition in the social sciences have been described.[36] It is from these two sources, which I refer to as radical social thought, that an interpretation of sociality is derived. In the next section, the notion of sociality found in radical social thought is introduced. It is later developed at length in Chapter IV.

Sociality and Radical Social Thought

Within radical social thought, human beings are assumed to be essentially social. Persons "are

7

constituted by one another and . . . achieve their identities through their relations with one another."[37] The understanding of persons-in-relation, and not persons as separate individuals interacting autonomously with one another, is an assumption basic to both the conflict tradition[38] and feminist writings.

Although some theorists, such as David Rasmussen, believe that the notion of persons-in-relation "is . . . just entering history,"[39] it is suggested here that the understanding of persons as essentially social has been a part of the underside of history for a long time. This interpretation of sociality is rooted in the reality of oppression, and expressed in feminist and third world social thought and spirituality. It is experienced as collective pain, collective presence and collective power.[40] Through revolutionary activity, new dimensions of this vision of sociality become further clarified; the notion of sociality which already exists as a revolutionary consciousness of what it means to be human, continues to unfold.

It is this interpretation of sociality--the notion of persons-in-relation--which serves as our criterion of adequacy in judging the anthropological presuppositions underlying the two ethical systems and approaches to social change.

In the preceding pages I have explained my reasons for selecting radical social thought as a source for developing the notion of sociality which serves as the criterion of adequacy in this work. I have provided justification for this selection since agreement with my evaluation of Niebuhr's and Ruether's ethical systems and approaches to social change depends primarily on the acceptance of the established criterion. I have argued, first of all, that my selection of the conflict tradition is based on the nature of the discipline to which it belongs. The focus of the social sciences is "human social experience." The selection of the conflict tradition is also related to its congruency with (1) the concerns of a study on the ethics of social change, and (2) a feminist perspective which is the basis of this work.

According to Thomas Kuhn, there is no way to prove the validity of a paradigm, or in this study the validity of radical social thought.[41] The choice of a tradition or perspective goes "beyond the assurance immediately available from the empirical evidence on hand."[42] "The sensed validity of a theory depends [ultimately] upon the sharing of experience and of the sentiments to which such experiences give rise, among those who offer and those who listen to the theory."[43] In the end, my selection of radical social thought for developing a criterion of adequacy is a matter of commitment.

Overview

To examine the relationship between anthropological presuppositions and ethics, I have chosen the works of Reinhold Niebuhr and Rosemary Radford Ruether. Both Niebuhr and Ruether stress the importance of their anthropology to the development of their work. Both writers give a place of prominence to the notion of sociality in their anthropology. Their writings also reflect a concern for social justice and social change, a concern that was validated in Niebuhr's life through political practice, as it presently is in Ruether's. Both ethicist-theologians discuss social change within the larger context of a socio-historical reality marked by systemic injustices and covert and/or overt violence. Although there are many similarities between their two positions, essential differences exist in their ethical systems and ethics of social change. I argue that these differences are due, to a large extent, to their differing interpretations of sociality.

The first two chapters immediately following focus on Niebuhr's work. Chapter II is a discussion of Niebuhr's interpretation of sociality. Chapter III traces the implications of this interpretation of sociality on Niebuhr's ethical system as a whole, and then more specifically on his approach to social change. Niebuhr's anthropology, with its vertical dialectic and transcendental dimension, includes an interpretation of the individual as ultimately discontinuous with and above society--a view that is not in keeping with the notion of sociality found in radical social thought. As a result of his anthropology, Niebuhr's ethical system as a whole, as well as his approach to social change is characterized by certain limitations.

In Chapter IV, an interpretation of sociality is developed at length, drawing upon radical social thought. It is this interpretation of sociality that serves as the criterion of adequacy.

9

Chapters V and VI address the work of Rosemary
Ruether. In Chapter V, the analysis of Ruether's
anthropology reveals an understanding of sociality
similar to the one described in Chapter IV. In Chapter
VI, Ruether's ethical system is developed, including
her approach to social change. Because Ruether's
ethical system is based on an understanding of the
human person as essentially social, it is judged to be
more adequate than Niebuhr's.

In the concluding chapter, the advantages of an
ethical system and an ethics of social change based on
an understanding of the person as essentially social
are clarified. Also, the ways in which Ruether's
ethical system and approach to social change overcome
the limitations found in Niebuhr's approach are
pointed out. Finally, I claim that for those seeking
an ethical system and approach to social change for
their pursuit of justice, Ruether's ethical system,
including her approach to social change, is an adequate
one.

Notes

[1]Robert McAfee Brown, Religion and Violence
(Philadelphia: The Westminister Press, 1973), p. 30.

[2]Denis Goulet, The Cruel Choice (New York:
Atheneum, 1971), p. 301.

[3]For example, the Catholic Worker is a movement
based on a personalist philosophy and advocates "Gospel
non-violence" for resisting the system (see, for
example, Pat Jordan, "Illuminating Dark Times," in The
Catholic Worker, December 1980, pp. 6-7). The United
Farm Workers is fighting for unionization of its
members in order to claim the power that is rightfully
theirs within the system. The Religious Task Force on
Central America supports those who are engaged in
armed struggle against unjust regimes.

[4]Clifford Geertz describes a people's world-view
as "their picture of the way things in sheer actuality
are, their concept of nature, of self, of society. It
contains their most comprehensive ideas of order" (The
Interpretation of Cultures [New York: Basic Books,
Inc., Publishers, 1973], p. 127). Geertz's description
of world-view is being used here.

[5]Although I use inclusive language in my own text,

I have chosen not to attempt to judge the intentions of other authors. Therefore, I have not made linguistic modifications in the quotations I cite. In a conversation with Rosemary Ruether, she initially suggested using "sic" to indicate the sexist language in her early works. However, rather than using "sic," I direct the readers to her statements concerning sexist language in the Preface to New Woman/New Earth. The one exception to my procedure, made in the light of Ruether's statements, is found in Chapter V, p. 127.

[6]Geertz, The Interpretation of Cultures, p. 141. Geertz sees this relationship as circular. Factual conclusions are also continually drawn from normative premises. Between one's ethics and world-view "there is conceived to be a simple and fundamental congruence such that they complete one another and lend one another meaning" (ibid., p. 129). Alan Dawe argues forcefully for this position in his article "Theories of Social Action" in A History of Sociological Analysis, ed. Tom Bottomore and Robert Nisbet (New York: Basic Books, Inc., Publishers, 1978), as does Gibson Winter, Elements for a Social Ethic (New York, New York: The Macmillan Company, 1968).

[7]Goulet, The Cruel Choice, p. 303.

[8]See, for example, George Sabine, A History of Political Theory, revised by Thomas Landon Thorson (Hinsdale, Illinois: Dryden Press, 1973); and Dawe, "Theories of Social Action."

[9]Dawe, "Theories of Social Action," p. 365.

[10]For a further discussion of the complementarity between the social sciences and social ethics see Winter, Elements.

[11]One of the limitations of simplifying sociology in such a way is the loss of minor, and in some cases major, distinctions among the various theorists who are placed in the same school. For an elaboration of the argument against dividing the discipline into two traditions, see Anthony Giddens, "Classical Social Theory and the Origins of Modern Sociology," American Journal of Sociology 81 (January 1976):703-29, especially pp. 714-18.

[12]Although this description of the discipline is based on knowledge of Western sociology, Robert

Friedrichs suggests that "sociology in the socialist world is facing the same essential split into 'system' and 'conflict,' 'priestly' and 'prophetic' polarities we witness within Western, essentially American [i.e., United States] sociology" (A Sociology of Sociology [New York: The Free Press, 1979], p. xxix).

[13]For an example of this approach, see Talcott Parsons, The Social System (Glencoe, Ill.: The Free Press, 1951). Parsons is considered the "founding father" and the most prominent representative of modern system theory (Alan Wells, "Contemporary Schools in Sociological Theory," in Contemporary Sociological Theories [Santa Monica, California: Goodyear Publishing Company, Inc., 1978], p. 10). For a more detailed description of system theory, see such works as Randall Collins and Michael Makowsky, The Discovery of Society (New York: Random House, 1972); Don Martindale, The Nature and Types of Sociological Theory (Boston: Houghton Mifflin Company, 1960); and Wells, ed., Contemporary Sociological Theories, as well as any other basic introductory sociology or social theory textbook. For a more critical approach to system theory, see Alvin Gouldner, The Coming Crisis of Western Sociology (New York: Avon Books, 1970); Joyce A. Ladner, ed., The Death of White Sociology (New York: Random House, 1973); C. Wright Mills, The Sociological Imagination (New York: Oxford, 1971); and Howard J. Sherman and James L. Wood, Sociology: Traditional and Radical Perspectives (New York: Harper & Row, Publishers, 1979).

[14]Friedrichs attributes a major portion of the popularity of the system paradigm to two factors: "The sudden hand-in-glove development of cybernetics and the electronic computer [and] the climate of the times [which was marked by an] unparalleled conformity and commitment to the status quo." This attitude "provided every kind of subtle support the system advocate might wish for a paradigm whose point of return was dictated by the relative equilibrium that was the image's unstated premise" (The Sociology of Sociology, pp. 16-17).

[15]Friedrichs, A Sociology of Sociology, p. 45. The increasing importance of the conflict tradition can be attributed, in part, to the social movements of the 1960s--e.g., civil rights, black power, La Raza, women's liberation, anti-war. Scholars and particularly activist and third world sociologists were discontent with a model that failed "to provide [a] central . . . place for fundamental social change" (Robert Friedrichs,

12

"Dialectical Sociology: Toward a Resolution of the Current 'Crisis' in Western Sociology," British Journal of Sociology 23 [September 1972]:281). Other factors include the revival of Marxist thought in the United States, and the rise of the Frankfurt school in Western Europe.

[16] I support using my own presuppositions in a way similar to Paul Ricoeur, when he writes: "I can readily see how one might take exception to the presuppositions of this study which I am formulating on its pre-critical level. But then, who does not begin an analysis without presuppositions or pre-judgments? The problem always concerns where we shall subsequently advance on the road of veracity, up to what point the presuppositions become critically elaborated, incorporated within a common endeavor wherein discussion may arise and thereby make explicit the implicit presuppositions" (in History and Truth, trans. Charles A. Kelbley [Evanston: Northwestern University Press, 1975], p. 223).

[17] By feminism I mean "the political theory and practice to free all women: women of color, working-class women, lesbians, old women, as well as white economically privileged heterosexual women" through the radical transformation of social relationships and structures (Barbara Smith, cited in Cherríe Moraga and Gloria Anzaldúa, eds., This Bridge Called My Back: Writings by Radical Women of Color, with a Foreward by Toni Cade Bambara [Watertown, Massachusetts: Persephone Press, 1981], p. 29).

[18] Lee Cormie, "Society, History and Meaning: Perspectives from the Social Sciences," p. 11 (Mimeographed.) See also Gouldner, Coming Crisis, pp. 8, 26.

[19] This view is in sharp contrast to the one found in system theory. For a thorough critique of academic social science and its contribution to the ongoing exploitation of women, see Marcia Westkott, "Feminist Criticism of the Social Sciences," Harvard Educational Review 49 (November 1979).

[20] As Forsythe writes, in radical sociology "'Class,' 'Race,' 'Technology,' 'Wealth,' 'Power,' 'Conflict,' 'Interests,' 'Ownership,' and 'Control' . . . become key areas of focus in trying to determine the nature of problems" ("Radical Sociology and Blacks," in The Death of White Sociology, p. 222).

[21]Sociologist Orlando Fals-Borda identifies types of counter-elements: (1) counter-values, (2) counter-norms, (3) rebel organizations, or "disorgans," and (4) technical organizations. These, according to Fals-Borda, are the elements of subversion within a society that challenge the established order. See Subversion and Social Change in Columbia, trans. Jacqueline D. Skiles (New York and London: Columbia University Press, 1969), p. 13.

[22]Ibid., pp. 20-21.

[23]Ibid., p. 203.

[24]See Forsythe, "Radical Sociology and Blacks," p. 26.

[25]Gouldner writes: "Every social theory facilitates the pursuit of some but not all courses of action, and thus encourages us to change or to accept the world as it is, to say yea or nay to it. In a way, every theory is a discreet obituary or celebration for some social system" (Coming Crisis, p. 47).

[26]This is in contrast to system theorists, who generally believe their work to be "strictly detached and neutrally analytic" (Dawe, "Theories of Social Action," p. 365). Forsythe claims that "a value-free sociology is impossible; values are forced underground only to be smuggled back into the discipline by various methods" ("Radical Sociology and Blacks," p. 216).

[27]Gouldner, Coming Crisis, p. 503. Fals-Borda describes this principle of methodology as "telic, projective, or anticipatory" (Subversion and Social Change, p. 205).

[28]Brian Fay, Social Theory and Political Practice, Controversies in Sociology, no. 1 (New York: Holmes and Meier Publishers, 1975), p. 110.

[29]Sherman and Wood, Sociology, p. 6.

[30]Fals-Borda, cited in Denis Goulet, The New Moral Order, with a Foreword by Paulo Freire (Maryknoll, N.Y.: Orbis Books, 1974), p. 59. In fact, Fals-Borda goes so far as to argue that it is only through such commitment that one can understand "the nature and characteristic of social processes . . . [and] arrive at the heart of the causal explanation of historical change"

14

(Fals-Borda, Subversion and Social Change, pp. 203, xi).

[31]For an extensive listing of books and articles which discuss the relation of social change to social practice, see Fay, Social Theory and Political Practice, pp. 47-48.

[32]Goulet, The New Moral Order, p. 60.

[33]Ibid., p. 67.

[34]Ibid. Robert Staples writes in reference to black sociologists: "The role of the Black sociologist should be as both theorist and activist. Not only must he develop the theories embodied in the discipline of Black sociology, he must also man the barricade" ("What is Black Sociology? Toward a Sociology of Black Liberation," in The Death of White Sociology, p. 172).

[35]Wells, "Introduction," in Contemporary Sociological Theories, p. 223. See also Gouldner, Coming Crisis, p. 503.

[36]This section has focused on the congruencies. It is also important to note that feminism contributes to the conflict tradition in a number of ways: e.g., its discussion of patriarchy and the hierarchical model of reality, its treatment of domestic labor in economic systems, its emphasis on the interrelationship between the personal and the political.

[37]David M. Rasmussen, "Between Autonomy and Sociality," Cultural Hermeneutics 1 (April 1973):22.

[38]See Dawe, Theories of Social Action," p. 410. In fact, conflict theorists criticize system theorists for what they consider to be the latter's assumption concerning the social dimension of human existence-- i.e., that "the relationship between self and other, the originary ground of sociality, is [a] quasi-contractual relationship of mutually independent selves [i.e., self-contained wholes] who agree, as it were, to be social" (Rasmussen, "Between Autonomy and Sociality," p. 41). Winter argues that the "debate between the two styles of social science has its roots in [their] differences over the understanding of man and social-ity"--a problem that "has continued to plague the development of the human sciences" (Elements, p. 85).

[39]Rasmussen, "Between Autonomy and Sociality,"

15

p. 4.

[40]See, for example, Carol B. Stack, <u>All Our Kin: Strategies for Survival in a Black Community</u> (New York, Evanston, San Francisco, London: Harper & Row, Publishers, 1974); and Anita Valeria, "It's in My Blood, My Face--My Mother's Voice, the Way I Sweat," in <u>This Bridge Called My Back</u>, p. 43.

[41]See Thomas Kuhn, <u>The Structure of Scientific Revolutions</u>, 2nd ed. (Chicago: The University of Chicago Press, 1970), pp. 198-204.

[42]Friedrichs, <u>The Sociology of Sociology</u>, p. 156.

[43]Gouldner, <u>Coming Crisis</u>, p. 8.

CHAPTER II

SOCIALITY: REINHOLD NIEBUHR'S INTERPRETATION

In his early work, Moral Man and Immoral Society, [1] Reinhold Niebuhr raises the following question--one which he subsequently asked throughout his life:

> How can [society] eliminate social
> injustice by methods which offer
> some fair opportunity of abolishing
> what is evil in society, without
> destroying what is worth preserving
> in it, and without running the risk
> of substituting new abuses and
> injustices in place of those
> abolished? [2]

Niebuhr understands the quest to find an adequate approach to social change as one of the major tasks of social ethics, and recognizes the need for this approach to be rooted in a sound anthropology. [3] For Niebuhr, the doctrine of human nature plays the determining role in the development of an ethical system. He consistently warns against mistaken notions of human nature which lead to incorrect interpretations of reality and to the selection of an erroneous course of action in society. [4]

A number of commentators stress the significance of the relationship between anthropology and ethics in Niebuhr's works. John Bennett writes: "In general we can say that Niebuhr's theological teaching about human nature determines the limits of what should be attempted in society and . . . it is one of the factors which determines the direction of ethical action." [5] Similarly, Bob E. Patterson states that Niebuhr's system "finds its beginning in the doctrine of man [and] this doctrine, his chief contribution to theology, is determinative for his ethics." [6]

The purpose of this chapter is to describe one aspect of Niebuhr's anthropology--his interpretation of sociality. I also discuss what Niebuhr calls the paradoxical or dialectical relationship between the individual and society as it relates to his notion of sociality, and conclude that in Niebuhr's anthropology, it is the individual above society that takes precedence. Then, in Chapter III, the effects of Niebuhr's

interpretation of sociality on his ethical system and
ethics of social change are examined. Although my concern is the notion of sociality, a brief overview of
Niebuhr's anthropology is provided first.[7]

Niebuhr uses various terms in his anthropology:
"man," "human nature," "self," and "individual."
Throughout my treatment of Niebuhr's works, I use the
terms "human beings" and "human person" to replace
Niebuhr's use of the term "man." "Man," for Niebuhr,
generally refers to the structure of human nature, the
basic elements of whatever is essentially human, and
the objective human condition. Niebuhr frequently uses
the two terms "man" (for us, "human beings" and "human
person") and "human nature" interchangeably. Although
never clearly defined, the "self" seems to refer to

> the dynamic, actional aspect of human
> life, the way its basic elements
> interplay one upon the other, the
> way in which these basic realities
> of life are subjectively appropriated,
> and with what a human being is
> essentially and in actuality.[8]

Niebuhr uses the term "individual" to emphasize the
person's discreteness and uniqueness. All of these
terms appear in this chapter.

An Overview of Reinhold Niebuhr's
Anthropology

Niebuhr characterizes the human person as a paradoxical being, "both strong and weak, both free and
bound, both blind and far-seeing [who] stands at the
juncture of nature and spirit."[9] The human person is
both

> a child of nature, subject to its
> vicissitudes, compelled by its
> necessities, driven by its impulses,
> and confined within the brevity of
> the years which nature permits its
> varied organic forms, allowing them
> some but not too much latitude [and]
> a spirit who stands outside of
> nature, life, himself, his reason
> and the world.[10]

Drawing upon the Biblical conception,[11] Niebuhr defines

the human person both as creature and as image of God; a complex unity of nature and spirit, of body and soul. This is what human beings truly are; it is "the essential nature and structure"[12] of all.

Focusing more specifically now on both of these dimensions, we find that for Niebuhr nature is characterized by "brevity and dependence."[13] Nature implies "contingency,"[14] "necessity,"[15] and "insufficiency."[16] In Niebuhr's anthropology, however, there is no such thing as "pure nature." Nature is always in relationship to spirit. Human beings, let us recall, live "at the juncture of nature and spirit."[17] To be human is to be made up of the "organic unity between the spirit of man and his physical life."[18]

Spirit is, for Niebuhr, the dialectical opposite of nature. It is the aspect of the human person which is independent, self-sufficient and self-determining. Spirit is "the self . . . in its awareness of its freedom over its functions."[19] Niebuhr uses the term "spirit" interchangeably with self-transcendence, self-consciousness, freedom, and the image of God.[20]

These two dimensions of the human person--nature and spirit--permeate the two aspects which characterize all creation: vitality and form.[21] Nature and spirit are not synonymous with vitality and form: there are vitalities of nature and vitalities of spirit, and forms of nature and forms of spirit. Vitality and form are resources for both nature and spirit.[22] Vitality refers to the energy or "force which carries life beyond itself, from one center of life to another. Form means the direction this energy takes and/or is given."[23] However all human activity--whether creative or destructive--involve the interplay of these four elements:

> (1) The vitality of nature (its impulses and drives); (2) the forms and unities of nature, that is the determinations of instinct, and the forms of natural cohesion and natural differentiation; (3) the freedom of the spirit to transcend natural forms within limits and to direct and redirect the vitalities; (4) and finally the forming capacity of spirit, its ability to create a new realm of coherence and order.[24]

Niebuhr's understanding of persons as social is directly related to the paradoxical essence of human beings described above. Sociality is rooted in the vitalities and forms of nature and spirit. These dimensions of sociality are described below.

The Notion of Sociality

Social Impulses

Human beings are endowed by nature with impulses, instincts, or drives. These are the vitalities of nature.[25] At the level of nature, human beings share with lower creatures social impulses which "carry life beyond itself."[26] At this level, sociality specifically takes the form of two impulses: survival and propagation. Humans are "creatures who have need of food and shelter, perhaps locomotion and communication in modern existence, and . . . are dependent upon each other for these goods."[27] Human beings also have "a sex impulse which seeks the perpetuity of [their] kind with the same degree of energy with which [they] seek the preservation of [their] own life."[28] For Niebuhr, these impulses are social insofar as they impel individuals to associate with one another and to live together in community in order to meet these basic needs.

Social impulses prompt individuals not only to reach out to others in the struggle for existence, but also to live together in society with "some achievement of harmony with other life."[29] In Moral Man and Immoral Society Niebuhr speaks of "a specific impulse of pity [which] bids [one] fly to aid of stricken members of his community."[30] In An Interpretation of Christian Ethics Niebuhr includes "the natural endowment of sympathy [and] paternal and filial affection"[31] among the social impulses.

Social impulses, as part of the vitalities of nature in humans, bring about social organization for survival and support; social impulses, as part of the vitalities of the spirit, lead to the formation of larger and more inclusive communities.[32] As Niebuhr explains:

> The individual cannot be a true self
> in isolation. Nor can he live
> within the confines of the community
> which "nature" establishes in the

20

minimal cohesion of family and herd.
His freedom transcends these limits
of nature and therefore makes
larger and larger social units both
possible and necessary.[33]

The development of "larger and larger social units" is
made possible by the potentialities which the spirit
creates for greater harmony in community.[34] Such a
development is necessary because the social impulses,
at the level of spirit, require that the self be drawn
out of itself into the lives of others in order to be
truly fulfilled. The self "can only find itself by
having an end beyond itself, for the self is too great
in its indeterminate freedom to be fulfilled within the
self."[35] Embedded in the essential being of the human
person is the impulse to reach out to others and to
enter into mutual and responsible relations with them.
This is the law of love and the fulfillment of life.[36]

     Sociality in Niebuhr's thought means then, first
of all, the social impulses at the levels of nature and
spirit. Sociality also refers to the concretization of
these impulses in the actual formation of societal
modes of existence. An individual may enter into
various kinds of relationships; for example, casual or
permanent; with one other or with several others, such
as the family; or with a whole community of others.[37]
Of particular interest to us here is Niebuhr's interpretation of sociality as it refers to the relationship
between the individual and his or her society.

The Individual and Society

     Individuals are in a paradoxical relationship to
their social world. This relationship is one of
dependence and independence, of fulfillment and frustration. It is symbolized by what Niebuhr calls the horizontal and vertical dimensions; that is, by persons
viewed as part of or in society (the historical self)
and by persons viewed as above or over society (the
transcendent self).[38] These two dimensions, which are
essential to Niebuhr's notion of sociality, and thus to
his ethics, are examined in turn.

Dependence, Fulfillment, and
the Horizontal Dimension

     Society is defined by Niebuhr as the "more or less
stable or precarious harmony of human vital

21

capacities."[39] Societies, like the individuals who comprise them, are characterized by the two dimensions of nature and spirit.[40] Individuals in society are dependent upon the natural elements in group existence for their particularity. Determining conditions such as family and ethnic kinship, national identity, racial origins, and geographic conditions provide this specificity.[41] Individuals are also dependent upon their society for a way of life organized around these determining conditions and around natural impulses. Language, customs, norms and other cultural forms give meaning and structure to the common life and provide individuals with a way of being in the world.[42]

Individuals emerge and develop in a given society with its regularized patterns of thought and behavior.[43] Through the socialization process individuals become integrated into a cultural system. They are united with the members of their society who share the system. The sharing of a common cultural experience contributes to the maintenance of society.[44]

Besides being dependent upon society for one's particularity and way of life, individuals are also dependent upon society for their fulfillment. As Niebuhr writes, a person is dependent upon society not only "for the stuff out of which particular and special forms of his vitality are created [but also] as the partial end, justification and fulfillment of his existence."[45]

Individuals cannot fulfill themselves within themselves; "they are not whole without the others." Because of the social impulses, or what Niebuhr also calls "the impulse for community," individuals need each other. Each individual self "seeks to complete itself . . . in its creative relations to its fellows." It is only in community that the law of love is realized. This fulfillment or realization is sought within a particular society--whether family, clan, nation, or culture--in history.[46]

This relationship of dependence and fulfillment is described by Niebuhr as the horizontal dimension of human existence. The horizontal dimension represents "the social substance . . . and the social character"[47] of human nature. It characterizes the individual as part of society, or the historical self. There is also a vertical dimension of human existence which represents the ability of human beings to transcend their society.

22

The vertical dimension is used to describe the independence and frustration that exists in the relationship between the individual and his or her society. It characterizes the individual as above society, or the transcendent self.

Independence, Frustration, and the Vertical Dimension

At the same time that individuals are dependent upon nature and society for their particularity, way of life and fulfillment,[48] they are engaged in the process of forming or creating their society. Human beings are not "prisoners of their respective cultures."[49] In Niebuhr's view, "the human self arises as an independent and self-determining force in the very social process and historical continuum in which it is also a creature."[50]

The capacity for transcendence is rooted in the human spirit and is the basis for freedom.[51] It is the spirit which enables the human person to rise above "nature, life, himself, his reason and the world,"[52] as well as be involved within them.[53] It is the spirit in human beings which enables them to create new and unique configurations of thought and action in history.[54]

It is this capacity for transcendence which creates the frustration in the relationship between the individual and society. Although society does have the capacity to partially transcend itself, it "is bound to nature more inexorably than [an individual]."[55] Society lacks a single organ of self-transcendence and so is not capable of transcendence to the same degree that the individual is.[56] "It knows nothing of a dimension of the eternal beyond its own existence."[57] For this reason, no society can totally contain the individual or provide complete fulfillment. As Niebuhr maintains, "the desires, hopes and ideals of an individual cannot be fitted with frictionless harmony into the collective"[58] enterprise. The impulse for perfection or complete fulfillment drives the individual to seek wholeness beyond the conditions of historical existence. Individuals are always able to conceive ends which transcend possibilities in history.[59] They yearn for the ultimate, search for the divine, and envision a "universal community concomitant with the universality of the human spirit."[60]

23

Thus far I have presented Niebuhr's understanding of the human person as a paradoxical creature of nature and spirit, and have described how this anthropological presupposition is related to his interpretation of sociality. The human person has social impulses which are rooted in and shaped by nature and spirit. The concretization of these impulses in the formation of societies in history results in a relationship between the individual and society that is marked by dependence and independence, by fulfillment and frustration; that is, by both a horizontal and a vertical dimension. A person is both a part of society and above society.

The relationship between the individual and society is a clear illustration of a paradox or of what Niebuhr calls a dialectical relationship. By a paradoxical or dialectical relationship Niebuhr means that the two poles of the relation are both in essential harmony and in inevitable conflict.[61] For Niebuhr, it is this type of relationship that appropriately describes "two partially incompatible and partially supplementary"[62] aspects of reality.

In his writings, Niebuhr continually struggles to incorporate both the harmony and the conflict that results from the individual being considered as a part of society and as above society. For example, he repeatedly stresses that "the highest reaches of individual consciousness and awareness are rooted in social experience and find their ultimate meaning in relation to the community."[63] The community is "the foundation upon which the pinnacle of uniqueness stands,"[64] and even though "there is a point in human freedom where the individual transcends both his own community and the total historical process,"[65] the individual always re-enters community and assumes responsibility for shaping its patterns and designs.[66] Given the permanence of freedom and finitude in human nature, this process of transcending community and then re-entering it will continue throughout history.[67] For Niebuhr, it is only at the end of history and outside of history that this conflict is resolved.

Apparent contradictions between the individual as a part of society and the individual as above society, between the horizontal dimension and the vertical dimension must not be explained away. Niebuhr states that solutions which identify or absolutely contrast these two elements are unacceptable. Types of monism[68] or dualism[69] must be avoided. If either the individual

24

above society or the individual as part of society is
ignored or dismissed, a form of collectivism which
denies the uniqueness of each individual or a form of
individualism which denies the inherent social dimension
of human nature results. According to Niebuhr, the
vertical and horizontal dimensions of human existence
must be kept in relation and tension.

Niebuhr's notion of sociality implies a number of
paradoxes in other areas, including: morality and
religion, time and eternity, the real and the ideal,
the self-in-action and the self-in-contemplation, and
the public sphere and the private sphere. These paradoxes interrelate, and have a significant influence on
Niebuhr's ethics. Therefore it is important to make
them explicit.[70]

Related Paradoxes

The horizontal dimension of the human person--the
historical self or the individual as a part of society--
represents the moral dimension of human existence.
This dimension is concerned with the principles of
human conduct and social relations within a historical
context.[71] Individuals, as a part of a particular
society, strive to achieve "proximate goals, determinate
ends and parochial interests."[72] The self-in-action
may bring about moral achievements, but these achievements never perfectly conform to the ideal. Reality is
in need of constant improvement and criticism by reference to the ideal.

This horizontal or moral dimension of human existence is public because it concerns the proximate ends
attainable in political life.[73] It is also communal or
social, for as Niebuhr insists, "we are members of
communities and civilizations whose fate is intimately
bound up with our brethren."[74]

The vertical dimension of the human person--the
transcendent self or the individual above society--
represents the religious dimension of human existence.[75]
The transcendent self strives for the ideal or the
absolute and "yearn[s] after values and truth which
transcend the partial, the relative and the historical."[76] Transcendence enables the self to "reach . . .
into eternity"[77] and encounter God, the one who completely transcends the limitations of finiteness and
history. In the vertical dimension of the individual's
relation to God, the self-in-contemplation recalls its

25

original righteousness, recognizes its failings and
guilt, experiences remorse or repentance, and receives
mercy and forgiveness.[78]

This vertical or religious dimension of human
existence is private because it concerns the "private
hopes and [ultimate] fulfillments which transcend any
communal attainments and realizations."[79] It is the
concern of the individual. As Niebuhr writes: "There
can be no question but that the ultimate heights of
religious faith are uniquely individual. . . . Our
final contact with God is made in solitariness."[80]

These polarities, which are derived "primarily
from the amphibian character of man,"[81] are as integrally related as nature and spirit, or as the individual as a part of society and the individual above
society. These polarities, like the elements of all
paradoxes, must always be held in relation and tension.

The dialectical relationship between these elements, and in particular the relationship between the
individual and society, is difficult to express in
clear, descriptive language. No simple schema can "do
justice to both the private and the collective drama in
which human beings are involved."[82] Although religious
myths and symbols come closest to expressing the exact
relationship between the horizontal and vertical
dimensions, even these are limited. For Niebuhr, no
form of language is adequate.

Summary

Thus far I have examined Niebuhr's understanding
of sociality, including the relationship between the
individual and society. I have described how, for
Niebuhr, this relationship is a paradoxical or dialectical one. I have also shown how Niebuhr's interpretation of sociality is related to other paradoxes that
are of significance to his ethics.

Niebuhr is not concerned that his understanding of
the relationship between the horizontal and vertical
dimensions of existence has been described by critics
as "more than a little ambiguous," "inconsistent,"
"rationally incoherent," and "self-contradictory."[83]
Rather, one of Niebuhr's main concerns is that of keeping both dimensions intact, as well as in relationship.
Thus, as we have seen in his interpretation of sociality, Niebuhr treats the individual and society as two

26

distinct, though definitely related, entities acting on each other, and often opposing each other,[84] rather than as one organically related whole--i.e., persons-in-relation--such as is found in radical social thought. For Niebuhr, the individual is both continuous and discontinuous with society; the individual is both a part of society and above society.[85]

This observation must be expressed with caution, for as I have already frequently noted, one of Niebuhr's basic anthropological presuppositions is that a person, characterized by social impulses, enters into social life because of his or her very nature. "The community _is_ as primordial as the individual,"[86] and the two "are so interlaced in each other's life that where one begins and the other ends is indeterminable."[87] But for Niebuhr, the human person remains ontologically separated from others and thus able to rise above society, because of the uniqueness and individuality of his or her own free spirit.[88]

Not only does Niebuhr maintain discontinuity between the individual and society in his interpretation of sociality, he also ascribes primary importance to the individual above society and the vertical dimension. As Hammar maintains, "ultimately, the _individual_ and not the group is of decisive importance."[89] One reason why it is difficult to detect the primacy of the individual is because, in Niebuhr's numerous articles focusing on the issues of his day, he emphasizes _either_ the individual or society, depending on what he perceives to be the need.[90] But, as Minnema argues, the existential individual is Niebuhr's starting point whether this is explicitly stated or not.[91] Evidence of these two aspects of Niebuhr's interpretation of sociality-- the discontinuity between the individual and society, and the distinctive importance of the individual above society--is found most clearly in Niebuhr's ethics.

In the next chapter, I provide this evidence by showing how Niebuhr's interpretation of sociality, which has been described in this chapter, affects his ethical system, including his ethics of social change. In discussing the various components of his ethical system, I point out how repeatedly the individual above society, or the vertical dimension takes precedence. Because of an inadequate interpretation of sociality, Niebuhr's ethical system and approach to social change are marked by certain limitations. In subsequent chapters I demonstrate how these limitations are overcome by Ruether's communal social ethics which is based on an adequate interpretation of sociality.

Notes

[1] Reinhold Niebuhr, Moral Man and Immoral Society (New York: Charles Scribner's Sons, 1932), hereafter cited as MMIS.

[2] Ibid., p. 167.

[3] Ibid., p. xxiv.

[4] Reinhold Niebuhr, Reflections on the End of An Era (New York and London: Charles Scribner's Sons, 1934), p. 48, hereafter cited as REE.

[5] John Bennett, "Reinhold Niebuhr's Social Ethics" in Reinhold Niebuhr: His Religious, Social and Political Thought, eds. Charles W. Kegley and Robert W. Bretall (New York: The Macmillan Company, 1956), p. 48.

[6] Bob E. Patterson, Reinhold Niebuhr (Waco, Texas: Word Books, Publishers, 1977), p. 63. See also Theodore Minnema, The Social Ethics of Reinhold Niebuhr (Grand Rapids, Michigan: Wm. B. Eerdmans Publishing Company, 1958), pp. 35, 115-16; Ronald Stone, Reinhold Niebuhr: Prophet to Politicians (Nashville: Abingdon Press, 1972), p. 170; Kenneth Thompson, "The Political Philosophy of Reinhold Niebuhr," in Kegley and Bretall, eds., Reinhold Niebuhr, p. 163; and William John Wolf, "Reinhold Niebuhr's Doctrine of Man," in ibid., p. 230.

[7] This overview of Niebuhr's anthropology is drawn primarily from his Gifford lectures which he significantly entitled The Nature and Destiny of Man: A Christian Interpretation, 2 vols. (New York: Charles Scribner's Sons, 1941 and 1943), hereafter cited as NDM. Although Niebuhr's anthropology is often explicitly expressed and always implicitly presupposed in all his works since Moral Man and Immoral Society, his exploration of the human person is developed in detail for the first time in these lectures. Wolf points out that "later works have more amply illustrated, but not essentially modified his basic contentions in the Gifford lectures" ("Reinhold Niebuhr's Doctrine of Man," p. 231). Stone supports Wolf's position and adds that "the differences between the analysis of man's nature in Man's Nature and His Communities and in The Nature

and Destiny of Man are due primarily to the disappearance of the theological vocabulary" (Reinhold Niebuhr, p. 133). Stone's statement is based on Niebuhr's "Introduction: Changing Perspectives," in Man's Nature and His Communities (New York: Charles Scribner's Sons, 1965), pp. 23-24, hereafter cited as MNHC. There are a number of excellent secondary sources available which provide more extensive overviews than the one that is given here. See the bibliography for a listing.

[8]Peter Homans, "The Meaning of Selfhood in the Thought of Reinhold Niebuhr and Sigmund Freud" (Ph.D. dissertation, University of Chicago, 1964), p. 19.

[9]NDM, 1:181.

[10]Ibid., p. 3. Dr. Shirley Caperton Guthrie writes that "Niebuhr never tires of reiterating this paradox. It is the beginning point of every doctrine he considers" (The Theological Character of Reinhold Niebuhr's Social Ethics [Winterthur: Verlag P. G. Keller, 1959], p. 97). This understanding of human nature results in what Ruurd Veldhuis considers to be unfounded criticism. Critics "obscure one side of the paradox which Niebuhr uses to describe reality" when in fact, what is believed to be missing "proves to be there at a second look" (Realism Versus Utopianism? [The Netherlands: Van Gorcum, Assen, 1975], p. 126).

[11]Niebuhr also refers to the Biblical conception as prophetic religion, biblical religion, biblical faith, Judeo-Christian tradition, Christian faith, and the Hebraic strain.

[12]NDM, 1:266, 269.

[13]Ibid., p. 169.

[14]Reinhold Niebuhr, Faith and History (New York: Charles Scribner's Sons, 1949), p. 77, hereafter cited as FH.

[15]Ibid., p. 79.

[16]NDM, 1:169.

[17]Ibid., p. 181.

[18]Ibid., p. 123.

¹⁹Reinhold Niebuhr, The Self and the Dramas of History (New York: Charles Scribner's Sons, 1955), p. 29, hereafter cited as SDH.

²⁰Peter Homans argues in his dissertation that "the relation between spirit and these concepts are so close . . . that the latter are really alternative ways in which the various meanings of spirit can be expressed" ("Meaning of Selfhood," p. 41).

²¹"All creatures express an exuberant vitality within the limits of certain unities, orders and forms" (NDM, 1:26).

²²Ibid., p. 27.

²³Homans, "Meaning of Selfhood," p. 49.

²⁴NDM, 1:27.

²⁵Niebuhr recognizes the number of interpretations given to these terms. By impulses, instincts, or drives Niebuhr means organic mechanisms, the "mechanisms of impulse with which nature has endowed him [i.e., the human person]" ("The Truth in Myths," in The Nature of Religious Experience: Essays in Honor of Douglas Clyde Macintosh, ed. J. S. Bixler, R. L. Calhoun, and H. R. Niebuhr [New York & London: Harper & Brothers Publishers, 1937], pp. 126-27).

²⁶MMIS, p. 27.

²⁷Reinhold Niebuhr, Justice and Mercy, ed. Ursula M. Niebuhr (New York: Harper and Row, Publishers, 1974), p. 107, hereafter cited as JM. See also Niebuhr's opening paragraph in "Morality," in The Search for America, ed. Huston Smith (Englewood Cliffs, N.J.: Prentice-Hall, Inc., 1959). Agreeing with Aristotle, Niebuhr writes: "We need one another to expedite the creation of life's physical necessities and social amenities" (p. 147).

²⁸MMIS, p. 26. Niebuhr explains: "The individual is a nucleus of energy which is organically related from the very beginning with other energy but which maintains nevertheless its own discrete existence. Every type of energy in nature seeks to preserve and perpetuate itself and to gain fulfillment within terms of its unique genius. The energy of human life does not differ in this from the world of nature" (ibid.,

p. 25).

[29]Ibid., p. 26.

[30]Ibid.

[31]Reinhold Niebuhr, An Interpretation of Christian Ethics (Harper & Brothers, 1935; reprint ed., New York: Meridian Books, 1956), p. 183, hereafter cited as ICE.

[32]NDM, 2:95.

[33]Reinhold Niebuhr, The Children of Light and the Children of Darkness (New York: Charles Scribner's Sons, 1944), p. 5, hereafter cited as CLCD.

[34]Niebuhr, "Morality," p. 147.

[35]Reinhold Niebuhr, Pious and Secular America (New York: Charles Scribner's Sons, 1958), p. 120, hereafter cited as PSA. See also NDM, 1:244; CLCD, p. 3; and Niebuhr, "Morality," p. 150.

[36]The law of love cannot be proven for "one's ultimate 'ought' always pivots on a faith that cannot be scientifically validated." For Niebuhr, the law of love is the one "timelessly valid ethical norm" ("Morality," pp. 150-51).

[37]As Niebuhr remarks: "There are endless nuances and levels of the dialogue of the self with others" (SDH, p. 4). Niebuhr devotes most of his analyses to large groups such as classes, nations, and even the world community.

[38]Niebuhr understands that "this double relation-ship [of being dependent and independent, etc.] naturally causes great perplexities and gives rise to some rather contradictory theories which emphasize either one or the other" (SDH, p. 41).

[39]NDM, 2:257.

[40]Ibid., p. 312.

[41]See, for example, Reinhold Niebuhr, Christianity and Power Politics (New York: Charles Scribner's Sons, 1940), p. 155, hereafter cited as CPP, also REE, p. 99; and NDM, 1:54-55.

[42]Although "the most immediate limitations of [people] as creature[s] of nature are immutable, . . . any particular historic expression of them is mutable" (FH, p. 183) through the forming capacity of the spirit--thus the endless variety of cultural differences within and among societies.

[43]Recognizing the influence of these cultural elements on individuals, Niebuhr writes: "Without the company of men we would not be human. The mind and personality of the individual requires the social 'field' of the community to be brought into being, to say nothing of perfecting themselves" ("Morality," p. 147).

[44]Niebuhr identifies two types of cohesive forces which members of society experience and which serve to bind a community together: organic and artifactual. These forces are also related to nature and spirit. Organic forces are "those which are least subject to conscious . . . manipulation and control. They are the 'given' forces [such as ethnic kinship and race]. . . . The forces of cohesion dependent on natural necessity are most clearly organic" (The Structure of Nations and Empires [New York: Charles Scribner's Sons, 1959; reprint ed., Fairfield: Augustus M. Kelley, Publishers, 1977], p. 260, hereafter cited as SNE). Artifacts are those forces which are subject to a more conscious contrivance or control. They are the "creation of the human will and reason" (SDH, p. 165) such as customs and laws. In the modern era, organic forces have become of less importance--a condition which Niebuhr laments. "The completely modern man has no social relations sufficiently organic to give his life real significance" (REE, p. 100). For a further discussion of organism and artifact see FH, p. 20; SDH, p. 163; and SNE, p. 149.

[45]CLCD, p. 55. See also SDH, p. 35.

[46]PSA, pp. 113-22 passim.

[47]JM, p. 106.

[48]Niebuhr insists that the natural and social environments are integrally related. "In history human contrivance is always mixed with nature" (SNE, p. 40). See also FH, p. 55.

[49]SDH, p. 42.

[50]Reinhold Niebuhr, Christian Realism and Political Problems (New York: Charles Scribner's Sons, 1953; reprint ed., Fairfield: Augustus M. Kelley, Publishers, 1977), p. 6, hereafter cited as CRPP.

[51]NDM, 1:55.

[52]Ibid., p. 3.

[53]Minnema explains the three levels of transcendence in Niebuhr's thought. "There is first the awareness of transcending natural processes. At this level of transcendence 'man stands outside of nature' and manifests this as a tool-making animal. A higher level is consciousness of the conceptual or the ability of making general concepts. This ability enables man to transcend not only nature but the world. The height of transcendence goes beyond tool-making consciousness and conceptual consciousness to self-consciousness. On this level man stands not only outside of nature and the world, but outside himself. . . . Here the subject, or self, meets no object, form or boundaries, but faces freedom, the eternal and the infinite" (Social Ethics, p. 4).

[54]See, for example, SNE where Niebuhr, summarizing his position, writes: "Man is that curious creature who, though partly determined and limited by the necessities of nature, also possesses a rational freedom which enables him to harness the forces of nature in the world and to transmute the natural appetites and drives in his own nature so that he can conceive ends and entertain ambitions which exceed the limits which pure nature sets for all her creatures except man. Man's freedom consists not only of the rational capacity for analysis and conceptual understanding which enables human beings to transcend the flux of temporal events by conceiving the patterns which give meaning to the flux. It consists, in addition, of the unique capacity to transcend himself and the flux of finite causes in which he, himself, is involved. Therefore he is able to choose between various alternative ends which present themselves to him and also choose between the various forces which presumably determine his actions. This freedom prevents any one of the causal sequences in which man is involved from finally determining his actions" (pp. 287-88; see also p. 124).

[55]SDH, p. 35. Societies do have the capacity "to stand beyond themselves, observe and estimate their

behavior, and trace the course of their history in
terms of some framework of meaning which gives them a
sense of continuing identity amidst the flux of time"
(Reinhold Niebuhr, The Irony of American History [New
York: Charles Scribner's Sons, 1952], p. 83, hereafter
cited as IAH). Niebuhr attributes a much greater
capacity for transcendence to societies in his later
works than in his earlier ones. The change is evident
in The Nature and Destiny of Man, but becomes increas-
ingly clearer in subsequent books.

[56]This assumption is crucial to Niebuhr's ethical
system and will be treated in greater depth below, see
pp. 53-54.

[57]SDH, p. 35.

[58]June Bingham, Courage to Change (New York:
Charles Scribner's Sons, 1961), p. 69.

[59]At times throughout this work the word
"history" is used interchangeably with "society."
This term, according to Homans, "unifies and contains
Niebuhr's other concepts describing the social life of
man" ("Meaning of the Self," p. 69).

[60]MNHC, p. 83. Transcendence enables the human
person "to seek after unique fulfillments of its own,
to consider the plight of its frustrations which no
communal activity can overcome, and to inquire after
the meaning of its existence in terms which are finally
irrelevant to any sense of meaning which the community
may have" (SDH, p. 223).

[61]Reinhold Niebuhr, Does Civilization Need
Religion? (New York: The Macmillan Company, 1927), p.
209, hereafter cited as DCNR.

[62]REE, p. 296.

[63]CLCD, p. 50.

[64]Ibid., p. 55.

[65]Ibid., p. 79.

[66]See Minnema, Social Ethics, pp. 36-37.

[67]See MNHC, pp. 90-95; and Langdon Gilkey, "Reinhold Niebuhr's Theology of History," Journal of

Religion 54 (October 1974):369-70.

[68]Niebuhr, "Truth in Myths," p. 122.

[69]Guthrie, Theological Character, pp. 8-9; see also DCNR, p. 200.

[70]This is not to infer that these are the only paradoxes that have relevance for Niebuhr's ethics, but that these are the major ones. For an extensive listing of the polarities in Niebuhr's writings, see Robert E. Fitch, "Reinhold Niebuhr's Philosophy of History," in Kegley and Bretall, eds., Rienhold Niebuhr, pp. 299-300.

[71]FH, p. 12.

[72]PSA, p. 118.

[73]SNE, pp. 130, 133.

[74]Niebuhr, "Individual and Social Dimension," Episcopal Churchnews 120 (October 16, 1955):9.

[75]See, for example, NDM, 1:179; and PSA, p. 114.

[76]REE, p. 183. See also CPP, p. 19.

[77]NDM, 1:154.

[78]Ibid., pp. 255-260.

[79]SNE, p. 133.

[80]Reinhold Niebuhr, "Individual and Social Dimension," p. 9. See also REE, p. 92; SDH, p. 230; and SNE, pp. 120-30.

[81]Fitch, "Philosophy of History," p. 299.

[82]SDH, p. 218. Niebuhr considers it "practically impossible" to conceive a frame of meaning that will adequately capture both of these dimensions because the two dramas "are so disparate and incommensurate . . . that either the one or the other is unduly subordinated to the other" (ibid.).

[83]For these descriptions of Niebuhr's thought, see Guthrie, Theological Character, p. 67; George Hammar, Christian Realism in Contemporary American Theology

(Uppsala: Appelbergs Boktryckeriaktiebolac, 1940), p. 192; and Wolf, "Reinhold Niebuhr's Doctrine of Man," p. 231.

[84]This interpretation leads critics to claim that "dialectical" is an inappropriate description of the interacting elements in Niebuhr's thought. For example, Wolf describes Niebuhr's thought as "relational" rather than "dialectical" (ibid., p. 232). And Veldhuis argues that "paradox" is the appropriate term, rather than "dialectical," since Niebuhr is interested only in calling attention to conflicting factors in human nature, society, and history and not in removing the tension by developing a new concept in which the two old ones are synthesized. (Realism Versus Utopianism?, pp. 13-16.

[85]See Minnema, Social Ethics, p. 118.

[86]SDH, p. 165, emphasis added.

[87]Minnema, Social Ethics, p. 37.

[88]NDM, 1:271.

[89]Hammar, Christian Realism, p. 193. Hammar supports his position, in part, by references to Niebuhr's discussion on the importance of the individual and his or her attitudes in solving social problems in REE, p. 257.

[90]See Hammar, Christian Realism, p. 192; and Dan Rhoades, "The Prophetic Insight and Theoretical-Analytical Inadequacy of 'Christian Realism,'" Ethics 75 (October 1964):1-15.

[91]Minnema, Social Ethics, p. 119.

CHAPTER III

REINHOLD NIEBUHR'S ETHICAL SYSTEM
AND SOCIAL CHANGE

Reinhold Niebuhr's interpretation of sociality has decisive consequences for his ethical system, and thus for his approach to social change. Given his understanding of the individual as above society and the individual as a part of society, and the consequent relationship between the individual and society, Niebuhr finds it necessary to develop what he calls personal ethics (or the independent Christian ethic) and political or social ethics. It is these two types of ethics that make up Niebuhr's ethical system. Niebuhr's commitment to interrelate the two ethics in his system never wavers; but, consistent with his notion of sociality, there is both continuity and discontinuity between the two ethics, with personal ethics assuming primary importance.[1]

In the first part of this chapter, the effects of Niebuhr's understanding of sociality on his ethical system are discovered by examining three major components: (1) the ethical agent, (2) ethical norms, and (3) the failure to achieve ethical norms. In each of these areas I indicate how the personal ethics of the individual above society assumes the place of prominence in Niebuhr's ethical system. Niebuhr's system provides the framework for his approach to social change. In the second part of this chapter I discuss the implications of Niebuhr's ethical system for his approach to social change. A consideration of his approach reveals certain limitations due to an interpretation of sociality marked by a discontinuity between the individual and society, with primary importance being given to the individual. As I demonstrate in later chapters, these limitations are overcome by an approach to social change developed within an ethical system based on an adequate notion of sociality.

The Ethical System

Ethical Agents: The Individual
and Society

Given Niebuhr's distinction between the individual above society and the individual as a part of society, Niebuhr treats the individual and society as two distinct, though definitely related, ethical agents. In

37

considering the first aspect of Niebuhr's ethical
system, the two types of agents are described and the
relationship between them pointed out.

The Individual as Ethical Agent

Niebuhr defines the individual as a free and
autonomous agent of his or her own actions. Freedom
gives each human being the capacity, or the will "to
choose between contrasting ends of action and conflicting motives which prompt [these] . . . ends."[2] A person chooses to act in either a creative or destructive
way, for good or for evil. The possibilities for self-
giving or self-aggrandizement in human relationships
are indeterminate within history.[3] Niebuhr calls this
view of the individual ethical agent the interior view
of moral responsibility.[4]

For Niebuhr, the interior view of moral responsibility is established introspectively. Individuals
know through contemplation that they "stand above the
flow of causes and are [them]selves the cause of
[their] own actions."[5] This knowledge is affirmed by
the remorse or repentance which usually accompanies
evil or sinful actions.[6]

This interior view of moral responsibility--the
understanding of the individual as a free and autonomous ethical agent--coexists in Niebuhr's system with
the exterior view which understands human actions to be
socially determined.[7] The ethical agent is also a part
of society; thus, moral judgments are not made in a
vacuum. They are, to a certain extent, relative to
one's particular historical and social context. As
Niebuhr writes, "the community in which [one] lives
sets the standards by which he judges himself."[8] However, the sense of moral obligation cannot be reduced
to a purely social phenomenon.[9] The transcendent self
has "the ability to determine its actions despite the
determining influences upon these actions in the environment."[10] Society does "provide the historical locus
from which the self can scan the historical process and
make individual decisions."[11] But, illustrating the
predominance of the vertical dimension in Niebuhr's
interpretation of sociality, the individual above
society is ultimately morally responsible for him or
herself.

Society as Ethical Agent

Society, like the individual, is made up of a unity of nature and spirit, vitality and form.[12] Society is characterized by natural necessities--dynamic forces and static conditions--which are transformed by the vitality of the spirit into new forms beyond the boundaries of nature. This process gives society its dynamic character as well as creates the tension and anxiety "which corresponds to the larger tension of all human existence between nature and spirit."[13]

This tension can be resolved by society in creative or destructive ways. But the ability of a society to choose among alternatives is significantly limited when compared to that of individuals. Although societies "do have the capacity to stand beyond themselves [and] observe and estimate their behavior,"[14] they do not have, as has been previously stated, a single organ of transcendence which allows them to confront and be critiqued by the eternal and the infinite.[15] Freedom, for society, is always more conditioned. It is freedom in terms of finiteness and historical structures.[16] Thus society, as an ethical agent, is limited in its capacity for making moral judgments. Its ethical perspective remains conditioned by its own locus in history.

It is the individual above society who provides the leavening influence for society. For Niebuhr, the moral sense of the community is constituted "of the competitive ideas of its various citizens as individuals about what the conduct of the community should be."[17] Sometimes individuals agree with the moral judgment of society and accept it as their own position. At other times, however, individuals disagree. Then they may choose to go along with the judgment of society out of inertia, ignorance or self-interest; or else they may rise in indeterminate freedom to defy society--a defiance which may be motivated by destructive and/or creative impulses. Finally, it is only the individual who can transcend society "in some act of heroism and sacrifice which defies all rational calculations and points to an ultimate if not eternal end."[18]

In the same way that Niebuhr distinguishes between the individual and society in his discussion of ethical agents, so too does he differentiate between the norms which each type of ethical agent is capable of achieving. According to Niebuhr, only the individual--i.e., the individual above society--is capable of realizing the highest ethical norm of love. For society, the ultimate ethical norm is justice. In the next section, the types of ethical norms and the relationship among them are discussed. A study of this component of Niebuhr's ethical system again reveals his emphasis on the individual above society, and thus on personal ethics in his system.

Ethical Norms: Sacrificial Love,
Mutual Love, and Justice

Niebuhr identifies three ethical norms that guide human action: (1) divine love which becomes, in history, sacrificial, (2) mutual love, and (3) justice. These norms are considered levels of perfection. The trans-historical pinnacle of perfection and Niebuhr's absolute, ultimate norm is sacrificial love. Mutual love is the first level below perfect, sacrificial love and is the highest good of the individual from the standpoint of history. Justice is one level below mutual love and is the only norm society can achieve. A description of each of these norms follows.

Sacrificial Love

The pinnacle of perfection in Niebuhr's ethical system is divine love, revealed in history through the New Testament as sacrificial love or agape. Niebuhr uses Christological assertions to symbolize and clarify this ultimate norm.

Christ is the "Second Adam" whose "essential good-ness . . . is sacrificial, suffering and self-giving love."[19] For Niebuhr, the Cross best expresses Christ's heedless self-sacrifice; "the Cross symbolizes the perfection of agape."[20] Niebuhr also uses the relevant teachings of Jesus to demonstrate that in the gospel "the love ideal is stated unqualifiedly."[21]

For Niebuhr, sacrificial love involves a "heedless-ness towards the interest of the self,"[22] an utter giving of oneself without weighing the consequences to anyone, a disinterestedness that reflects the perfect disinterestedness of divine love. The motive that underlies sacrificial love is obedience to God; that is, conformity to divine love.[23] Unity and frictionless harmony of life with life occurs when the norm of sacrificial love is achieved.[24]

40

Such disinterested love, when it exists in this life, inevitably results in self-sacrifice. As Niebuhr explains:

> The perfect disinterestedness of the divine love can have a counterpart in history only in a life which ends tragically, because it refuses to participate in the claims and counterclaims of historical existence. It portrays a love "which seeketh not its own." But a love which seeketh not its own, is not able to maintain itself in historical society. Not only may it fall victim to excessive forms of the self-assertion of others, but even the most perfectly balanced system of justice in history is a balance of competing wills and interests, and must therefore worst anyone who does not participate in the balance.[25]

The disavowal of power and the refusal to participate in the power struggles of historical existence results in crucifixion. Without power, no force can maintain itself in the world. "The perfect love which [Christ's] life and death exemplify is defeated, rather than triumphant, in the actual course of history."[26] It is the resurrection which symbolizes an ahistorical fulfillment of love.

For Niebuhr, "complete powerlessness, or rather . . . a consistent refusal to use power in the rivalries of history"[27] is the only possible way to symbolize divine goodness. Any participation in power struggles "means the assertion of one ego interest against another"[28]—an act which is contrary to perfected disinterestedness and self-sacrificial love.

According to Niebuhr, Christ's powerlessness gives a trans-historical dimension to his existence which is evident in his attitude and actions. Because Christ is above the vitalities and powers of history, his attitude toward social and political issues is that of complete indifference.[29] His actions are motivated purely by agape and performed irrespective of their personal, social or political consequences.[30] The independent Christian ethic challenges individuals to love in the same way.

41

> We are asked to love our enemies,
> not because the social consequences
> of such love will be to make
> friends of the enemies, but because
> God loves with that kind of impar-
> tiality. We are demanded to forgive
> those who have wronged us, not
> because a forgiving spirit still
> proves redemptive in the lives of
> the fallen, but because God forgives
> our sins. We have a right to view
> the social and political consequences
> of our action in retrospect, but if
> we view it (sic) in prospect, we have
> something less than the best.[31]

Sacrificial love as symbolized by the Cross and expressed in gospel teachings is a revelation of divine love. It is also an expression of human fulfillment.[32] By his death on the cross, Christ indicates the final perfection of human beings.[33] The Cross of Christ is an expression and clarification of the norm given by the very nature of personhood. "The same Christ who is accepted by faith as the revelation of God is also regarded as the true revelation of man."[34]

It is the transcendent self, or the individual above society, who becomes conscious of love as the ab-solute ultimate goal.[35] This contemplative moment of consciousness is a solitary and private one, and leads to a sense of obligation and lack.[36] As Niebuhr writes, "the moral urge [to conform to the law of love] issues out of religious experience"[37] which, as I have already noted, is an individual's experience separate and apart from--that is, above--nature, society and history.[38]

Sacrificial love is the absolute ethical norm of personal ethics which corresponds to the vertical dimen-sion of human existence and the individual above society in Niebuhr's interpretation of sociality. As individ-uals enter into relationship with others, as they become a part of society, the possibility of realizing sacri-ficial love becomes extremely rare. Sacrificial love is history's "impossible possibility."[39] For Niebuhr, mutual love, which is a level below "the pinnacle of love," is the highest good of history[40] and the link between sacrificial love and justice.

42

Mutual Love

Mutual love resembles sacrificial love insofar as it is directed toward the harmony of life with life; but unlike sacrificial love, mutual love is marked by the condition that it be proportionally reciprocated.[41] Although characterized to some degree by "being-for-the other," mutual love is based on considerations of prudence more than on spontaneity and heedless self-giving. This level of love involves the calculation of mutual interests and advantages.[42]

Because a relationship of mutual love is subject to human calculation, it is always tainted by self-interest. As Niebuhr writes, mutual love "is always arrested by reason of the fact that it seeks to relate life to life from the standpoint of the self's own happiness."[43] In mutual love, elements of sacrificial or selfless love and self-love are inextricably mingled.

It is possible for the individual to reach the norm of mutual love in relationship with one other or several others, but attainment of this norm is not possible for society.[44] Self-interest is the basis for the action of society. Given society's inability to act selflessly or sacrificially,[45] justice is the ultimate norm for society.[46]

Justice

Niebuhr identifies two dimensions of justice: "The first is the dimension of rules and laws of justice. The second is the dimension of structures of justice, of social and political organization."[47] It is these two components or dimensions of justice in Niebuhr's social ethics that guide the historical self, or the individual as part of society.

According to Niebuhr, "every society needs working principles of justice."[48] Niebuhr describes these as "definite principles, upon which as upon a loom, the fabric of pragmatic decisions is woven."[49] They are the "rational formulations . . . designed to arbitrate and adjudicate competing claims and competing rights."[50]

Principles of justice are based on experience and reason, as well as Biblical faith. Drawing upon these resources, Niebuhr identifies liberty and equality, achieved within a framework of order, as the regulative principles of justice.[51] The principles of liberty,

43

equality and order permeate the customs and mores of particular historical communities through the ages. These principles are found so frequently in history that they seem to be, for Niebuhr, the common experience of humankind.[52]

Liberty, as a regulative principle of justice, requires that individuals be free to use their unique and creative powers for the good of themselves and society. Liberty is based on an understanding of the human person as having "the capacity for indeterminate transcendence over the processes and limitations of nature."[53] The individual "has a source of authority and an ultimate fulfillment transcending the community."[54] Society must allow for this creativity in its laws and structures.

Equality, as a regulative principle of justice, requires impartiality in the determination of human needs and rights.[55] Based on an appreciation of the worth of each unique individual, this principle asserts that all persons are "to be treated equally, within the terms of the gradation of functions which every healthy society uses for its organization."[56]

Liberty and equality are sought within the framework of a given social order. By social order Niebuhr means the hierarchical organization or arrangement of "the mutually dependent and partially conflicting vitalities" in a particular society. Social order is maintained through organic and artifactual forces of cohesion. Niebuhr equates order with unity, stability, harmony and peace.[57]

These principles of justice are in paradoxical relation to each other. One cannot be applied wholly or in isolation from the others without destroying the community. One cannot be achieved except at the price of another. For example, order is necessary to ensure some degree of equality for men and women with competing interests; but order contradicts, to some extent, the liberty of community members.

Social philosophers throughout history have frequently regarded liberty, equality and order as able to be achieved more easily than, in fact, they are. In contrast, Niebuhr stresses that these principles are not simple possibilities. They are always compromised in practice. Given the limitations of the human condition, "community is not possible without a certain degree of subordination and without a modicum of coercion."[58] How these principles are actually related to each other in concrete situations is as varied as each society is unique.

The second dimension of justice requires that the principles of liberty, equality and order become as historically concrete in the "structures and systems, the organizations and mechanisms of society"[59] as possible. For Niebuhr, the social structures which most effectively assure and promote justice are the ones characterized by "the equilibrium of power."[60] By the equilibrium of power, Niebuhr means "the balance of vitalities and forces in any given social situation."[61] From Niebuhr's perspective there has never been a scheme of justice which did not have a balance of power at its foundation. Conversely, injustice is basically due to irresponsible, inordinate and uncontrolled power. As Niebuhr stresses: "It may be taken as axiomatic that great disproportions of power lead to injustice, whatever may be the efforts to mitigate it."[62]

Equilibrium of power does not develop in society, however, unless there is "a conscious control and manipulation of the various equilibria which exist in it." In order to ensure equilibrium there must be a government, or what Niebuhr calls "the central organizing principle and power." As "organizing center within a given field of social vitalities," government must fulfill the following functions:

> [It] must arbitrate conflicts from
> a more impartial perspective than
> is available to any party of a
> given conflict; it must manage and
> manipulate the processes of mutual
> support so that the tensions
> inherent in them will not erupt into
> conflict; it must coerce submission
> to the social process by supreme
> power whenever the instruments of
> arbitrating and composing conflict
> do not suffice; and finally it must
> seek to redress the disproportions
> of power by conscious shifts of the
> balances whenever they make for
> injustice.[63]

Like the regulative principles of justice, the equilibrium of power and government are in paradoxical relation to each other. Equilibrium of power, without government, "degenerates into anarchy." Government, without an equilibrium of power, becomes tyrannical, "destroy[ing] the vitality and freedom of component elements in the community in the name of 'order.'"[64] It is in the process of developing structures that can prevent anarchy and tyranny, and promote liberty and equality in social life, that a relative justice is achieved in society.

In the preceding pages I have described the norms of sacrificial love, mutual love, and justice in Niebuhr's ethics. In the next section I point out how Niebuhr's interpretation of sociality affects his understanding of the relationship among the norms in his ethical system.

The Relationship Between Ethical Norms

For Niebuhr, the relationship between sacrificial love, mutual love, and justice is a dialectical one which reflects the relationship between the individual above society and the individual as a part of society, between the individual and society.

Sacrificial love, the absolute norm of ethical perfection "has a three-fold relation of transcendence"[65] to mutual love and justice--the norms of history. First, sacrificial love clarifies the historical possibilities of mutual love and justice. Second, it negates the achievements of the norms of history insofar as they contain an admixture of selfishness. When mutual love and justice are confronted with sacrificial love, their failures become clear. From its transcendent perspective, sacrificial love judges the norms of history and finds them lacking.[66] Third, sacrificial love fulfills mutual love and justice. Redemptive and forgiving love closes the chasm between its own ultimate harmony of life with life and the incomplete harmony achieved through mutual love and justice.

This three-fold relationship between sacrificial love and the norms of history is a counterpart to the relation between mutual love and justice. Mutual love clarifies the possibilities of justice. It negates the achievements of justice because all systems, rules and laws governing social relations involve egoism and power conflicts which are a compromise of mutual love.

Finally, mutual love partially completes the incompleteness of justice. Final completion requires sacrificial love.

Although sacrificial love is related to the proximate norms of social ethics and the historical individual in the three ways described, it cannot be achieved in history. This final norm is realized only by the individual above society, outside of history. It is a law for the individual at the transcendent level "which suffers in purity when taken into the intricacies and complexities of social relations."[67] For Niebuhr, "real love between person and person is . . . a relationship between spirit and spirit [which] is a possibility only by way of the love of God."[68]

Freedom provides the individual with the possibility and the capacity for realizing the ethical norms of sacrificial love, mutual love and justice; it also allows for the failure to achieve these norms. There are "unlimited possibilities for good and evil in every human life."[69] In the next section I examine the notions of sin and injustice in order to show how Niebuhr's interpretation of sociality affects his understanding of the failure to achieve ethical norms. Given the ultimate importance of the individual above society in Niebuhr's anthropology, sin, or the failure to achieve the ultimate norm of personal ethics takes precedence in his system over injustice, or the failure to achieve the ultimate norm of social ethics.

The Failure to Achieve Ethical Norms: Sin and Injustice

The paradoxical character of human existence—the fact that human beings are both nature and spirit, the fact that they are both limited by forms and boundaries and free to transcend these limitations—results in persons feeling anxious. Anxiety is an inevitable and permanent dimension of the human condition. Niebuhr repeatedly emphasizes that the human situation is not in itself evil. Anxiety can be a source of creative actions as well as destructive ones, or what in religious terms Niebuhr calls sin.[70]

Sin occurs when individuals are unwilling to put up with the basic ambiguity which is intrinsic to their nature.[71] Although the individual above society recognizes, in contemplation, love as the ultimate norm and thus "feels obligated to conform to the 'law'

47

written in its nature,"[72] the individual as a part of society inevitably "use[s] his freedom to make himself falsely the center of existence."[73]

Sin is, according to Niebuhr, primarily a religious phenomenon which occurs when individuals fail to subject themselves to God in faith and trust in order to cope with anxiety.[74] This lack of faith and trust results in the transcendent self's refusal "to admit 'creature-liness' and acknowledge [it]self as merely a member of the total unity of life."[75] In the effort to escape from the weakness, dependence and insufficiency of the human situation,[76] a person "makes pretensions of being absolute,"[77] of being in the center of the universe, and thus "usurp[s] the prerogatives of God."[78] This is, for Niebuhr, the "original sin"--"the universal inclination of the self to be more concerned with itself than to be embarrassed by its undue claims."[79]

Although sin is primarily a religious phenomenon related to personal ethics, it does have social and moral implications. In order to make the pretensions of being absolute plausible, individuals must control their own destinies by mastering the conditions of finitude--nature, other members of society, history, and even death. To achieve this mastery, persons become involved in the struggle for power in their social relations, and "inevitably subordinate other life to [their] own will[s] and thus do injustice to other life."[80] Injustice, the horizontal dimension of sin, is the failure to achieve the proximate norms of social ethics.

Every relationship is contaminated by sin and in-justice. Some simple relations--e.g., husband and wife, a family, two friends--may come closer to approx-imating the law of love than other more complex ones, but all relationships are "always to some degree an extension of the self."[81] "Common sense," writes Niebuhr, "takes human egotism for granted in all forms of human relations."[82]

Niebuhr argues that "the ethical capacity of the individual is correlated inversely with the size of the group."[83] A social, economic or national group is more arrogant, hypocritical, self-centered and ruthless in the pursuit of its ends than the individual, dyads, or small groups.[84] Niebuhr presents several reasons for this correlation.

First, a group "cumulates the egoism of individuals
and transmutes their individual altruism into collective
egoism so that the egoism of the group has a double
force."[85] Collective self-interest "is a compound of
individual egoism collectively expressed, and the spirit
of loyalty and self-sacrifice of the individual which
the community easily appropriates for its own ends."[86]

Second, the absence of personal and intimate relations between or among the groups which make up society
contributes to the society's predatory inclinations.
In fact, the more powerful a group within society
becomes, the more likely it is to act on its socially
destructive tendencies.[87]

Finally, the lack of a single organ of self-
transcendence which would allow a group to judge its
motives and actions in the light of an ultimate norm
makes human communities more inclined than individuals
to claim perfection, and more prone to absolutize their
accomplishments.

Even though Niebuhr speaks of collective egoism
and social sinfulness, and identifies a number of
factors that strengthen unethical attitudes and actions
in group relations, the individual above society is
still responsible for social injustice. As a member of
the group, it is the individual's own selfishness that
contributes to collective egoism. As is stated in the
discussion on ethical agents,[88] it is the individual's
own choice whether to act in conformity with collective
decisions or to challenge them.[89] In Niebuhr's words:

> While all particular sins have both
> social sources and social conse-
> quences, the real essence of sin can
> be understood only in the vertical
> dimension of the soul's relation to
> God because freedom of the self
> stands outside all relations, and
> therefore has no judge but God. It
> is for this reason that a profound
> insight into the character of sin
> must lead to the confession, "Against
> thee, thee only, have I sinned, and
> done this evil in thy sight."[90]

Even if a person chooses to act morally, in a
moment of transcendence he or she "discovers" that some
degree of conscious dishonesty accompanied the act."[91]

49

The motivation for human choice is never as perfect as it is often assumed to be. This moment of awareness, when the transcendent self understands that "its will is not free to choose between good and evil,"[92] is the ultimate proof of the freedom of the human spirit. This is, for Niebuhr, the ultimate paradox.

> the final exercise of freedom in the
> transcendent human spirit is its
> recognition of the false use of that
> freedom in action. Man is most free
> in the discovery that he is not free.[93]

The individual finds release from this "bondage of the will" in faith and trust in God; release is found in the belief "that only God is able to resolve the conflict between what man is and what he ought to be, a conflict in which all men stand."[94] Thus inevitable and universal sinfulness is ultimately resolved at the transcendent level of divine mercy and forgiveness. "The good news of the gospel is that there is a resource of divine mercy which is able to overcome a contradiction within our own souls which we cannot ourselves overcome."[95] The resurrection of Christ symbolizes triumph over sin and death. It is this assurance of grace which allows individuals some semblance of inner peace while acting in the world.

In the discussion of sin, the distinctive position of the individual separate and apart from society has once again been demonstrated.[96] The primary cause of sin involves a transaction between the individual and God. The choice of sinful actions takes place at the level of the transcendent. The experiences of guilt, remorse or repentance are solitary experiences which occur in confrontation with the absolute. And finally, the awareness of one's ultimate unfreedom and the need for God's mercy and forgiveness for salvation, is a religious profession of faith made by the individual above society.

Summary

In the preceding section the importance of Niebuhr's interpretation of sociality for his ethical system has been discovered by examining three aspects: (1) ethical agents, (2) ethical norms, and (3) the failure to achieve ethical norms. I have shown that, at the horizontal level of human existence, individuals as part of society make decisions together and act together to achieve their goals. Guided by the ethical norm of justice, members of society struggle to establish "tolerable harmonies of life on all levels of community"[97] given the limitations of historical existence and the conditions of sin. I have also indicated the prominent place given to the individual because of the vertical dimension of human existence, or the ability to rise above society. It is the individual who, though operating within a social context, is ultimately responsible for his or her ethical decisions and actions. It is the individual who is capable of achieving the ultimate norm of love which lures, negates and fulfills justice. Finally, it is the individual who is free to fail, be forgiven and redeemed.

Niebuhr consistently maintains the relationship between the two types of ethical agents, between the ultimate and proximate norms, and between sin and injustice. However, in the end, given the discontinuity between the individual and society and the distinctive importance of the individual above society in Niebuhr's interpretation of sociality, it is the elements related to personal ethics--the individual as ethical agent, sacrificial love, and sin--that take precedence in his ethical system.

Within this ethical system, Niebuhr pursues his quest for an acceptable approach to social change.[98] The ethical question he addresses is how to eliminate social injustice in a way that is compatible with the ethical norms of love and justice. In the second major part of this chapter, Niebuhr's approach to social change is described by focusing on three main areas: (1) non-resistance as it relates to sacrificial love, (2) the struggle for social change as it relates to justice, and (3) the relationship between non-resistance and the struggle for social change. Niebuhr's interpretation of sociality, which shapes his ethical system, is evident in his approach to social change as well. It is the individual above society who engages in non-resistance in conformity with the absolute norm of sacrificial love. The individual as a part of society participates in the process of social change according to the proximate norm of justice. This chapter concludes by noting certain limitations in Niebuhr's position. The following description of Niebuhr's approach to social change also serves as preparation for the critical appraisal of Niebuhr's and Ruether's ethics in the concluding chapter.

The Approach to Social Change

Sacrificial Love and Non-resistance

Sacrificial love, let us recall, is a rigorous ethical ideal; it is "an over-arching principle which confronts the Christian in all his relations."[99] However, sacrificial love cannot be immediately applied to socio-political situations because of its disavowal of power and refusal to participate in power struggles. More specifically, though related, sacrificial love is not <u>directly</u> applicable to social ethics and an approach to social change.[100] Sacrificial love is selfless; therefore any form of self-assertion, even if it is on behalf of another or for a "worthy cause" is a compromise of this ultimate ethical norm.[101] Furthermore, sacrificial love, according to Niebuhr's understanding, is ahistorical and universal; therefore, one cannot draw upon this norm for guidance in distinguishing between just and unjust claims of particular groups in history. Sacrificial love does not allow a person to take sides because <u>any</u> "expression of devotion to a parochial community is an expression of imperfection."[102] Niebuhr concludes that the norm of sacrificial love "uncompromisingly enjoins non-resistance."[103]

A life-style of non-resistance, based on sacrificial love, "can be realized only in very limited circles; in ascetic withdrawal from the world and in disavowal of political responsibility."[104] Those who sincerely live according to Christ's rigorous ethic are religious pacifists,[105] and must be prepared for the martyrdom that will most likely come.[106]

For Niebuhr, the importance of non-resistance is symbolic.[107] As Niebuhr writes, non-resistance "as a part of a general ascetic and symbolic portrayal of love absolutism in a sinful world, has its own value and justification."[108] Though symbolically important, those who adopt a stance of non-resistance remove themselves from the political sphere and become individuals separate from or above society. Since the struggle for justice necessarily includes some types of self-assertion and resistance to power, advocates of non-resistance are summoned to renounce "all responsibility for justice which depends upon coercion, explicitly or implicitly."[109]

Furthermore, Niebuhr stresses, any attempt to apply the absolute demand of the Gospel to the morally

ambiguous realities of socio-political life results in
confusion and error, and "may actually imperil the
interests of justice."[110] Niebuhr identifies two
errors[111] which occur when attempting to use non-
resistance in history.

The first error is to weaken the gospel message by
reducing the meaning of non-resistance to non-violent
resistance. In contradistinction, Niebuhr argues that
"there is not the slightest support in Scripture for
this doctrine of non-violence."[112] Christ forbids not
merely violent resistance and coercion but all resistance and coercion. As Niebuhr explains, sacrificial
love in the ethic of Jesus

> expresses itself in terms of a per-
> fectionism which maintains a critical
> vigor against the most inevitable
> and subtle forms of self-asser-
> tion. . . . When . . . the doctrine
> of non-resistance becomes merely an
> injunction against violence in con-
> flict, it ceases to provide a per-
> spective from which the sinful element
> in all resistance, conflict and
> coercion may be discovered.[113]

The second error is that of completely disregard-
ing non-resistance in the political arena; of developing strategies of action totally apart from the gospel
message. Niebuhr rejects this position as well,
stressing that "Christianity is not a flight into
eternity from the tasks and decisions of history."[114]
Rather for Niebuhr, the relationship between non-resistance and the struggle for social change is analogous
to the relationship between love and justice. Before
examining this relationship, however, Niebuhr's understanding of the relationship between justice and the
struggle for social change is discussed.

Justice and the Struggle
for Social Change

The struggle for social change and the elimination
of injustice occurs in society and history where
justice is the norm. Let us recall that "justice is
basically dependent upon a balance of power."[115] In
order to achieve this equilibrium, "the centers of
excessive power which are the bases of injustice"[116]
must be leveled. Niebuhr understands politics to be "a

dangerous game"[117] because "only coercion will effect
this redistribution of privilege and only opposing
power [will] cause a balance of power."[118] But politics
is a necessary game because "all justice that the world
has ever known has been established through tension
between various vitalities, forces and interests in
society."[119]

It is the primary function of government to
balance power; to "redress radical disproportions of
power without . . . becoming the source of new tyrannical power."[120] But, Niebuhr cautions, every government
is always in danger of serving the purpose of the
powerful rather than the common good. The government's
impartiality may be subverted in the interest of and by
the power of the ruling group or groups, and legal
instruments used on behalf of the privileged. When
government aligns itself with the ruling group, an
equitable distribution of power becomes even more
difficult.

Although some morally sensitive individuals may be
persuaded "to grant to others what they claim for themselves,"[121] this is, according to Niebuhr, an impossi-
bility for groups. Those who occupy the dominant positions in society resist efforts to achieve a more equal
redistribution of power and privilege. "It is a fact
of history . . . that no privileged group has every
voluntarily divested itself of power or privilege without pressure from below."[122] Given this pressure from
below, the oligarchs of society may yield certain
privileges . . . but they will not yield the power
which is the source of their privileges without a
struggle."[123]

Ruling groups maintain their positions "by the
covert use of force and their hypocritical pretensions
of virtue."[124] Niebuhr warns that those in power "will
use every device and exploit every policy to escape the
inevitable."[125] These devices include such measures as
economic power, propaganda, the police power of the
state, and traditional processes of government.[126] If
the pressure for redistribution of power continues,
covert use of force may erupt into overt violence.

Another tactic of groups in power is to condemn
disturbances of the peace, while using instruments of
coercion and violence to maintain their own positions
and gain their own ends. Niebuhr remarks ironically:
"So persistent is the cry of peace among the ruling

classes and so strong the seeming abhorrence of every
form of violence and anarchy that one might imagine
them actuated by the purist pacifist principle."[127]
All too often, Christian liberals, moralists and church
leaders support the ruling groups in this approach
(even if unsuspectingly) because of their failure "to
recognize the elements of injustice and coercion which
are present in any contemporary social peace."[128]
These persons, whom Niebuhr calls "nice people,"[129]
seldom experience the reality and brutality of systemic
injustice and thus, for the most part, are unaware of
it.[130]

Within such a social context, there are six major
ethical considerations which guide individuals acting
in society and as a part of society in the development
of a program of action for the pursuit of justice.
These considerations include: (1) the motivation of
the individuals engaged in the process of social change;
(2) the seriousness of the situation; (3) the avail-
ability of human resources; (4) the selection of means
to achieve the desired ends; (5) pragmatic considerations concerning the selection of means; and (6) an
evaluation of the possible consequences of the political activity. Each of these areas are considered in
turn.

Motivation of the Individual

Love[131] intent on justice must be the motive of
individuals participating in the struggle for social
change. Niebuhr writes:

> It is obviously wrong for either the
> individual or the group to pursue
> its interests consistently without
> regard for the interest of other
> individuals or groups who are bound
> to it in the bundle of life.[132]

Even the fact of systemic injustice and the use of
covert force or overt violence by those in power "does
not cancel the element of love [in persons] of conscience who really give themselves to the task of making human relations a little . . . more just."[133]

Individuals must search their hearts and judge
their own motives as carefully as possible in the light
of the standard of love. For Niebuhr, "honesty, or
freedom from self-deception is a most important

instrument of justice."[134]   There are a number of self-
deceptions and unacceptable motives that must be
avoided in the struggle for justice. Victimized and
exploited persons and those supporting them must not be
"driven by blind fury . . . or by false idealism which
gives them an excuse for cruel and unjust methods for
the realization of their goals."[135]   Revolutionaries
must be wary of their claims to love humanity while
"'block[ing] out' the individual."[136]   Intolerance,
vengeance, self-interest, messianism, abstract humanism
combined with hatred for concrete individuals are all
evil or misguided motives and are, therefore, unacceptable motives for persons seeking to eliminate injustice.

     Consideration of motivation is crucial in the
process of decision-making because, according to
Niebuhr, only goodwill or ill-will can be judged as
intrinsically moral or immoral.[137]   Decisions concerning social change cannot be based solely on an individual's motivation, however, for several reasons. First,
motives are basically inaccessible, and also ambiguous
because every political stance involves some degree of
self-interest and will-to-power. Second, the historical context in which one acts is a "bewildering confusion of coercion, conflict of self-interests, domination and subordination."[138]   Regardless of how pure
one's own motives may be, action in the political
sphere results in moral ambiguity. Given this ambiguity and complexity, a relatively pure motive provides a
moral base for participation in the struggle for
justice, but goodwill and the desire for justice are
not enough.

     Besides motivation, Niebuhr suggests other areas
for ethical consideration. Political activists must
ask themselves: (1) how serious is the present social
situation; and (2) are there human resources available
to bring about the needed changes. In order to answer
the first of these two questions, there is a need to
determine "the degree of crisis in which a society
finds itself,"[139] and therefore, according to Niebuhr,
there is a need for social analysis.[140]

The Social Situation

     An analysis of the situation is shaped by the kinds
of facts which a person is willing to consider.[141]
Given the vast array of social data, Niebuhr provides
the following criterion for selecting the facts for
analysis. A person must be "willing to take all

56

elements of experience into account, while particularly stressing those elements which offer resistance to moral norms."[142] For Niebuhr, analysis should focus on existing injustices to the disinherited, the oppressed and the poor. Niebuhr bases this directive on the teachings of "the Old Testament prophets who were the spokesmen of a biased justice in favor of the victims of corrupted power."[143] Consideration of the social situation from the perspective of those suffering from the disequilibrium of power often helps persons to see more clearly the injustices of the present situation.

Niebuhr calls for caution when undertaking social analysis because it may become "an ideological reflection and rationalization of contentious and contending practical politics."[144] Persons must critically appraise analyses--both their own and others--with religious humility joined with skepticism in order to determine if the description of the social situation is, in fact, accurate.

Availability of Human Resources

In addition to consideration of the social situation, available human resources must be studied in order to judge if and to what degree they might be able to mitigate social conflict and contribute to social change. Within any given situation, Niebuhr warns, the process of social change must "do justice to the moral resources and possibilities in human nature and provide for the exploitation of every latent moral capacity in man."[145] For Niebuhr, these resources include social impulses, reason, a moral sense, and religion.

The social impulses, as we have seen, include an impulse of pity and the sense of community. An appeal to the social impulses for harmony in the social order does justice to the law of love which is an essential aspect of human nature.

A second resource for securing a just society is reason. Reason places restraints on human desires and interests, and enables persons to view the claims of others from the wider perspective of the total community. As Niebuhr notes:

> The measure of our rationality deter-
> mines the degree of vividness with
> which we appreciate the needs of
> other life, the extent to which we

> become conscious of the real char-
> acter of our own motives and
> impulses, the ability to harmonise
> conflicting impulses in our own
> life and in society, and the
> capacity to choose adequate means
> for approved ends.[146]

Education is an important tool for enhancing rationality
and increasing the range of human sympathies.[147]

A third resource is a moral sense--that is, "the
peculiar phenomenon of the moral life, usually called
conscience." Conscience is "a sense of obligation
toward the good, however [persons] may define it." As
Niebuhr writes: "Among many human desires, there is a
unique desire, 'the desire to do right.'"[148]

Religion provides the fourth resource. Religion,
with its sense of the absolute, fosters a spirit of
contrition and humility as individuals come to recognize
their own selfishness and finitude.[149] These sentiments
may motivate an individual to move away from self-seek-
ing as a goal of life. Religion, with its emphasis on
love as the highest virtue, "gives transcendent and
absolute worth to the life of the neighbor and thus
encourages sympathy toward him."[150] Love challenges an
individual to affirm life other than his or her own.

Although these resources may be used to bring
about justice, they are limited in their effectiveness.
For example, social impulses are infused with selfishness and the will-to-power. Reason is subject to
partiality and susceptible to "ideological taint."
Education can only do so much to convert oppressors
from selfishness to unselfishness. Moral sentiment may
be the "oil which reduces the frictions of a given
system of social relationships, but it changes the relationships only in the rarest instances."[151] And religion, with its sense of the absolute, may lead an
individual to withdraw from the world or to despair.
Religious introspection "may involve the soul in hopeless obsession with self."[152]

For Niebuhr, an approach to social change must
first "exploit every available resource of altruistic
impulse and reason to extend life from selfish to
social ends."[153] If these resources prove to be in-
sufficient in establishing a just equilibrium of power,
which Niebuhr predicts they will because of their

limitations, "political power and political coercion become a necessity."[154] In the selection of strategies and tactics for a program of action, all methods, short of violent conflict must first be explored.

The Selection of Means

Violence is, for Niebuhr, the "ultima ratio," a matter of last resort. Even though coercion is the core of both violent and non-violent means for social change,[155] non-violence has a moral priority over violence.[156] As part of the law of love, human beings have a duty not to harm each other. The rule of non-violence "is seen as binding although not as conclusive as one's actual obligations in particular situations which may well present conflicting claims."[157] If in certain circumstances this rule must be suspended, it should still "affect the way the act is performed and what the agent does later. . . . Certainly [it] should affect his mental attitude, as expressed in regret and perhaps remorse."[158]

There are times when it is judged necessary to violate the moral duty not to harm anyone, and to suspend the immediate and less inclusive values of respect for life and property in order to achieve the more ultimate and inclusive value of justice.[159] At this point, an ethical consideration becomes: "What are the political possibilities for establishing justice through violence?"[160] Pragmatic justification must be given for the means selected.

Pragmatic Considerations

Pragmatically there are a number of reasons for preferring non-violence to violence. Niebuhr identifies this position as pragmatic pacifism. It is "the attempt to mitigate the contest between opposing forces by means of social imagination, intelligence and arbitration. [It] utilize[s] political arguments to demonstrate that violence should be avoided."[161]

Niebuhr's pragmatic reasons for preferring non-violence include the following. Violence tends to destroy, or at least lessen, the amount of social cooperation.[162] Therefore, there is a greater possibility of social disintegration once persons resort to violent means.[163] Violence also "stiffens the moral conceit of dominant groups and gives a measure of plausibility to their insistence that the challenge of

their dominance is a threat against law and order."[164]
Violence allows oppressors to play the role of
defenders of society.[165]

In addition, the use of violent means creates
greater resentment and animosities, leading to an
escalation of violence by both sides and frequently
resulting in an undue use of force by the ruling
majority against the minority.[166] Thus violence is a
particularly dangerous weapon "for an oppressed group
which is hopelessly in the minority and has no possibility of developing sufficient power to set against
its oppressors."[167] The use of violence must also be
judged inappropriate if there are too few persons in
society who feel hopeless.[168]

There must also be sufficient leadership, intellectual depth, moral purpose, strategic skills, technical efficiency, and physical strength if violent means
are to be used. Without these components, violence is
not a justifiable alternative and non-violence is to be
preferred. For Niebuhr, once violent means are justified, they may be used; but "the terror [of violent
tactics] must have the tempo of a surgeon's skill and
healing must follow quickly upon its wounds."[169]

Possible Consequences

The last area for ethical consideration in the
process of social change is the possible consequences
of a program of action. Even though "political action
proceeds in small steps of which the consequences can
either not be foreseen at all, or are only visible in
the vaguest and dimmest outline,"[170] some speculation
concerning the cost--especially in terms of lives lost
and social chaos created--must be attempted. Niebuhr
recognizes, however, that there are times when

> peoples and nations which face an
> imminent threat of enslavement do
> not make nice calculations of
> alternative consequences. There
> are critical moments in history
> when such calculations become
> irrelevant. Every instinct of
> survival and every decent impulse
> of humanity becomes engaged and
> prompts resistance, no matter what
> the consequences.[171]

60

These then, according to Niebuhr, are the ethical considerations which shape an approach to social change. An acceptable program of action must be based on and include the following: (1) a motive of (at least relative) goodwill; (2) an adequate analysis of the situation; (3) the use of available human resources to ease the conflict and bring about social change; (4) an option for non-violence whenever possible; (5) a careful consideration of pragmatic matters; and (6) the weighing of the consequences of political action.

This process must be employed for every social situation because "empirical reality is too complicated to determine once and for all what is the right application of moral norms in all cases."[172] Political activists must continually reassess the social situation to determine which factors have varied, and which have remained constant, in order to revise their program of action in the light of the new social data.

There are many dangers involved in the struggle for social change. By considering a program of action in relationship to non-resistance, some of the risks can be minimized. This relationship between non-resistance and the process of social change is analogous to the relationship between love and justice in Niebuhr's ethical system.

Non-resistance and the Struggle for Social Change

Non-resistance challenges Christian activists to remember "the 'dignity' of the person which makes it illegitimate for any community to debase the individual into a mere instrument of social process and power and try to obscure the fact of his ultimate destiny."[173] Non-resistance is a constant reminder that "the true end of man is brotherhood and love is the law of life."[174]

Non-resistance also stands in judgment "over all the elements of coercion and conflict which destroy [this] . . . fellowship."[175] It reveals the moral ambiguity--the self-interest and the will-to-power-- involved in the power struggles to bring about a just society. Niebuhr maintains that a pure pacifist position, or a position of non-resistance, reminds political activists "not to regard the pressures and counter-pressures, the tensions, the overt and covert conflicts by which justice is achieved and maintained as finally and ultimately normative."[176]

Non-resistance also serves as a corrective for the romantic illusion that any program of action in society can have redemptive effects; that it can create a new social order free from all forms of injustice--"a social order in which conflict of interest and selfish impulses [are] finally and completely abolished."[177] Confronted with the ideal of non-resistance, men and women are reminded to pursue justice in terms of achievable moral ends and not utopian ideals, because "every solution . . . gives rise to a new form of the particular problem."[178] "Human egoism and collective will-to-power will reduce the justice actually achieved by every new society to something less than perfect justice."[179]

Finally, non-resistance "helps keep alive an uneasy conscience."[180] It allows a person "to transcend a conflict while standing in it,"[181] to engage in the struggle for justice but without self-righteousness and pride and "with a religious reservation in which lie the roots of the spirit of forgiveness."[182]

Conclusion

In the second part of this chapter I have been concerned with Niebuhr's approach to social change as it relates to his ethical system. Niebuhr's approach provides further evidence of his struggle to relate personal and social ethics in his ethical system, and the vertical and horizontal dimensions of being human in his interpretation of sociality.

In Niebuhr's approach to social change, ethical considerations concerning motivation pertain to personal ethics and the vertical dimension--the individual above society. The transcendent self, having contemplated original righteousness and inevitable sinfulness, having recognized the ultimate end of existence and the inability to realize this norm in history, enters into social relations and political activity with humility and trust in God's mercy and forgiveness.

Other ethical considerations apart from motivation, pertain to social ethics and the horizontal dimension-- the individual as a part of society. These areas, as I have already noted, involve careful calculation and consideration of self-interest and power within a given social situation. Regardless of what decisions are made by a group of individuals, acting in history as a part of society, non-resistance, an expression of sacrificial love, stands as a judge against all programs of action for social change. The non-resistance of an individual above society is a reminder that a perfect social order characterized by frictionless harmony and pure disinterestedness is realized only in God.

Niebuhr interrelates personal ethics and social ethics in his ethical system, and non-resistance and the struggle for justice in his approach to social change. However, because of the distinction between the individual above society (the transcendent self) and the individual as part of society (the historical self), and because of the primacy of the vertical dimension of human existence, Niebuhr's ethical system and approach to social change is limited in its understanding of (1) the moral responsibility of persons-in-relation, (2) the place of love and the heroic in political action, (3) social sin, and (4) the realization of the absolute ultimate norm through the struggle for justice. These notions require an integration of the elements in Niebuhr's ethical system--an integration which is not possible given Niebuhr's interpretation of sociality. In an ethical system based on an interpretation of sociality drawn from radical social thought, these limitations are overcome. Before presenting such an ethical system, the notion of sociality which serves as the criterion of adequacy is developed, and its congruency with Ruether's interpretation is shown.

Notes

[1]In his earlier writings, Niebuhr insists on a much greater disjunction between the two ethics. In his later works he lessens the gap by focusing on the persistent egoism of individuals as well as the creative possibilities of communities. Niebuhr describes this change as one which allows for "a more consistent 'realism' in regard to both individual and collective behavior" (MNHC, p. 22). Although Niebuhr comes to emphasize the limitless possibilities of both individuals and communities, he continues to warn against the complexity, impersonality and mechanization of modern society which tend to diminish personalities, lessen social cohesion and aggravate the vices which dehumanize life. See, for example, Reinhold Niebuhr on Politics, ed. Harry R. Davis and Robert C. Good (New York: Charles Scribner's Sons, 1960), p. 4; REE, pp. 70, 116;

and DCNR, pp. 5, 13-14, 17.

[2]PSA, p. 127.

[3]See SDH, pp. 91, 139-40.

[4]NDM, 1:255.

[5]PSA, p. 127.

[6]NDM, 1:255. Self-deception and/or habit may lessen the ability to feel remorse or repentance but can never completely destroy the uneasy conscience (ibid., p. 256).

[7]NDM, 1:255.

[8]SDH, p. 14.

[9]The ability of individuals to defy their communities is one proof of the irreducibility of moral obligation. Niebuhr qualifies this proof by stating that this defiance is usually done in the name of another community, even if it exists only in the imagination. But for Niebuhr, even the fact of "competition between communities for the loyalty of the individual serve[s] to bring . . . individual decision into sharp relief" (ibid., pp. 15, 38).

[10]Ibid., p. 128. And, Niebuhr adds in response to psychoanalytic theorists, "despite the possible inhibiting forces in [the self's] own sub-rational nature upon the power of its will" (ibid.). Niebuhr's position resembles the description of ethical individualism submitted by Steven Lukes in Individualism (Oxford: Basil Blackwell, 1973). Lukes writes that a "relevant feature of human beings which marks them out as persons in the context of moral judgments . . . is the capacity to form intentions and purposes, to become aware of alternatives and make choices between them, and to acquire control over their own behavior by becoming conscious of the forces determining it, both internally, as with repressed or subconscious desires and motives, and externally, as with the pressures exerted by the norms they follow or the roles they fill" (p. 131; see also p. 52). This and other portions of Lukes' writings give support to the argument of this study that Niebuhr is, ultimately, an ethical individualist.

[11]Minnema, Social Ethics, p. 36. See also SNE,

64

p. 134.

[12]Minnema writes: "Society is a reflection of the structure of man. Society is a historical magnitude which Niebuhr approaches through the nature of man" (Social Ethics, p. 116).

[13]Ibid., p. 29. For Niebuhr, "the most important similarity between the life of individuals and collective organisms is that the latter, like the former, have the same sense of the contingent and insecure cnaracter of human existence and they seek by the same pride and lust for power to overcome that security" (FH, p. 218; see also Dennis McCann, Christian Realism and Liberation Theology [Maryknoll, New York: Orbis Books, 1981], p. 63).

[14]IAH, p. 82, emphasis added.

[15]See SDH, p. 40; also see above, p. 37. To state this difference simply, in their transcendence societies may look "down upon" themselves in history, but not "up at" the ultimate.

[16]NDM, 2:78. For Niebuhr, "when individuality turns into plurality there are postulated limitations and boundaries. Freedom can no longer be experienced as the limitlessness of infinity and eternity, but must come closer to nature with its limits and demarcations" (Minnema, Social Ethics, p. 34).

[17]SDH, p. 235.

[18]SNE, p. 138.

[19]FH, p. 171.

[20]NDM, 2:40. As John Bennett emphasizes: "Niebuhr's ultimate reference in ethics is always to the perfect love revealed in the Cross of Christ, the suffering love of one who sought nothing for himself, the love directed toward all neighbors" (Bennett, "Reinhold Niebuhr's Social Ethics," p. 52). Gordon Harland also emphasizes the importance of the Cross in Niebuhr's ethical system. He writes: "The Christocentric character of Niebuhr's thought is of paramount significance for his ethics. His concern is ever to show how the agape of the Cross illumines the whole meaning of our existence and provides both insight and resource for the responsible living of our life. At

the cross we discern that love which is the norm, the
law of human life" (The Thought of Reinhold Niebuhr
[New York: Oxford University Press, 1960], p. 3).

[21]REE, p. 211. See also ICE, chapter 2, pp. 43-62.

[22]FH, p. 171.

[23]NDM, 2:74.

[24]Ibid., p. 81.

[25]Ibid., p. 72.

[26]FH, p. 135.

[27]NDM, 2:72.

[28]Ibid.

[29]Reinhold Niebuhr, "The Ethic of Jesus and the
Social Problem," Religion in Life 1 (Spring 1932):199-
200; see also REE, p. 214. Hammar expresses Niebuhr's
position on the trans-historical dimension of Jesus in
these terms: "Jesus does not deal with the immediate
moral problems, with politics, economy and social relations. The ethic of Jesus does not regard the horizontal plane; it deals with the vertical plane. The per-
fectionist ethic of love does not compromise with 'the
natural self-regarding impulses' or with 'the necessary
prudent defenses of the self, required because of the
egoism of others'" (Christian Realism, p. 212). Hammar
criticizes Niebuhr for his essentially non-historical
image of Christ.

[30]Niebuhr, "Ethics of Jesus," p. 200.

[31]Ibid., pp. 199-200.

[32]SDH, p. 232.

[33]NDM, 2:68.

[34]NDM, 1:146.

[35]Niebuhr also speaks of this as the moral intui-
tion of original righteousness. See SDH, p. 14.

[36]Harland explains this sense of lack in these
words: "Man's essential nature is . . . not an immanent

possession of the historical self. It is apprehended
by virtue of the self's capacity for self-transcendence
as that which it lacks but which is nevertheless the
law of its being" (The Thought of Reinhold Niebuhr, p.
18).

[37]DCNR, p. 116.

[38]Minnema, reflecting on Niebuhr's position,
writes: "The individual believer is the one who, in
the final analysis, mysteriously touches the sphere
where an undialectical and unambiguous fulfillment can
be momentarily sensed" (Social Ethics, p. 90).

[39]See ICE, chapter 4, pp. 97-123, especially pp.
97-99; also NDM, 2:76.

[40]NDM, 2:68-69; and Minnema, Social Ethics, p. 58.

[41]See NDM, 1:68-70, 78; FH, p. 185; CRPP, p. 160;
and Bennett, "Reinhold Niebuhr's Social Ethics," p. 57.

[42]This is true, for Niebuhr, even for a small
number of individuals such as a family or group of
friends.

[43]NDM, 2:82.

[44]In Niebuhr's words: "A relation between the
self and one other may be partly ecstatic; and in any
case the calculation of relative interests may be
reduced to a minimum. But as soon as a third person is
introduced into the relation even the most perfect love
requires a rational estimate of conflicting needs and
interests" (ibid., p. 248).

[45]Because society lacks an organ of transcendence
it is unable to "sacrifice its life." There is no
central power that can be identified with all the members which allows for such a decision. (See Veldhuis,
Realism Versus Utopianism?, p. 49).

[46]It is important to note that Niebuhr's use of
the term "justice" is complex. At times Niebuhr uses
justice in a general sense to refer to the whole field
of human relations. More often, Niebuhr uses justice
to refer "both to the ends of politics, the general
principles and standards according to which society
ought to be organized, and to the social structures,
techniques and institutions through which such ends may

best be achieved" (Harry Davis, "The Political Philosophy of Reinhold Niebuhr" [Ph.D. dissertation, University of Chicago, 1951], p. 143).

[47]NDM, 2:247. Niebuhr goes on to describe three levels of the first dimension of rules and laws: (1) laws and principles abstractly conceived; (2) ideal and abstract principles which have been compromised by "the hopes and fears, the pressures and counter-pressures of living communities"; and (3) the embodiment of these diluted ideals of justice in historical or "civil" law (ibid., pp. 247-250, 257).

[48]CLCD, p. 71.

[49]Reinhold Niebuhr, "The Problem of a Protestant Social Ethic," Union Seminary Quarterly Review 15 (November 1959):9.

[50]FH, p. 189. It is important to note that these principles are not universal-eternal ideals in the sense, for example, of the natural law tradition. As Stone points out: "The notion that there are laws of any kind which can be relied upon to furnish universal-eternal ideals is rejected by Niebuhr. Scripture, reason and nature do not provide universally valid concepts of justice for all time" (Reinhold Niebuhr, p. 232). For Niebuhr, the natural law tradition, with its norms drawn from classical ontology and the notion of "essence," obscures the complex relation of human freedom and historical possibilities. Furthermore, it erroneously exempts reason from finiteness and/or sin and then confidently derives universal rational norms from reason. For a further development of Niebuhr's position on natural law, see SDH, pp. 101-102; Reinhold Niebuhr, "Reply," in Kegley and Bretall, eds. Reinhold Niebuhr, pp. 434-36; and Veldhuis, Realism Versus Utopianism?, p. 111.

[51]Although, as Davis points out, "Niebuhr seems never to have attempted to relate these three concepts to each other in systematic fashion, they recur again and again in his books and articles--so often that they emerge quite clearly as the major elements which comprise his interpretation of justice" ("Political Philosophy," p. 152).

[52]CRPP, p. 148. Niebuhr counts heavily on the fact that liberty, equality and order are recognized as principles of justice in practically all theories of

natural law, including the Stoic, medieval and modern. See NDM, 2:245; as well as Ramsey, "Love and Law," in Kegley and Bretall, eds., Reinhold Niebuhr, p. 94.

[53]CLCD, p. 3.

[54]PSA, p. 68.

[55]Bennett, "Reinhold Niebuhr's Social Ethics," p. 58.

[56]PSA, p. 77. Niebuhr resists positions on equality which fail to recognize that "arbitrary and contingent factors of natural inequalities and social heritages" ("Christian Faith and the Common Life," as cited in Davis, "Political Philosophy," p. 157), as well as "differences of need or of social function make the attainment of complete equality in society impossible" (NDM, 2:255).

[57]See, for example, Reinhold Niebuhr, "The Nation's Crime Against the Individual," Atlantic Monthly, November 1916, pp. 609-14; and PSA, chapter 5, pp. 61-77.

[58]Niebuhr, Reinhold Niebuhr on Politics, p. 327. Niebuhr continues with this comment: "Naturally the debate on how much or how little of either subordination or coercion is necessary or desirable is endless" (ibid., p. 327).

[59]NDM, 2:257.

[60]Ibid.

[61]Ibid. Niebuhr's understanding of power is threefold. First, power is morally neutral. It is "simply the vitality of human life and is synonymous with energy." Secondly, however, given the human condition, power is primarily understood as "an outgrowth of man's pride and his false attempt to gain security by dominating other men. . . . It [is] the capacity to impose one's will upon the other." Finally, power is "a necessary expression of social organization and coercion" (Stone, Reinhold Niebuhr, p. 176).

[62]NDM, 2:262. See also Reinhold Niebuhr, Beyond Tragedy (New York: Charles Scribner's Sons, 1937), p. 102, hereafter cited as BT; and CLCD, p. 174.

[63]NDM, 2:266.

[64]Ibid., pp. 266-67.

[65]NDM, 2:258.

[66]ICE, pp. 128, 206.

[67]CRPP, p. 168.

[68]NDM, 1:294. See also NDM, 2:296-97.

[69]SDH, p. 91.

[70]NDM, 1:182-85.

[71]Reinhold Niebuhr, Love and Justice, ed. D. B. Robertson (Gloucester, Mass.: Peter Smith, 1976), p. 47, hereafter cited as LJ; and FH, p. 118.

[72]SDH, p. 14.

[73]CRPP, p. 131. Human beings sin inevitably due, in part, to the anxiety and temptation that lie in the human condition. But, Niebuhr claims, "the situation of finiteness and freedom would not lead to sin if sin were not already introduced into the situation." One must conclude, then, that evil has existed in the world prior to any human action and that "evil brings forth evil." The devil in Biblical thought symbolizes the evil that has been a part of history since the beginning. Therefore, for Niebuhr, even though freedom is the basis of both creative and destructive acts, the latter have been predominant; even though love is the law of existence, sin is the law of history (NDM, 1:251, 254).

[74]NDM, 1:252.

[75]Ibid., p. 16. As Niebuhr succinctly states: "Man is mortal. That is his fate. Man pretends not to be mortal. That is his sin" (BT, p. 29).

[76]NDM, 2:253.

[77]ICE, p. 74. As Niebuhr writes: individuals make "abortive efforts to hide their insignificance by various forms of self-worship" (SNE, p. 90).

[78]FH, p. 121.

[79]<u>SDH</u>, p. 18.

[80]<u>NDM</u>, 1:179.

[81]Reinhold Niebuhr, "A Christian Philosophy of Compromise," <u>The Christian Century</u> 50 (June 7, 1933): 746.

[82]<u>SDH</u>, p. 135.

[83]Thomas R. McFaul, "Reinhold Niebuhr: An Alleged 'Individualist,'" <u>Religion in Life</u> 42 (Summer 1973):199.

[84]<u>NDM</u>, 1:208.

[85]George A. Coe and Reinhold Niebuhr, "Two Communications," <u>The Christian Century</u> 50 (March 15, 1933): 363.

[86]Niebuhr, <u>Reinhold Niebuhr on Politics</u>, pp. 332-33. Even if the individual members are persons of the greatest goodwill, their virtue is channeled into loyalty to the group, increasing the group's selfishness.

[87]McFaul, "Reinhold Niebuhr," p. 199; see also <u>NDM</u>, 1:208.

[88]See p. 39.

[89]Niebuhr regrets that "those who possess the courage to assert themselves against the community are few in number" ("Morality," p. 149).

[90]<u>NDM</u>, 1:257.

[91]Ibid., p. 255.

[92]Ibid., p. 258.

[93]Ibid., p. 260.

[94]Reinhold Niebuhr, "Ten Years That Shook My World," <u>The Christian Century</u> 56 (April 26, 1939):544.

[95]<u>CPP</u>, p. 2. See also <u>CRPP</u>, pp. 183-84; and <u>PSA</u>, pp. 137-40.

[96]Niebuhr emphasizes this point by quoting

Kierkegaard: "The concept of sin and guilt presupposes the individual as individual" (NDM, 1:263).

[97]Niebuhr, "Nation's Crime," p. 81.

[98]Although there is a consistency in Niebuhr's ethical system that allows for a continuity in his approach to social change, there are also several major shifts in Niebuhr's thinking regarding pacifism and revolution, that influence the way he applies his ethics to the particular events of his day. The focus of this study is on the continuities in Niebuhr's approach to social change. For extensive discussions of the shifts in Niebuhr's position, see Paul Merkley, Reinhold Niebuhr: A Political Account (Montreal and London: McGill-Queen's University Press, 1975); and Stone, Reinhold Niebuhr. Several articles are also useful: Bennett, "Reinhold Niebuhr's Social Ethics," especially pp. 64-67; James Childress, "Reinhold Niebuhr's Critique of Pacifism," The Review of Politics 36 (October 1974):467-91; and Dennis McCann, "Reinhold Niebuhr and Jacques Maritain on Marxism: A Comparison of Two Traditional Models of Practical Theology," Journal of Religion 58 (April 1978):140-68.

[99]Angus Dun and Reinhold Niebuhr, "God Wills Both Justice and Peace," Christianity and Crisis 15 (June 13, 1955):75.

[100]Ibid.

[101]Franklin I. Gamwell, "Reinhold Niebuhr's Theistic Ethic," in The Legacy of Reinhold Niebuhr, ed. Nathan A. Scott (Chicago and London: The University of Chicago Press, 1974), p. 67.

[102]PSA, p. 116.

[103]CPP, p. 10. This interpretation of Jesus' ethic is controversial. There are those who maintain that the gospel ethic is that of non-violent resistance as well as those who propose that Jesus came to overthrow the system of his day and advocated revolutionary tactics to do so. For various discussions of this issue see Richard J. Cassidy, Jesus, Politics, and Society (Maryknoll, New York: Orbis Books, 1978); Jean Lasserre, War and the Gospel (Scottdale, Pa.: Herald Press, 1974); and John H. Yoder, The Politics of Jesus (Grand Rapids, Michigan: William B. Eerdmans Publishing Company, 1972).

[104]REE, p. 178.

[105]Religious pacifism differs from pragmatic pacifism, which is described on pp. 59-60.

[106]CPP, p. 89.

[107]Stone, Reinhold Niebuhr, p. 175.

[108]ICE, p. 168; see also p. 167.

[109]Stone, Reinhold Niebuhr, p. 75.

[110]ICE, p. 147. See also Reinhold Niebuhr, "Idealists as Cynics," Nation, 150 (January 20, 1940): 73.

[111]Niebuhr also calls these errors, heresies (see CPP, pp. 1-32).

[112]Ibid., p. 10.

[113]ICE, pp. 53, 52.

[114]Niebuhr, "Ten Years," p. 545.

[115]CPP, p. 104.

[116]REE, pp. 230-31.

[117]Niebuhr, as cited in Davis, "Political Philosophy," p. 111.

[118]Frederick W. Gunti, "Conflict and Reconciliation in the Thought of Reinhold Niebuhr," The American Ecclesiastical Review 168 (April 1974):227.

[119]LJ, p. 276.

[120]Harland, The Thought of Reinhold Niebuhr, p. 52.

[121]Niebuhr, "Ethic of Jesus," p. 203.

[122]Reinhold Niebuhr, "Socialism and Christianity," The Christian Century 48 (August 19, 1931):1039.

[123]Reinhold Niebuhr, "Making Radicalism Effective," The World Tomorrow 16 (December 21, 1933):682.

[124]Niebuhr, "Ethic of Jesus," p. 207.

[125]Reinhold Niebuhr, "A New Strategy for Social-ists," The World Tomorrow 16 (August 31, 1933):492.

[126]MMIS, p. 333.

[127]Ibid., p. 139.

[128]Ibid., p. 233.

[129]REE, p. 142.

[130]Reinhold Niebuhr, "Is Peace or Justice the Goal?" The World Tomorrow 15 (September 21, 1932):275.

[131]Here I am using love to mean mutual love in dialectical relationship to sacrificial love.

[132]SNE, p. 30.

[133]Bennett, "Reinhold Niebuhr's Social Ethics," p. 58. See also LJ, pp. 218-22.

[134]Reinhold Niebuhr, "The Quality of Our Lives," The Christian Century 77 (May 11, 1960):569.

[135]Bennett, "Reinhold Niebuhr's Social Ethics," p. 60.

[136]D. R. Davies, Reinhold Niebuhr: Prophet from America (5 Wardrobe Place, Carter Lane, London, E.C. 4: James Clarke & Company, 1945), pp. 80, 82. Niebuhr considers this tendency to be "the abiding sin of reformers and revolutionaries" (ibid., p. 80).

[137]MMIS, pp. 170-75.

[138]John A. Hutchinson Christian Faith and Social Action (New York, London: Charles Scribner's Sons, 1953), p. 236.

[139]MMIS, p. 230.

[140]Theodore Gill suggests that Niebuhr's emphasis on social analysis and the use of the social sciences is one of his greatest contributions to Christian thought (as cited in Stone, Reinhold Niebuhr, p. 93). Throughout Niebuhr's career, the observation and inter-pretation of social data is always an important compon-ent of his work (see, for example, Davies, Reinhold Niebuhr, p. 72).

For Niebuhr, social analysis is most useful when it is only "a modest undertaking." Niebuhr recommends low-level, empirically-oriented social science in which "the field of inquiry is reduced to some manageable set of uniformities or recurrences in the behavior of individuals subject to the same set of natural or historical circumstances." These empirical studies are most apt to take into account "the uncalculable freedom of man . . . [and] variable conditioning circumstances." It is this type of social analysis that Niebuhr sees as contributing to the accuracy of pragmatic considerations concerning the use of violent means (SDH, p. 46).

Niebuhr is wary of the broad generalizations in social analysis because they are "hazardous and speculative" (ibid., p. 45; see also Stone, Reinhold Niebuhr, p. 102). Although cycles, recurrences and analogies do occur in history, "endless contingencies supervene upon the recurrences [due to] the complexity of the causal chain and the fact that human agents intervene unpredictably in the course of events" (CRPP, pp. 84, 91). Therefore, no scientific investigations of past behavior can become the basis of predictions of future behaviors" (SDH, p. 47). If social scientists claim to have understood the meaning of history or comprehended its pattern, they have falsified or negated some of the facts (ibid., p. 49).

Niebuhr also describes social analysis simply as paying attention to the empirical situation in which people find themselves. At times Niebuhr takes into account the effect of basic presuppositions and conceptual schemes on the interpretation of reality, especially when he speaks of "ideological taint." More often this type of relationship is not made explicit.

[141] In Niebuhr's words: "Every moral decision very much depends on the facts which one is willing to take into account, besides the moral norms to which one refers" (as cited in Veldhuis, Realism Versus Utopianism?, p. 117).

[142] Ibid., p. 108.

[143] Ibid., p. 115. See also PSA, pp. 91-94; and SNE, p. 173.

[144] CRPP, p. 82.

[145] MMIS, p. xxiv.

[146] Ibid., pp. 27-28.

[147]Ibid., p. 28.

[148]Ibid., pp. 37-38.

[149]The introspective character of religion makes this recognition more likely.

[150]MMIS, p. 57.

[151]REE, p. 232.

[152]MMIS, p. 60.

[153]REE, p. 229.

[154]MMIS, pp. 32, 164.

[155]Niebuhr distinguishes between violent and non-violent means in the following way. "The distinguishing marks of violent coercion and conflict are usually held to be its intent to destroy either life or property. This distinction is correct if consequences are not confused with intent. Non-violent conflict and coercion may also result in the destruction of life or property and they usually do. The difference is that destruction is not intended but the inevitable consequence of non-violent coercion. The chief difference between violence and non-violence is not in the degree of destruction which they cause, though the degree is usually considerable, but the aggressive character of one and the negative character of the other. Non-violence is essentially non-co-operation. It expresses itself in the refusal to participate in the ordinary processes of society" (MMIS, p. 240).

[156]Violence is not, however, intrinsically evil unless it proceeds from ill-will; and violence is not considered a "natural and inevitable expression of ill-will" (ibid., pp. 171-72). "The type of power used by the will to effect its purposes does not determine the quality of the purpose or motive" (NDM, 2:261, n. 3). Niebuhr emphasizes that the motives of those who opt for violent means to bring about justice certainly need "not [be] less moral than the motives of those who defend special privileges by more covert means of coercion" (MMIS, p. 170).

[157]Childress, "Critique of Pacifism," p. 488.

[158]Ibid., pp. 488-89. Childress argues persua-

sively for this _prima facie_ interpretation of non-violence in Niebuhr's thought.

[159]Niebuhr is very clear that he is suggesting a _qualified_ means-end argument. "Any end does not justify any means, for every possible value does not deserve the subordination of every other possible value to it" (_MMIS_, p. 174).

[160]Ibid., p. 80.

[161]Stone, _Reinhold Niebuhr_, p. 75.

[162]_MMIS_, p. 251.

[163]_ICE_, p. 169.

[164]Niebuhr, "Peace or Justice," p. 276.

[165]Hammar, _Christian Realism_, p. 198.

[166]_ICE_, p. 169.

[167]_MMIS_, p. 252.

[168]Niebuhr maintains that there must be a large enough segment of the population who "disavow[s] the slow method of political action for the quicker but dubious method of violence" ("Political Action and Social Change," _The World Tomorrow_ 12 [December 1929]: 493).

[169]_MMIS_, p. 220.

[170]Hans J. Morgenthau, "The Influence of Reinhold Niebuhr in American Political Life and Thought," in _Reinhold Niebuhr: A Prophetic Voice in Our Time_, ed. Harold R. Landon (Greenwich, Connecticut: Seabury Press, 1962), pp. 105-06.

[171]_CPP_, pp. 43-44.

[172]Veldhuis, _Realism Versus Utopianism?_, p. 116.

[173]Reinhold Niebuhr, "Theology and Political Thought in the Western World," _The Ecumenical Review_ 9 (April 1957):258.

[174]_CPP_, p. 31.

[175]Ibid., p. 22.

[176]NDM, 2:72.

[177]REE, p. 210.

[178]Davies, Reinhold Niebuhr, p. 63.

[179]Niebuhr, "Marx, Barth and Israel's Prophets," p. 140.

[180]Childress, "Critique of Pacifism," p. 474.

[181]Reinhold Niebuhr, "Christian Faith and Natural Law," Theology 40 (February 1940):93.

[182]Niebuhr, as cited in Hammar, Christian Realism, p. 223.

CHAPTER IV

ESSENTIAL SOCIALITY: THE CRITERION
OF ADEQUACY

In tracing the development of the human self,
studies in anthropology indicate that in primitive
societies a sense of the individual apart from the
group was limited or non-existent. In these early
societies, the primary unit was the tribe, clan, or
extended family. A similar understanding characterizes
medieval thinking in which "'individual' meant 'inseparable'. . . . [T]o describe an individual was to give
an example of the group of which he was a member."[1]
Changes in the social fabric of medieval society, and
new political and religious doctrines which challenged
medieval orthodoxy, contributed to the emergence of a
different understanding of human nature. The human
self was no longer identified with his or her role in
society, but was considered an "individual in his own
right."[2]

Since the development of this conception of "the
individual in his own right," sociality, or the social
dimension of the human condition has come to be interpreted in a number of ways. For some philosophers,
sociality refers to the external relations of radically
separate individuals. These relations may be viewed as
precarious and threatening, and/or as contractual or
quasi-contractual relationships of persons "who agree,
as it were, to be social."[3] Although the degree of
animosity among individuals may differ,[4] those who
ascribe to this interpretation agree that social bond-
ing occurs among mutually autonomous and independent
entities.

Another interpretation of sociality depicts human
beings as innately social and destined to live in
community. Persons require membership in society by
virtue of their dignity and their needs. In this view,
social relations are essential for survival and fulfillment, but the individual is still considered as existing prior (perhaps not temporally, but ontologically)
to social life. It is the relatively autonomous pre-
constituted person who enters into social relations.[5]
As I have demonstrated in Chapters II and III, Reinhold
Niebuhr interprets sociality in this manner, giving
primacy to the individual in his understanding of the
human condition. Because of his emphasis on transcendence and the vertical dimension of human existence, a

79

clear and steady vein of individualism runs throughout Niebuhr's notion of sociality, his ethical system and approach to social change.

There are also those who believe that human beings are social in a stronger sense than the two interpretations just mentioned. Advocates of this position argue that human beings are essentially social in a strict sense; apart from social interaction there can be no human person. Human nature and sociality are synonymous. This understanding of the individual as essentially social can be seen as part of a general social ontology which maintains that to be is to be interrelated. This view of reality "emphasizes wholeness, connectedness and interdependence, and a different consciousness of self, others, human society and the natural world."[6]

The final interpretation of sociality to be mentioned is that of collectivism. Collectivism views society: (1) as an entity in itself, distinct from the individuals who compose it; and (2) as the whole for which the individuals exist only as parts. As I demonstrate in the course of this chapter, the understanding of human beings as essentially social, which is posited here as the most adequate position among the various interpretations, differs significantly from a collectivist stance.

In the first part of Chapter IV an interpretation of sociality, which defines the human person as essentially social, is developed at length based on radical social thought. Then, in the second part, it is argued that social contexts, characterized by domination and false consciousness, mask this understanding of sociality. It is only in and through the transformation of alienating social conditions that the concrete meaning of sociality can be more sharply revealed. To complete this chapter, the notions of freedom, self-realization, and human fulfillment, as they relate to essential sociality, are briefly described.

The Notion of Sociality in
Radical Social Thought

Karl Marx, perhaps the most prominent figure among radical social scientists, continually argues: "Man is, in the literal sense of the word, a zoon politikon, not only a social animal, but an animal which can develop into an individual only in society."[7] One cannot

80

understand the individual in isolation from the whole of which he or she is a part. Human nature is that which "resides in the totality of relations [individuals] have with nature, with others, and with themselves."[8]

Human beings, then, are constituted in their personhood by relationality. "Social relations are not external factors but the very essence of the personality."[9] Social relations are so much a part of an individual, that when a relation alters so does that individual; he or she becomes someone else.[10] As Carol Gould explains in her critical reconstruction of Marx's system:

> All relations between concretely existing individuals are internal relations. Internal relations are those in which the individuals are changed by their relations to each other, that is, where these relationships between individuals are such that both are reciprocally affected by the relation.[11]

In their social relations, individuals interact not only to produce their means of survival, but also to produce themselves, society, and history.

Human Activity

For all finite entities, existence is the activity of interrelating. For human beings, it is in the process of interacting with other persons that certain capacities which are peculiar to the human species are developed. That is, human beings become who they are only through activity with others in the world in which they find themselves.[12] These capacities, which develop through interaction, differentiate humans from the rest of the animal world.[13] As Plamenatz writes: "What is peculiar to man consists in the capacities revealed and developed when he acts with other men to satisfy his needs."[14] Consciousness and freedom are the uniquely human capacities of social individuals.[15] Briefly these two capacities are described.

Human Activity and the
Development of Consciousness

Consciousness is the human capacity to become

81

aware of experience.[16] "Consciousness is experience;
. . . one's consciousness is what one experiences."[17]
It includes "the ability to have the experience of
oneself."[18] Through interaction, persons become aware
of and experience themselves in relationship with
others, recognize the similarities and differences
among existing, relating entities, and identify themselves as being of a certain kind in relationship with
those of similar and different kinds.[19]

Consciousness also includes the experience which
humans have of: (1) the way their relations with
others and the world has been organized; and (2) the
meaning this organizational schema has been given.
Consciousness is, in fact, a world-view,[20] the specific
content of which is conditioned by the social arrange-
ments of a given society.

One of the major aspects of consciousness is the
development of a sense of individuality. By individuality is meant the unique configuration of relations
which are formed and transformed in an individual's own
life-process, given the conditions posed by biological
and social factors, as well as species-limitations.[21]
The particular pattern of social relationships which
distinguishes one person from another results in the
actualization of human potentialities in a unique and
unrepeatable way.[22] Because sociality is the distinctive mark of human experience, individuation is a twofold process of identification involving both differentiation and integration.[23]

Individuation necessarily involves differentiation
or the consciousness of one's own unique being in
society. Using Gould's words, differentiation is the
recognition of the "being of the relata" which is oneself; the "'that which' stands in relation to something
else."[24] Differentiation--an essential aspect of
identification--is easily susceptible to illusions of
self-sufficiency and independence unless one understands
that it is only one phase of the process of individuation.[25]

Individuation also involves integration or the consciousness of oneself as essentially related to others,
and as realized in and through social interaction.
True individuation leads to an experience of interde-
pendency; it is a profoundly participatory process.

Human Activity and Freedom

The second capacity which distinguishes humans from other beings is freedom. Because of "the limited hold [that] the instincts have over human nature,"[26] individuals "have an open-ended, quasi-infinite [potential] for relating to other existents."[27] This is true even though, as finite beings, "the scope of this relatedness to other entities is quite limited"[28] at any given moment. Freedom is the capacity of persons to co-create themselves as well as the society, world, and cosmos of which they are a part; it is the ability to co-determine what reality becomes. Freedom is only realized interdependently. Shlomo Avineri states this principle in this way: ultimate freedom is based "on a universal recognition of man's dependence upon each other. The very alteration of circumstances [is] accomplished through co-operation with other human beings."[29] As with consciousness, human beings become free in relationship with others. It is in and through social interaction that one's capacity for creativity is actualized.

Activity, then, which is conscious and free is the distinctive activity of human beings; that is, their species-activity. Through human activity, and in particular, through the development of practical skills for survival, social relations are given a specific structure or form. Besides producing patterns of social interaction, human beings also develop "organized systems of significant symbols"[30] to represent and give meaning to these patterned processes of social life.[31] These symbol systems--e.g., language, political doctrine, religious ritual--which are

> man-created, shared, conventional,
> ordered and indeed learned, provide
> human beings with a meaningful
> framework for orienting themselves
> to one another, to the world
> around them, and to themselves.[32]

As Dawe notes, emphasizing the collaborative nature of human activity: "We coauthor the social world as an active human relationship between us."[33]

Thus far we have seen that according to a notion of sociality suggested by radical social thought, "the self emerges in social process."[34] Persons-in-relation form and transform themselves, society and culture, the

83

human species, history and the world through their activity, and according to the human capacity for relating to other existents. Through social interaction, human beings have the ability to freely and consciously participate in the production of social life.

Human activity occurs, however, within a previously determined social context. Individuals are given the conditions for their activity. Individual consciousness arises in a particular society where patterns of social relations have already been established and meaning constituted. As Rasmussen emphasizes, "Everyone is born into an institutional context of meaning in which the patterns of thought and activity are already given."[35] Through socialization individuals assimilate these cultural patterns and develop their specifically human capacities in the process. In Cormie's words: "The very core of our being is shaped by the collectively-held culture into which we are born and in which we live."[36] Culture is a person's social heritage, providing "the conditions which then present possibilities for new choices and purposes and new modes of action"[37] in the present moment.[38]

In summary, a notion of sociality developed from radical social thought includes the understanding of: (1) individuals-in-relation and (2) a mutually formative relationship between these individuals and society with its particular culture. Marx describes this relationship in these words: "As society itself produces man as man, so is society produced by him."[39] This understanding of the relationship between the individual and society is a dialectical one, "in which the individual and the social group interact with one another and are selectively and causally determinative of both each other and the environment."[40] Let us look now more closely at this relationship.

The Individual and Society

For many radical social theorists, the basic entities of social reality are individuals, understood as individuals-in-relation, or social individuals.[41] Human beings, socially related to one another, constitute society. Society exists in and through the individuals who compose it and "expresses the sum of interrelations, the relations within which these individuals stand."[42] Society is not, however, simply an aggregate of its parts; it "cannot be understood simply by understanding the individuals who compose it.

84

It requires . . . an understanding of the interrelations among them."[43] In Joseph O'Malley's words, society is also "a complex of relationships among men, and of institutions which embody, express and regularize these relationships."[44]

This understanding of society does not correspond to either of two "major interpretations of man and society represented by . . . collectivism . . . and individualism."[45] Collectivism assigns primacy to society and views it as an entity with <u>independent</u> existence irreducible to the lives of <u>its members</u>."[46] An understanding of society found in radical social thought provides a counterbalance to collectivism.[47] Society exists <u>in</u> and <u>through</u> social individuals and "cannot be understood apart from these individuals and their activities."[48]

The relationship between the individual and society suggested by radical social thought also avoids a position of individualism because, as has been repeatedly stated, individuals cannot be separated from their relations—the relations which form society. The individual does not exist as an entity separate from or over and above society. In fact, it is the ensemble of social relations which, taken as a whole, constitutes the matrix in which individuals are formed.

Thus, the understanding of sociality described in this chapter is not one of "the imperialism of 'society' over 'the individual' on the one hand; [or] on the other, the pervasive reification of individual singularity, the private self, the solitary 'ego.'"[49] Rather, the individual and society are integrally related—neither one exists as an entity distinct from the other.

Theories which give preponderance to the society over the individual, or the individual over society are "engrossed in the imaginary antinomy of . . . [the] individual versus society."[50] These theories reflect the relationships of domination characteristic of the societies in which they are formulated.[51] Systems of hierarchy based on relations of domination and subordination mask the essential sociality of the human person through ideologies of individualism and collectivism. Within such systems, individuals and groups seem "split up and in opposition to one another."[52] Society appears as an autonomous entity with the power to control its members in the public sphere. The

interrelationships which, in fact, comprise society
become difficult if not impossible to ascertain; there
is little or no sense of communal personhood.[53] In the
next part I briefly describe relationships of domination, and the alienation and false consciousness which
they generate. Examples of these social phenomena are
drawn from Western capitalist society. It is by understanding, struggling against, and seeing through
alienation and false consciousness that an interpretation of humans as essentially social is further clarified.

Domination, Alienation and
False Consciousness

Kathy Ferguson defines domination in the following
way:

> To be dominated is to be in a sit-
> uation that has been defined by
> another person or group and to be
> forced to operate within this
> situation without being able to
> effect one's own definition of it.[54]

Gould's definition expands that of Ferguson. Drawing
upon Marx, she defines domination as "the exercise of
power by one individual (or group of individuals) over
another (or others), that is, the direction or control
of their actions by means of control over the conditions of their activity."[55] Through the unjustified
use of power, the dominant deprive the dominated of
their ability to determine, in relationship with others,
what reality becomes--the dominant deprive the dominated
of their freedom--thus preventing self-realization
through transformative activity.[56] Relationships of
domination are non-reciprocal, and therefore unfree.

Relationships of domination give rise to social
structures which provide members of society with an
unequal amount of and unequal access to power. Thus
positions of domination and subordination become institutionalized and perpetuated through the social system.
In Ferguson's words: "Institutions express and maintain
the distribution of power in society."[57]

Individuals, born into and living within a given
society, are assigned positions of dominance or subordination according to certain roles or characteristics,
and the meaning ascribed to them.[58] Historically,

differences such as those of kinship, class, gender, ethnicity, race, religion, and sexual preference have had a significant effect on the distribution of power. Given the importance of human activity directed towards survival, the distribution of power in relationships of production in both the family and the workplace, critically influences the complex network of institutional structures within which people live and interact. Those who own and/or control the means of production, and determine the conditions of labor occupy the positions of dominance in economic relationships, and frequently in a society's other institutional structures as well.[59]

Consciousness, as it emerges from social conditions marked by cultural patterns and institutional structures which encompass relationships of domination, "finds itself in a situation of alienation."[60] Domination is a perversion of the mutuality characteristic of persons-in-relation. Thus consciousness, formed and developed in a social context which "falsifies" reality, becomes itself distorted and false.[61] As a manifestation or reflection of existing social conditions, consciousness becomes "a mystified interpretation of reality, the true nature of which remains misunderstood, thus enclosing man in illusion, alienation and dependence."[62]

False consciousness, as it exists in Western capitalist society, dissolves the human world into a world of atomistic individuals in social classes confronting each other with mutual hostility.[63] The experience of alienation is not solely related to productive activity, however. Given the interstructuring of divisions in capitalist society based on class, sex, race, sexual preference and age, all human relationships and interaction are distorted.[64] Workers and owners, women and men, people of color and white people, homosexuals and heterosexuals, old and young are set over and against one another. What it means to be human is lost from view. People

> do not know themselves and others
> as social beings whose needs demand
> mutual cooperation but as private
> and competing entities, an anarchis-
> tic galaxy of selfish worlds . . .
> [P]eople are siphoned off into
> partial communities based on
> shared antagonisms.[65]

87

This false consciousness, which is a manifestation of relationships of domination, aids and abets the continuance of a dehumanizing social situation.[66]

In order to restore an understanding of individuals as essentially social, it is necessary to overcome the historical situation which is alienating. Through the transformation of relationships and structures of domination, the awareness of essential sociality is discovered or rediscovered. Revolution or revolutionary practice--the transformation of humans and the human collectivity through the radical transformation of society in history[67]--is both a form of and a basis for creative activity and the reclamation of one's humanity.[68]

The goal of revolution is twofold: (1) freedom from existing oppressive relationships and structures which hold socially-generated human capacities in bondage; and (2) freedom for self-realization and human fulfillment.[69] However, freedom, self-realization, and human fulfillment are not understood in the same way as within false consciousness. To conclude this chapter, the different meanings of these three terms when, through a liberating process, the social dimension is recognized, are briefly described.

Revolution, Social Transformation, and Sociality

Freedom

Within the form of false consciousness described above, freedom, which is accorded to the discrete individual, refers "positively . . . [to] the power to pursue one's goals without human interference. Negatively, it is the condition in which one does not have to submit to someone else's will."[70] Freedom is "the abstract capacity for choice and its correlative requirement for freedom from constraint."[71]

Through revolutionary practice and the radical transformation of relationships and structures of domination, an understanding of freedom, such as the one stated earlier in this chapter, is rediscovered: the capacity of persons to co-create themselves as well as the society, world, and cosmos of which they are a part.[72]

Within a social context of domination, the human

capacity for freedom can only be realized through struggle. The freedom one has is "earned freedom."[73] Humans actualize their freedom, they <u>become</u> free as they rebel against alienation, and <u>work with</u> others to create relations and structures of mutuality in which to co-determine reality.

Self-realization

In a social world divided into groups with unequal access to and unequal amounts of power, an individual's self-realization is limited by the definitions which the dominant groups determine and enforce.[74] Even though humans have a wide range of creative potentialities, individuals know and interact with one another according to the role-definitions which have been prescribed <u>for</u> them (and not <u>by</u> them) within the social system.[75]

Through revolutionary practice and the struggle to transform relations of domination into those which are mutually enhancing, the forms of self-realization <u>imposed</u> by others are recognized. Oppressive definitions, and stereotyped roles and categories which impede individuation are rejected.[76] Although still limited by time, energy and socio-historical conditions, self-realization is understood as the cultivation of a vast array of human potentialities, given an individual's own unique and ever-varying pattern of mutual relationships.[77]

Human Fulfillment

Finally, through the transformation of alienating social conditions, human fulfillment is understood in terms that reflect essential sociality. Relationships of domination among individuals and groups perpetuate a false consciousness of one's own fulfillment as separate and apart from the fulfillment of others.[78] Insofar as dominance exists, any supposed social understanding of human fulfillment such as the "common good" is manipulated by the dominators to mean their own good or fulfillment. Under conditions of domination, human fulfillment ceases to stand for something universal about humanity.[79]

Through revolutionary practice, an awareness emerges of human fulfillment as shared fulfillment reflective of a humanity which each person expresses in a unique way in and through mutual relationships with others, and which is contained within each person through his or her essential sociality. Humankind contains innumerable possibilities which can only be realized and expressed through concrete, historical individuals.[80] Each person, given his or her individuality, actualizes certain potentialities in a way that no other person is capable of doing. In Unger's words, "each person is a unique, particular expression of the universal that is the species."[81] But no one person is able to exhaust the potentialities of the human species in the course of a life-time. Since each one "represents in [only] a limited [though] distinctive fashion the possibilities open to the entire species,"[82] persons are mutually dependent on one another for the full expression or representation of their humanity. Together persons-in-relation form and continually transform the human species by their participation in history,[83] and, because of their essential sociality, experience this fullness of humanity within themselves.[84]

A social understanding of freedom, self-realization and human fulfillment is produced by and in turn produces social relations and social structures marked by communal control over the processes of social life. The central value and animating principle of such a social world is "positive freedom, understood as the fullest self-realization of social individuals."[85] The transformation of alienated social life and the false consciousness which accompanies it, through revolutionary practice, is in Gibson Winter's words, "the coming to be of that humanization which is . . . the truly human."[86] It is the recognition, further clarification, and concretization of essential sociality.

In the preceding pages I have presented an interpretation of sociality drawn from radical social thought which describes the human person as in-relationship. This being-in-relation constitutes what it means to be human. Through interaction, that is through activity with others, the human capacities for consciousness and freedom are realized and in this process, society, humanity and history are created and transformed.

Persons-in-relation, living in a particular society and historical era both shape and are shaped by their reality. Throughout history, relations of domination have determined social life, effecting a distorted

consciousness of what it means to be human. It is
therefore only in and through revolutionary practice
that the true meaning of humanness--that is, social
individuality--is clarified and a social understanding
of freedom, self-realization and human fulfillment is
restored. In the next chapter I show how Rosemary
Ruether's interpretation of sociality parallels that of
radical social thought. Ruether's treatment of dualisms
is of particular importance to her theological anthropology and, after a brief introduction, is the major
focus of the discussion. It is Ruether's understanding
of sociality which serves as the basis for the ethical
system and approach to social change developed in
Chapter VI.

Notes

[1]Dawe, "Theories of Social Action," p. 376.

[2]Raymond Williams, The Long Revolution (London:
Chatto and Windus, 1961), cited in ibid. For a further
discussion of this historical development, see Dawe's
article, pp. 376-78; and Wayne Proudfoot, God and the
Self (Cranbury, New Jersey: Associated University
Presses, Inc., 1976), pp. 203-205.

[3]Rasmussen, "Between Autonomy and Sociality," p.
41.

[4]Thomas Hobbes, for example, "depicts the self as
an aggregation of desires, a solitary individual who is
locked with others in an increasing struggle for power"
(Kathy E. Ferguson, Self, Society, and Womankind: The
Dialectics of Liberation, Contributions in Women's
Studies, no. 17 [Westport, Connecticut; London, England:
Greenwood Press, 1980], p. 14). John Locke, on the
other hand, "view[s] man as a pretty decent fellow, far
removed from the quarrelsome, competitive, selfish
creature found in Hobbes" (Thomas P. Peardon, Introduction to Second Treatise of Government, by John Locke
[Indianapolis: The Bobbs-Merrill Company, Inc., 1952],
p. xii).

[5]See Rasmussen, "Between Autonomy and Sociality,"
p. 5.

[6]Elizabeth Dodson Gray, Green Paradise Lost
(Wellesley, Massachusetts: Roundtable Press, 1979),
p. 127.

[7]Karl Marx, Introduction to A Contribution to the Critique of Political Economy, trans. N. I. Stone, cited in Bertell Ollman, Alienation: Marx's Conception of Man in Capitalist Society, 2d. ed. (Cambridge: Cambridge University Press, 1976), p. 105. Rasmussen writes: "If there is one fundamental insight which appears in the writing of Marx it is that man is social" ("Between Autonomy and Sociality," p. 18).

[8]Unger, Knowledge and Politics (New York: The Free Press, 1975), p. 247.

[9]Lucien Sève, Man in Marxist Theory and the Psychology of Personality, trans. John McGreal (Sussex: The Harvester Press, 1978), pp. 141-42.

[10]Ollman, Alienation, p. 15.

[11]Carol C. Gould, Marx's Social Ontology: Individuality and Community in Marx's Theory of Social Reality (Cambridge, Massachusetts, and London, England: The MIT Press, 1978), p. 37. This social and dynamic understanding of human nature has much in common with process philosophy. From a Whiteheadian perspective, an actual entity "exists only because of its interrelatedness with the other actual entities in the world at the same moment" (Joseph A. Bracken, S. J., "God and World Reconsidered: Principles for a New Synthesis," Marquette University, Milwaukee, Wisconsin, 1981, p. 6).

[12]See Rasmussen, "Beyond Autonomy and Sociality," p. 20; also Karl Marx, "Economic and Philosophical Manuscripts," in Karl Marx: Early Writings, trans. and ed. T. B. Bottomore, with a Foreword by Erich Fromm (New York: McGraw-Hill Book Co., 1964), p. 158. With reference to the sixth thesis on Feuerbach, Sève states: "What makes man essentially man in developed humanity is not a natural given in each isolated individual but a product of human activity--forces of production, social relations of all kinds, cultural heritage--built up in the social world in the course of history" (Man in Marxist Theory, p. 443).

[13]Ollman, Alienation, p. 74.

[14]John Plamenatz, Karl Marx's Philosophy of Man (Oxford: Clarendon Press, 1975), p. 47.

[15]These two capacities correspond to those

identified by Marx. Plamenatz observes: "Marx, speaking of man and what he calls his life activities-- meaning, presumably, the activities by which man sustains his life--is at pains to make two points: that man is both self-conscious and self-directing, and could not be either unless he were the other as well" (Karl Marx's Philosophy of Man, pp. 67-68. See also Unger, Knowledge and Politics, p. 199).

[16]See Gray, Green Paradise Lost, p. 110.

[17]Lewis Perelman, "Elements of an Ecological Theory of Education" (Ph.D. dissertation, Harvard University, 1973), p. 134, cited in ibid.

[18]Ferguson, Self, Society, and Womankind, p. 25.

[19]Many descriptions of consciousness use the distinction between subject/object, but these categories are being avoided in this work. Embodiment--that is, the condition of presence in the world--provides some margins for personal identity, but the human person is not "set apart from objects." Although "man [i.e., the male] has wanted to see himself as the creator and experiencer of history and culture--set apart from objects (lesser men, women, slaves, nature, things) which he could act upon, observe, manipulate with detachment as though 'above and apart'" (Gray, Green Paradise Lost, p. 67), the argument of this study is that reality is not necessarily perceived in this manner. Subject/object, and the accompanying notion of the self above or apart from "the other," are man-made structural patterns which have resulted in "metaphysical one-upmanship," oppression, and destruction (See Sheila Collins, A Different Heaven and Earth [Valley Forge: Judson Press, 1974], p. 25).

[20]See Chapter I, p. 10, n. 4 for the definition of world-view.

[21]Sève warns against "biologising historico-social individuality" (Man in Marxist Theory, p. 145). Since persons do not pre-exist their social world but become human in and through social relationships, it is here we must look for personal individuality. Although biological facts play a part in shaping personality, "individuality is to be seen as formed of social elements" (Lukes, Individualism, p. 151). As Sève notes in a later part of his book, a person "assumes

individuality in the historical process and not in spite of it or only marginally related to it" (Man in Marxist Theory, p. 239).

[22]According to Unger, "the form of our individuality is determined by the character of our sociability" (Knowledge and Politics, p. 271). In the next section I discuss how one's inability to realize his or her individuality impoverishes reality.

[23]This description of individuation conforms to a tenet in process thought that "every actual entity is both a unique and individual occurrence, and an entity which is essentially related to the whole world" (Valerie Saiving, "Androgynous Life: A Feminist Appropriation of Process Thought," in Feminism and Process Thought: The Harvard Divinity School/Claremont Center for Process Studies Symposium Papers, Symposium Series, no. 6, ed. Sheila Greeve Davaney [New York and Toronto: The Edwin Mellin Press, 1981], p. 23.

[24]Gould, Marx's Social Ontology, p. 31. It is important to remember, however, that the "being of the relata" is in itself essentially social. Any one self is constituted by relations which are internal to it. Differentiation is the self-consciousness of a constituted self.

[25]Ollman argues that differentiation is an ambiguous process since the ways of dividing up the real world into distinct parts are, to a certain degree, arbitrary and endless. The categories that individuals use to differentiate themselves are culturally conditioned and, for the most part, culturally determined. See Alienation, pp. 37-39, 48, and 266-67; also John MacMurray, M.C., M.A., LL.D., Persons in Relation (London: Faber and Faber, 1961; reprint ed., Atlantic Highlands, N.J.: Humanities Press, 1979), pp. 75-85.

[26]Unger, Knowledge and Politics, p. 199.

[27]Bracken, "God and World Reconsidered," p. 17.

[28]Ibid.

[29]Shlomo Avineri, The Social and Political Thought of Karl Marx (Cambridge: Cambridge University Press, 1968), p. 92.

[30]Geertz, The Interpretation of Cultures, p. 46.

[31]Unger, Knowledge and Politics, pp. 108-109.

[32]Geertz, The Interpretation of Cultures, p. 250.

[33]Dawe, "Theories of Social Action," p. 411.

[34]Winter, Elements, p. 18.

[35]Rasmussen, "Beyond Autonomy and Sociality," p. 21. Rasmussen further describes this pre-determined social situation: "Individuals . . . find themselves in a situation where they have been pre-defined apart from their own rational intentions, where specific roles have already been determined by culture and history, and where these contexts slowly will be made apparent" (ibid., p. 17).

[36]Cormie, "Society, History and Meaning," p. 8. Anthropologist Clifford Geertz emphatically argues that culture is fundamental to human beings and their development as a species. "The innate, generic constitution of modern man (what used, in a simpler day, to be called 'human nature') now appears to be both a cultural and biological product." By producing culture, human beings "quite literally, though quite inadvertently, created [themselves]." Culture "is not just an ornament of human existence but . . . an essential condition for it." It is "necessary not merely to . . . survival but to existential realization." For Geertz, "the standard procedure of treating biological, social and cultural parameters serially--the first being taken as primary to the second, and the second to the third-- is ill-advised" (The Interpretation of Cultures, pp. 67, 48, 46, 83 and 74 respectively; see also p. 35).

[37]Ferguson, Self, Society, and Womankind, p. 30.

[38]Similar to Geertz's conclusions, Marx maintains that "we have to be produced as living substantial beings before we can begin to act. This is true both of the individual and the species. The individual cannot determine the historical period or the class he is born into--which fundamentally limits his possibilities. The species itself at the dawn of history already had a certain mode of life before it could begin to recreate itself through solving the problems which faced it with solutions also conditioned by given circumstances" (Karl Marx and Frederick Engels, The German Ideology: Part One with selections from parts 2 and 3 and supplementary texts, ed. and intro. C. J.

Arthur [New York: International Publishers, 1977], p. 37).

[39]Marx, "Economic and Philosophical Manuscripts," p. 349. See also Gould, Marx's Social Ontology, p. 36; and Plamenatz, Karl Marx's Philosophy of Man, p. 71.

[40]Ferguson, Self, Society, and Womankind, p. 24.

[41]See, for example, Marx, "Economic and Philosophical Manuscripts," pp. 350-51.

[42]Karl Marx, The Grundrisee, cited in Sève, Man in Marxist Theory, p. 90. As Gould states: "Society is a constituted entity and not a basic entity" (Marx's Social Ontology, p. 36).

[43]Gould, Marx's Social Ontology, p. 36.

[44]Joseph O'Malley, Introduction to Critique of Hegel's "Philosophy of Right," by Karl Marx, cited in Gibson Winter, "Human Science and Ethics in a Reflective Society." (Mimeographed.), pp. 5-6. For a further discussion of the dialectical relationship between human beings and their circumstances, see Karl Marx, "Theses on Feuerbach" in The Marx-Engels Reader, ed. Robert Tucker (New York: W. W. Norton & Company, Inc., 1972), pp. 107-109; Avineri, Social and Political Thought, pp. 66-69; and Sherman and Wood, Sociology, p. 392.

[45]Martindale, Prominent Sociologists, p. 76.

[46]Unger, Knowledge and Politics, p. 82, emphasis added.

[47]As Sève writes, Marx's view of society "puts an end to the myth of this ideological mystification . . . [and] reveal[s] the fundamental relations and processes through which each singular society becomes what it is. This is not to erect a substantial model of society but to identify the typology of the production, reproduction and transformation of concrete social formations, a typology which is not itself a universal generality but which alters in the course of history" (Man in Marxist Theory, pp. 453-454).

[48]Gould, Marx's Social Ontology, p. 36.

[49]Dawe, "Theories of Social Action," p. 410, see

also p. 363; and Unger, Knowledge and Politics, p. 136.

[50]Avineri, Social and Political Thought, pp. 94-95.

[51]As Anthony Giddens observes, a person "is first and foremost a social being and the very notion of the isolated individual is one which is created as part of the ideology of a specific form of society (and is itself an expression of alienated consciousness)" (Studies in Social and Political Theory [New York: Basic Books, Inc., Publishers, 1977], p. 222).

[52]Marx, The German Ideology, p. 91.

[53]See Unger, Knowledge and Politics, p. 229; and Plamenatz, Karl Marx's Philosophy of Man, p. 141.

[54]Ferguson, Self, Society, and Womankind, p. 105. See also Unger, Knowledge and Politics, p. 167; and Carol Ehrlich, "The Unhappy Marriage of Marxism and Feminism: Can It be Saved," in Women and Revolution: A Discussion of the Unhappy Marriage of Marxism and Feminism, South End Press Political Controversies Series, no. 2, ed. Lydia Sargent (Boston: South End Press, 1981), p. 114.

[55]Gould, Marx's Social Ontology, pp. 135-36. Domination implies an extensive use, or misuse of power. The use of power does not, however, necessarily imply domination. As is seen when I consider Ruether's writings, when relationships of mutuality exist, "power is effective action. Power is the ability to create" (Rosemary Ruether, "Black Theology and Black Church," America 120 [June 14, 1969]:686).

[56]See the description of freedom, p. 83.

[57]Ferguson, Self, Society, and Womankind, p. 94.

[58]This is not to suggest that in all relationships and structures, positions that have the greater power and authority are necessarily those of domination; but that relationships and structures characterized by legitimate authority and the just use of power are those in which the various positions have been co-determined by free, interacting members. Given this process, the positions are no longer understood as dominant or subordinate, but simply as different roles with varying tasks and responsibilities.

⁵⁹As Cormie writes: "The economy is especially important . . . because the ways in which people organize themselves to produce and to allocate all that they need to survive affect every aspect of life" ("Society, History and Meaning," p. 21).

⁶⁰Rasmussen, "Between Autonomy and Sociality," p. 19. In a well-known passage, Marx describes a situation of alienation specifically as it exists within capitalism: "The worker is related to the product of his labour as to an alien object. . . . Alienation appears not only in the result but also in the process of production and productive activity itself. The worker is not at home in his work which he views only as a means of satisfying other needs. It is an activity directed against himself, that is independent of him and does not belong to him. Thirdly, alienated labor succeeds in alienating man from his species. Species-life, productive life, life creating life, turns into a mere means of sustaining the worker's individual existence, and man is alienated from his fellow men" ("Economic and Philosophical Manuscripts," cited in David McLellan, The Thought of Karl Marx: An Introduction [New York, Evanston, San Francisco, London: Harper & Row, Publishers, Harper Torchbooks, 1974], p. 107; see also "Economic and Philosophical Manuscripts," in Karl Marx: Early Writings, trans. Rodney Livingstone and Gregor Benton, with an Introduction by Lucio Coletti [New York: Vintage Books, 1975], pp. 322-31). This situation of alienation produces an alienated or false consciousness in which human beings experience themselves as estranged from and in conflict with (1) their own work, (2) the products they produce, (3) the human species, and (4) other human beings.

⁶¹False consciousness includes false conceptions about humans, what they are and what they ought to be. See Marx and Engels, The German Ideology, p. 37.

⁶²Sève, Man in Marxist Theory, p. 352. Gould distinguishes between a strong sense and a weak sense of false consciousness, or what she calls ideological distortion. The strong sense is "the deliberate use of ideological distortion as an instrument for domination." The weak sense--which is for Gould more significant because it is more pervasive--is the "ideological distortions which come from the uncritical acceptance of whatever partial view is expedient or current" (e.g., the identification of essential human traits such as rationality with dominant and male social roles). See

"The Woman Question: Philosophy of Liberation and the Liberation of Philosophy," in Women and Philosophy: Toward a Theory of Liberation, ed. Carol C. Gould and Marx Wartofsky (New York: G. P. Putnam's Sons, Capricorn Books, 1976), pp. 21-25. These two forms of false consciousness are complementary and both forms reflect a system of domination and subordination.

[63]Karl Marx, "On the Jewish Question," in On Religion, The Karl Marx Library, vol. 5, ed. and trans. Saul K. Padover (New York: McGraw-Hill Book Company, 1974), p. 191; see also Unger, Knowledge and Politics, p. 155.

[64]As Ollman observes: "The indifference and hostility which characterize relations between workers and capitalists have their counterpart throughout society" (Alienation, p. 203).

[65]Ibid., p. 208.

[66]See, for example, Christine Riddiough, "Socialism, Feminism and Gay/Lesbian Liberation," in Women and Revolution, p. 78.

[67]This definition of revolution is drawn from Robert Tucker, "The Marxian Revolutionary Idea," in Why Revolution? Theories and Analyses, ed. Clifford T. Paynton and Robert Blackey (Cambridge, Massachusetts, U.S.A. and London, England: Shenkman Publishing Company, Inc., 1971), especially pp. 215-16 and 227-29; as well as excerpts from Marx's writings on revolution cited in McLellan, The Thought of Karl Marx, pp. 203-11. Defining revolution in such a way "makes quite irrelevant the question whether change in individuals will precede change in circumstances or vice versa." The changes are concurrent. Since "'society' does not exist as an entity distinct from the 'individual,' change in individuals is ipso facto also change in society, and change in social circumstances is also change in individuals" (Avineri, Social and Political Thought, p. 92).

[68]See Unger, Knowledge and Politics, p. 247.

[69]See Tucker, "The Marxian Revolutionary Idea," p. 221.

[70]Unger, Knowledge and Politics, p. 84. For Unger, "the positive and negative definition is interchange-

able, given the qualification attached to the former, 'without human interference'" (ibid.).

[71]Gould, Marx's Social Ontology, p. 171. See also Rasmussen, "Between Autonomy and Sociality," pp. 8-9.

[72]See p. 83.

[73]Rasmussen, "Between Autonomy and Sociality," p. 22.

[74]See Ferguson, Self, Society, and Womankind, p. 12.

[75]See Unger, Knowledge and Politics, p. 184; Ollman, Alienation, pp. 205-206; Rasmussen, "Between Autonomy and Sociality," pp. 8-9; and Marx and Engels, The German Ideology, pp. 83-84.

[76]Mary Daly refers to this process as "burning/melting/vaporizing the constricting walls imposed upon the Self" (Gyn/Ecology: The Metaethics of Radical Feminism [Boston: Beacon Press, 1978], p. 380).

[77]Marx and Engels, The German Ideology, p. 83. See also Plamenatz, Karl Marx's Philosophy of Man, p. 108; and Sève, Man in Marxist Theory, p. 377.

[78]This individualistic understanding of human fulfillment is accompanied by such conduct as competitiveness (see Ollman, Alienation, pp. 206-207), avarice, exploitation (see Gould, Marx's Social Ontology, pp. 154-58), manipulation (see Unger, Knowledge and Politics, p. 153), and consumerism (see Heidi Hartmann, "The Unhappy Marriage of Marxism and Feminism: Towards a More Progressive Union," in Women and Revolution, p. 10). These, notes Hartmann, must be recognized "as the dominant values of capitalist society" (ibid.).

[79]See Unger, Knowledge and Politics, pp. 238-48, especially p. 242.

[80]See Unger, Knowledge and Politics, pp. 143, 144, and 246.

[81]Ibid., p. 214.

[82]Ibid., p. 240. See also Sève, Man in Marxist Theory, pp. 256, 274.

[83]Avineri, *Social and Political Thought*, p. 85;
and Ollman, *Alienation*, p. xii.

[84]See Marx, "Economic and Philosophical Manu-
scripts," pp. 350-51; David McLellan, *Karl Marx: His
Life and Thought* (New York, Hagerstown, San Francisco,
London: Harper and Row, Publishers, Harper Colophon
Books, 1977), p. 120; Avineri, *Social and Political
Thought*, pp. 88, 189; and Ollman, *Alienation*, p. 61.

[85]Gould, *Marx's Social Ontology*, p. 163.

[86]Winter, "Human Science and Ethics," p. 8.

CHAPTER V

SOCIALITY: ROSEMARY RUETHER'S
INTERPRETATION

Rosemary Radford Ruether, a feminist and a prominent representative of North American liberation
theology, engages in what she calls "liberation
scholarship." Ruether's writings are born out of a
struggle with the dominant world-view and the social
structures which give rise to it. Her work reflects a
passionate commitment "to the survival of the children
and the earth"--"to the future of life"[1] "through the
total abolition of the social pattern of domination and
subjugation and the erection of a new communal social
ethic."[2]

Ruether's theological anthropology is an affirmation of the essential sociality in which individuality
is grounded. In the first part of this chapter,
Ruether's interpretation of sociality is described. It
is shown how her notion of communal personhood is an
exemplification and further explanation of the understanding of sociality described in Chapter IV. Similar
to the position found in radical social thought,
Ruether maintains that relationships and structures of
domination, alienation, and false consciousness mask
this essential sociality. Thus, in the second part of
the chapter, Ruether's treatment of the "systems of
ruling-class male power which have dominated human
history and self-understanding"[3] is presented. For
Ruether, religious myth is one of the main symbol
systems that legitimates and perpetuates domination and
alienation. In the third part, Ruether's criticism of
religious myth as an expression of false consciousness
is discussed. The discussion includes a consideration
of Reinhold Niebuhr's theological anthropology as a
part of the religious ideology which supports a system
of domination. In the fourth and concluding part of
this chapter, Ruether's description of an alternative
consciousness, which further clarifies her understanding of essential sociality, is offered.

Communal Personhood

Ruether believes that "women have traditionally
cultivated a communal personhood."[4] Communal personhood implies, for Ruether, a holistic understanding of
the self which extends not only to the collective body
of human beings, but to the whole of creation.

103

Ruether's understanding of reality is one in which "each part has an equally vital part to play in maintaining the renewed harmony and balance of the whole."[5] In such a system of interdependence "no part is intrinsically 'higher' or 'lower.'"[6] Each part must be accorded respect and dignity and "no part can long flourish if the other parts are being injured or destroyed."[7] All parts form a single community of life.[8]

This community of life or of creation, as I have noted, encompasses the integration of nature and humanity.[9] As Ruether explains: "In relation to humanity, nature no longer exists 'naturally,' for it has become part of the human social drama. . . . Humanity as a part of creation is not outside of nature but within it."[10] It is "not a question of nature over and against society, but rather nature and society together, the human and the non-human cosmos as one."[11] According to Ruether, "human survival depends on the renewal of this holistic vision that perceives the interdependence of all living things in a global community."[12] A holistic and communal world-view must be realized in "how we live our lives with our fellows, even on the other side of the earth, or how we situate our social and economic systems in relation to the organic life systems of animal and plant, earth and sky, air and water."[13]

Within this community of creation, the model for relationships is communal, empathetic, supportive and participatory. Such relationships foster "authentic creativity"[14] and "authentic cooperation."[15] Power, or the ability to act, is defined as "participation in the making of one's destiny."[16] Human activity itself, including work, is identified "with creative self-expression within a framework of a community of mutual affirmation."[17]

Ruether's position, similar to the one described in Chapter IV, is that relations of domination and subordination mask essential sociality. For Ruether, "community consciousness"[18] is, for the most part, overshadowed by a false consciousness with its "antagonistic concept of self and social and ecological relations."[19] In the next part I focus on: (1) Ruether's treatment of the hierarchical system of domination and alienation which creates this false consciousness; and (2) the dualistic consciousness which, Ruether argues, "is rapidly destroying mankind and the earth,"[20] and

104

"threatening the very survival of the planet."[21]

Domination, Alienation and False Consciousness

Domination and the Hierarchical System

The "shaping of history has resulted in misshapen social relations."[22] As Ruether argues: "In the beginning there develops a social structure of injustice and oppression."[23] The first exploitative social relations in history were between men and women.[24] Ruether's explanation for this phenomenon is as follows:

> From the dawn of history the physical lightness of woman's body (which has nothing to do with biological inferiority) and the fact that the woman is the childbearer have been used to subordinate the woman to the man in a chattel status and to deprive women of the leadership possibilities and the cultural development of the dominant group.[25]

According to Ruether, societies developed structures based on reproductive differences that led to oppression of women in the family and in the productive arena.[26] This pattern of dominance and subordination served and continues to serve as "the ideological model for all subsequent exploitative relations."[27] Thus the hierarchical paradigm is incorporated in social structures and engrained in culture and tradition.

Within a hierarchical system some orders of being are established "above" others. Groups of people in power--that is, those who occupy superior positions-- are "able to define other groups of people over against themselves."[28] Those in power identify themselves as subjects while defining those "below" as others, aliens, or objects. Groups in power become the norm for what is considered truly human, and everyone outside those groups is thereby defined in a dehumanized way.[29] In this process, dictated by the dominant, a situation of alienation is created. The power of the dominated to define themselves and the world is suppressed,[30] the possibility for relationships of mutuality and inter-subjectivity between individuals and between groups is

105

eliminated,[31] and oppression and exploitation of the "less-than-human" is legitimated.[32]

A hierarchical system "works," at least in part, because it creates vested interest in the status quo. "Those at the highest levels can 'buy off' those at the lower levels by offering them power over those still lower."[33] In the Western capitalist system, in which "the elite white patriarch rule[s] supreme, dominating a society divided by sex, race and class,"[34] sexism and racism function to keep oppressed groups from seeing their common exploitation.[35] The complexity of the interpenetration of racism and sexism[36] in a class society results in antagonism and alienation rather than solidarity among potential allies. In Ruether's words, "the ruling class typically puts minority groups at each other's throats."[37]

With hostility ingrained in a hierarchical system; and with groups of individuals set over and against each other, and in competition with each other, one's identity as an interdependent social being is concealed. As Ruether argues, a hierarchical system, based on domination and alienation, "distorts the character of man in community and in creation so fundamentally that it can be visualized as a false 'world'; an anti-society and anti-cosmos where man finds himself entrapped and alienated from his 'true home.'"[38] Community consciousness is lost and in its place dualistic consciousness is formed, reflective of the existing social divisions and inequities. For Ruether, "dualistic ideologies, sexist ideologies, etc. are ideological reflections of the social structures of injustice."[39] In the next section this false consciousness, with its various polarities, is explored.

Dualisms and False Consciousness

Alienated or false consciousness partitions reality--what Ruether calls "the basic dialectics of human experience"[40]--into a series of dualisms, the two halves of which are related to each other as superior to inferior.[41] Dichotomization becomes the cognitive basis for almost every conceivable relationship.[42] According to Ruether, the alienated sexual relation between men and women is the primary symbol, "the original model"[43] for dualistic thinking.

> Sexual symbolism is foundational to
> the perception of order and

106

relationship that has built up in
cultures. The psychic organization of consciousness, the dualistic
view of the self and the world, the
hierarchical concept of society,
the relation of humanity and nature,
and of God and creation--all these
relationships have been modeled on
sexual dualism.[44]

Basic dualities or polarizations within false consciousness include the following levels: (1) alienation from oneself; (2) alienation from others; and (3)
alienation from the world.[45] These three areas are
examined below.

Alienation from Oneself

According to a dualistic anthropology, the self is
divided into the polar elements of body/soul, or body/
mind. This understanding of the self is part of a
cosmology which splits the universe "into a dualism
between a transcendent spiritual principle and a lower
material reality."[46] "The world is viewed as a
hierarchy of mind over body, a noumenal world of spirit
over a phenomenal world of material existence."[47] Such
a cosmology is particularly representative of Western
tradition.

Describing the dichotomy between body and soul
found in classical philosophy, Ruether writes:

The intellect or "soul" sees itself
as an alien, lonely species which
originates in a spiritual world
beyond body, space or time, and
which has been dropped, either as a
testing place, or through some
error, into this lower, material
world. But space and time, body and
materiality, coming to be and
passing away, far from being its
natural vehicle, are totally anti-
thetical to it. The body drags the
soul down, obscuring its clarity of
perception and debasing its moral
integrity. Liberation is redemption
from the body, a flight from all
duality, matter and change, back to
the incorruptible spiritual world,

which is its true home.[48]

The authentic self is the soul or transcendent rationality; the body is an alien object that must be repressed, subjugated and mastered in order to develop the integrity of the true self.[49]

The division of reality into two separate realms of mind and matter continued with the birth of the modern era.[50] Today most individuals in the Western world are conscious of themselves "as isolated egos existing 'inside' their bodies."[51] Not only is the individual divided "into a dualism in which the ruling mind is seen as engaged in a struggle to subdue a recalcitrant body,"[52] so too, as is shown next, is humanity divided.

Alienation from Others

The sexual or male-female dualism is, as stated above, the fundamental symbol used to express relationships of domination and subordination within a society. Therefore alienation from others is considered first in relation to this dualism.

"Autonomous spiritual selfhood is imaged (by males, the culture creators of this view) as intrinsically masculine, while the feminine becomes the symbol of the repressed, subjugated and dreaded 'abysmal' side of man."[53] "Men identify themselves with the mind; women with dangerous carnality."[54] Typically, the male is active, rational, objective, logical, detached; the female is passive, irrational, subjective, intuitive, emotional. These and many other qualities which are, in fact, accessible to both males and females become separated according to gender, "socially projected upon men and women as their natures,"[55] and then culturally enforced. As Ruether argues: "Society, through the centuries, has in every way profoundly conditioned men and women to play out their lives and find their capacities within this basic antithesis."[56]

This "repressive view of the alien female [is] also the model for the inferiorization of other subjugated groups, lower classes, and conquered races."[57] In a society characterized by a patriarchal system of domination and supported by sexist ideology, subordinate groups are forced to play a "feminine" role--one of powerlessness, dependency and passivity. Society itself is frequently viewed as an alien object, a feminine

108

object, which must be acted upon--shaped, directed,
controlled and used--by men in positions of dominance.[58]
Society, like woman, is defined in terms of male needs
and negations; it is man-made.

Thus far we have considered one definition of
femaleness imposed on women by those in power. In the
nineteenth century, due to shifting social, political
and economic patterns, "a reshaping of the dominant
image of the feminine takes place."[59] Industrialization, one of the major factors contributing to this
shift,

> depriv[ed] women in the home of many
> of their traditional functions.
> [Even though] poor women were being
> drawn out of the home into the
> factory . . . the normative nature
> of women was . . . redefined in
> terms of the bourgeois housewife,
> who was primarily seen as a nurturer,
> rather than a productive labourer
> in a family business.[60]

The Romantic movement, a reaction against various social
revolutions of the period, supported this idealized
view of women.[61] Thus, the earlier typologies used to
characterize men and women were partially reversed."[62]

During this historical period and after, women are
defined as "religious, spiritual, asexual, virtuous,
altruistic, irrational, dependent and weak." Men, by
contrast, "are seen as secular, rational, egotistic,
combative, sexual, and oriented toward power and stren-
uous manipulation of the physical realities of the
world."[63] While women are still considered irrational
and men rational, "rationality loses its connections
with 'wisdom,' or moral and spiritual values, and comes
to be identified with the technological rationality of
science."[64] Rationality is directed toward "the manipulation [of] the material world, . . . rather than the
elevation of the spirit."[65] Men "now need women to
'uplift' them."[66] Women are able to "retain this
elevating role only by remaining in strict segregation
in the home."[67]

"Home and work, female and male . . . become complementary symbols in modern culture."[68] The female is
enshrined in the privacy of the home. Her primary, and
often only, functions are those of interpersonal

109

intimacy, extended child nurture, and house-keeping.
The male, thus freed, participates in the "real world,"
and comes home for relaxation and restoration. The
privatized feminine home is idealized as the antithesis
and bulwark of the public, masculine sphere of work; it
is everything that the modern industrial society is not.
Home is the repository for all the values denied in the
workplace--e.g., love, emotionality, intimacy,
aesthetics.[69]

Given these revised definitions of male and female,
the relationship between men and women is viewed as one
of complementarity rather than inferiority.[70] But, as
Ruether points out, even though "complementarity is
often designed to make women appear not only different,
but even superior to males . . . this ideology masks
the reality of dependency."[71] And, whether women are
defined as inferior or superior, they are "effectively
removed from the 'real world' of men and public
affairs"[72] and kept powerless.

Although the ideology of complementarity between
females and males, and between home and work, "has been
somewhat modified to accommodate the reality of working
women in the middle classes, the same contradictions
between the female domestic roles and the work world
remain largely unalleviated."[73] In fact, Ruether
argues:

> a woman who tr[ies] to occupy both
> spheres at once finds reality itself
> stacked against her, making the
> combination of maternal and masculine
> occupations all but impossible
> without extraordinary energy or
> enough wealth to hire domestic
> help.[74]

The basic form of complementarity remains the language
of modern ideology, and political and religious groups
defend it as the norm.[75]

In the preceding pages I have described two
apparently different understandings of the "true
nature" of woman; but, in essence, good femininity is
very much the counterpart to bad femaleness.[76] As
Ruether explains: "'Woman-as-body-sensuality' and
'woman-as-pure-altruistic-love' are both abstractions
of human potential created when one group of people in
power is able to define other groups of people over

110

against themselves."[77] Both ideologies condition women
to accept their dependency and powerlessness; both
ideologies prevent women and men from relating to and
cooperating with each other as equals in the creation
and transformation of society; both ideologies support
structures which keep women from "interfer[ing] with
the real business of running the world."[78]

Alienation from the World

Just as human beings are alienated from themselves
and from one another, so too, those conditioned by
Western tradition are alienated from the world--that
is, from nature.[79] Within false consciousness, the
organic interrelationship of humans and the natural
world is denied. "Earth, air, water, plants and
animals are not perceived as living beings who form a
single community of life" with all other existents;
rather "they are seen simply as 'objects to be used.'"[80]
The natural world is considered an inferior order of
creation which is to be dominated and subdued.

Since, as has already been shown, "inferiors" in
society--women, workers, etc.--are traditionally
identified with nature, it is not surprising that the
subjugation of nature is expressed in the same language
as the domination of women.[81] As Ruether illustrates:
"Nature is symbolized as female; the domination of
nature as the domination of a wife and the exploitation
of nature as the 'rape' of a woman."[82] Even when
"dominion over" is interpreted as "responsible stewardship," the latter notion remains embedded in a hierarchical view of reality with man conceived as
definitely "above" and in control of the rest of
nature.[83] A romantic or idealistic approach--a "back
to nature" approach--only serves to continue the isolation and exploitation of the natural world. In
Ruether's words, this approach is a "kind of conserva-
tism which amounts to the freezing of the present system
of injustice."[84]

Three types of alienated relationships--self,
social and ecological--which give shape to and are
expressed in false consciousness have been examined.
On each level the relationship is one of superior to
inferior, dominator to dominated rather than one of
mutuality. The relationship is one of separation and
opposition rather than cooperation, alienation rather
than communality. In the next part I describe
Ruether's position on the significance of religion in

111

maintaining a hierarchical system and enhancing false
consciousness. This part also includes a further
criticism of Niebuhr's work. I argue that his theological anthropology and interpretation of sociality which
serves as the basis for his ethical system and approach
to social change reflects, and is in fact a part of,
the very religious ideology that supports a hierarchical system of domination and alienation.

Religion and Alienated
Consciousness

In all societies, religious beliefs and rituals
serve as reinforcement for social life--its relationships, structures and consciousness. Where relationships and structures of domination comprise a social
system, religious symbols are used to sanction these
relationships and structures, making them "appear as
'natural'; not as social constructs but as the givens
of a necessary and divinely-created order of things."[85]

Drawing upon archaeological evidence, Ruether
suggests that although the first two millenia of
recorded history appear to have had a more holistic
world-view, "somewhere in the first millenium BC, . . .
alienations of civilization began to reshape the
religious world picture"[86] into a dualistic one.

> Classical religions were born through
> a breakdown of the unities of tribal
> culture and the appearing of a way
> of formulating a "religious dimen-
> sion" of life which split reality
> into distinct polarities: the sacred
> and the secular; the soul and the
> body; the material and the spiritual;
> "this world" and the transcendent
> world "to come" or "above."[87]

Religious symbols which support a hierarchical
system of the Western world are drawn primarily from
two traditions: Hebrew patriarchalism and Greek
dualism. Ruether describes the contributions of these
two traditions in the following way:

> In the Hebrew tradition God is
> imaged as . . . a male, a great
> patriarch of the sky, who like the
> patriarchs of the earth, dominates
> and rules a _familia_ of dependent

persons, women and slaves. The
creaturely as the creation and the
Community (Israel) of this divine
Patriarch are imaged either as a
community of sons (daughters are
completely invisible) or as a
community of servants or, collectively, as the wife of the Patriarch;
in other words, as the dependent
persons within the patriarchal family.
      In the Greek tradition, the
divine is imaged as a transcendent
male Mind which exists eternally
outside of and independent of matter.
This eternal male Mind creates the
material, visible world by a process
of devolution. This divinity retains
its purity and integrity by a process
of radical separation and flight from
the material to the immaterial, from
the visible to the invisible, from
sense to Mind, from the mutable to
the immutable.[88]

These two traditions were brought together in Western
religion and, in particular, Christianity. The subsequent religious symbols that developed encompass the
alienated relationships--self, social and ecological--
that have been considered above. These alienated relationships are expressed in religious language by three
types of interrelated dualisms: (1) body/soul or
matter/spirit; (2) male/female; and (3) man/nature.

Body/Soul or Matter/Spirit
Dualism

      The hierarchicalism of the dominant biblical view
provides a context for the body/soul dualism. Although
classical Christian writers struggled to reconcile the
spiritual and material realms, "both Greek and Latin
Christianity remained committed to a Platonized spirituality and eschatology that defined redemption as the
rejection of the body and the flight of the soul from
material, sensual nature."[89] Christian conversion is
"identified with withdrawal from all things 'of the
flesh' and the exclusive concentration upon the spiritual world of the soul where one lived literally as
though 'not in the body.'"[90]

      Medieval scholasticism deepened the notion of

113

Christian salvation as the suppression of "carnality" and the ascendence of the soul into the spiritual realm. Similar to the definition in patristic writings, the body continues to be defined as the inferior, if not always the evil, principle of human existence.[91]

Some historians and theologians claim that with the Reformation, a "fierce anti-asceticism" arose which tempered the condemnation of the body.[92] But the strength and effectiveness of anti-asceticism is questionable, however, when one considers that "organized witch craft persecution . . . [was] not a phenomenon of the patristic period or early Middle Ages, but of the late medieval and Reformation eras."[93] In modern theology, various expressions of this dualism between body and soul, and the inferiorization of the body remain.

Reinhold Niebuhr is careful to distance himself from a dualistic view of matter and spirit, body and soul, and from the condemnation of the finite. He explicitly rejects all Greek, idealistic and naturalistic dualisms,[94] maintaining that these various types of dualisms grow out of a misinterpretation of the conflict of spirit and impulse in human life.[95] Niebuhr claims as his own "the Biblical view," according to which "man is . . . a created and finite existence in both body and soul."[96]

Although, as we have seen in Chapter II, Niebuhr argues at length for a paradoxical relationship between nature and spirit, what Niebuhr considers dimensions of the spirit--consciousness, transcendence, self-consciousness, self-transcendence, reason, freedom and will--are, in the end, primary. The human person's "essential nature includes the freedom of his spirit, his transcendence over natural process and finally his self-transcendence."[97] In the hierarchical order of being[98] (which Niebuhr's vertical dialectic implies and which Niebuhr himself professes), the creature is lower than the "image of God" in the self; "the finite, partial, temporal, fragmentary, contingent"[99] self (i.e., the historical self) is subordinate to the transcendent self. Spirit is above and superior to nature.

Male/Female Dualism

In early church writings, the primary symbol of the carnality "which draws the soul down from its

114

'heavenly heights' to 'wallow in the flesh' is sex."[100]
Since woman, as I have already stated,[101] is identified
with the body, with carnality and sexuality, she
becomes "peculiarly the symbol of the Fall and sin."[102]
In the Christian tradition, woman is considered the
antithesis of the male who seeks "redemption through
denial of his roots in the mother, in matter, in
finitude and in mortality."[103] Woman is, in short,
inferior and ethically dangerous to man.[104] Religion
provides reasons, then, for the legitimation of a male-
dominated social order. These reasons for subjugating
and controlling women are considered "revealed truths"
rather than ideological reflections of existing relationships of domination, and "can be illustrated in the
entire line of classical Christian theology from
ancient to modern times."[105] As de Beauvoir writes:
"The Church sees to it that God never authorizes women
to escape male guardianship."[106]

Protestantism rejected, to some degree, the
ascetic of anti-sexuality promoted by Catholicism and
by Catholicism's negative view toward marriage, and
"restored the Biblical patriarchal view of the family
as a realm of religious nurture."[107] Protestantism did
not, however, challenge the patriarchal view of the
role of women. "The marital relation for women was
[and is] still defined as that of bearing children and
being under the domination of their husbands."[108]

These dimensions of Protestantism are reflected in
Niebuhr's position. First, Niebuhr clearly asserts
that sex is not in _itself_ inherently sinful.[109] The
sexual impulse, like every other physical impulse, "is
subject to and compounded with the freedom of man's
spirit."[110] Sexuality does not pull the soul down;
rather the spirit uses "the natural stuff of sex for
both the assertion of the ego and the flight of the ego
into another."[111] Responsibility for one's sinfulness,
as noted in Chapter III,[112] falls within the spiritual
realm.

Second, following his predecessors in the Protestant tradition, Niebuhr does not fundamentally challenge
the patriarchal view of women when writing about the
family. For Niebuhr, the two inexorable bounds set by
nature for relations in the family are: (1) sex
differentiation; and (2) dominion of the father.
Regarding sex differentiation, Niebuhr contends that
the primary function of a woman is motherhood. In his
words:

> The natural fact that the woman
> bears the child binds her to the
> child and partially limits the
> freedom of her choice in the
> development of various potential-
> ities of character not related to
> the vocation of motherhood.[113]

Furthermore, Niebuhr writes, the inclinations of "a
rationalistic feminism . . . to transgress inexorable
bounds set by nature" and the "efforts on the part of
the female to achieve such freedom [is] justified <u>as is
not incompatible with the primary function of mother-
hood</u>."[114] But, warns Niebuhr, "reason cannot transcend
the organic fact of sex so completely as to create the
kind of sex equality of which a utopian feminism
depends."[115]

Regarding the dominion of the father, Niebuhr
claims that "nothing in history, except perhaps the
authority of the father, belongs to the 'order of
creation.'"[116] "Every form of dominion except possibly
the first dominion of fatherhood, contains an embarrass-
ment to the moral conscious of man."[117]

The shift in socio-economic conditions during the
nineteenth century brought about a change in religious
ideology as well. Driven into the private realm of the
home by secularization, the rise of capitalism and
industrialization, religion becomes sentimentalized and
"feminized." Essential to this development is the
redefinition of woman "as the feminine; that is to say,
as submissive, docile, receptive, sublimated (unsexual)
body totally at the disposal of the divine male
demands."[118] As Ruether maintains, the woman is now
understood as

> the more natural bearer of the Christ-
> like virtues of love, altruism, and
> self-sacrifice. Spirituality, piety
> and self-abnegation [are considered]
> particularly appropriate for women
> (i.e., "good" domesticated women).[119]

"'Christian man' comes to mean primarily woman."[120]

At the same time that the home becomes "the realm
of piety and nostalgic religiosity"[121] with women as
"the high priestesses,"[122] society, in contrast, "loses
any official relation to God and the sacred."[123] It

becomes "a value-free public world,"[124] characterized
by competitive male egoism, power and functional
rationality.[125]

Morality is also, for the most part, privatized,
"feminized" and sentimentalized. Morality, as altruism,
is lodged in the private sphere "appropriate only to
person-to-person relations exemplified by marriage."[126]
Such "love morality is [considered] 'unrealistic' in
the public sphere."[127] The only possible morality in
the real world "is that of 'justice' defined as a
balancing of competitive egos."[128] According to
Ruether, this ethical split between the private and
public spheres, and between the home and work is "sanctified in . . . the theology of bourgeois society."[129]
Reinhold Niebuhr is one of the chief formulators of
this "theology of bourgeois society."

As we have already seen in Chapter II,[130] Niebuhr
associates religion, the ideal of love, and contemplation with the individual above society, and the private
sphere. Morality, the proximate goal of justice, and
action or activity he associates with the individual as
a part of society, and the public sphere. Niebuhr also
explicitly uses women to symbolize the private sphere;
to exemplify "moral man." For example, Niebuhr writes
that

> sacrificial love is a moral norm
> relevant to interpersonal relations
> (particularly family relations),
> and significant for parents (parti-
> cularly mothers, heroes and saints),
> but scarcely applicable to power
> relations.[131]

Or again, in a sermon delivered at Union Theological
Seminary, Niebuhr declares that "the extreme love ethic
is appropriate for 'mystics, monastics, martyrs, and
mothers."[132] Although the wide gap between private and
public morality narrows somewhat over time in Niebuhr's
writings, a dichotomy between the two moralities, and
between personal and social life remains. Private man
(i.e., woman) must be about "the problems which transcend the social struggle and historical situation,"
while public man sees to "the social and historical
task."[133] If a man applies private, "feminine"
morality to the real world, he is believed to be
unrealistic, naive, sentimental and ultimately effete,
i.e., effeminate.[134]

117

In the preceding section we have seen how religion, over the centuries, has reinforced the images of womanhood by using the female to symbolize both sin and purity.[135] Among the religious symbols which legitimate these images, the figures of Eve and the Virgin Mary are of particular importance.

Eve, the carnal sinful mother, represents bad femaleness; Mary, the virginal sinless Mother, represents good femininity.[136] As daughters of Eve, women learn "to expiate the disobedience of their first mother through constantly renewed gift offerings of obedience to fathers, husbands, pastors and rulers."[137] As daughters of the Virgin Mary, women are taught to "redouble [their] efforts to expiate their sinfulness by following her example of perfect obedience."[138] And, since "Mary is an exception to the general rule of femaleness," women are condemned to a sense of failure because, in the end, "no woman can really emulate her example."[139]

Together these symbols, along with the concomitant myths of the Virgin and the Whore, are used to divide women along class and racial lines into two spheres: one of sexual repression and idealization, and the other of brutalization and sexual exploitation. In Ruether's words:

> Spiritual femininity identified with
> the Virgin Mary and carnal femaleness
> identified with fallen Eve . . .
> divided into the middle class world
> of repressed decorum and into the
> lower class world exploited for work
> and sexuality.[140]

According to Ruether, white women were identified with spiritual nature; women of color with bestial nature. Historically, then, these religious symbols reinforce the domination and self-suppression of women, as well as women's separation not only from men but from one another.

Man/Nature Dualism

The alienation of the soul from the body, and the alienation of the male and "masculine" from the female and "feminine" form part of a religious world-view which also includes the separation of spiritual man from the natural world. This level of alienation has

118

received various religious expressions, including nature/grace, creation/redemption, earth/heaven, world/institutionalized church, time/eternity, and history/eschatology. Although theological interpretations vary greatly, in each one of these polarities the former element is in some way separate from, inferior to, and incomplete without the latter element.

According to Ruether, these dualisms, as they are found in Christian theology, are grounded in both classical Neo-Platonism and apocalyptic Judaism. Neo-Platonism, as has already been noted,[141] is characterized by the exaltation of spirit over matter, intellect over body, and the immutable over the mutable. Besides absorbing elements of Greek philosophy, apocalyptic Judaism was also influenced by Persian thought "with its view of world history as a struggle between a good and an evil power, ending in the overthrow of creation and the establishment of a new super-mundane world beyond history."[142] This position reflected a change from the original Hebrew messianic hope which was futuristic but this-worldly.[143]

The incorporation of classical Neo-Platonism and apocalyptic Judaism into Christian thought supports an interpretation of spacio-temporal creation as distinct from and "less-than" an eternal realm. Accompanying this notion is an interpretation of eschatology that places its ultimate hope in an Age-to-Come, in Heaven understood as either "another world into which we can escape" or "the confirming halo of existing creation."[144] Salvation involves the release, through death, of an individual soul from the natural world to a changeless, infinite world above and beyond nature, earth, and history. Both of these interpretations concerning socio-temporal creation and eschatology characterize Niebuhr's theology.

Following the Biblical tradition, Niebuhr insists that the world is "good," and therefore cannot be escaped from in the present or annihilated in the end. But the natural world is also a mystery and a threat. In Niebuhr's words, nature and society "are perennial problems of the human spirit."[145]

Niebuhr characterizes the natural world as mysterious and threatening because he sees the relation of nature to humans and their purposes as one of indifference and capriciousness. Referring to Niebuhr's position, Farley writes:

> Nature is not "reasonable" if
> "reasonable" means supporting the
> patterns and plans of human
> history. Nature often threatens
> such plans either by recalcitrantly
> resisting them, or by capriciously
> wiping them out, the final example
> being death.[146]

Niebuhr himself states (using a male/female analogy):

> Men will learn that nature can
> never be completely tamed to do
> man's will. Her blind caprices,
> her storms and tempests will con-
> tinue on occasion, to brush aside
> man's handiwork as a housewife
> destroys a cobweb; and her inexor-
> able processes will run counter to
> man's hopes and designs.[147]

Spacio-temporal creation--nature and society--"remain[s]
something of the jungle."[148] Therefore the sensitive
soul must "learn how to use the forces of nature to
defeat nature"[149]--that is, how to bring creation a
little nearer to the Kingdom of God.

Given this interpretation of nature, it is not
surprising that Niebuhr's eschatology places its ultimate hope in the full realization of the Kingdom of God
at the end of history. Reflecting the paradoxical
nature of human existence, "end," for Niebuhr, has a
double connotation. First,

> by reason of man's subjection to
> nature and finiteness this "end" is
> a point where that which exists
> ceases to be. . . . [Second,] by
> reason of man's rational freedom
> the "end" . . . is the purpose and
> goal of his life and work.[150]

The end is both finis and telos. But, it is important
to note that, in conjunction with Niebuhr's hierarchy
of spirit over nature, finis corresponds to nature and
finiteness, and it is the natural world which ceases to
be. Telos, on the other hand, corresponds to the
freedom-spirit dimension, which is above nature and
history, and remains into eternity.[151]

In some mysterious way, the permanent tension in history between spirit and nature is resolved at the end of and outside of spacio-temporal creation. God, a power outside of history, who has a freedom beyond all natural, social and rational coherences, is able to complete and culminate the whole moral and historical enterprise. But this fulfillment occurs in a trans-historical, spiritual realm; i.e., eternity. According to Niebuhr, perfect unity and ultimate harmony are realized at the cost of nature.

Thus far we have seen how religion is used to help shape and reinforce the alienated consciousness which masks essential sociality, and how Niebuhr's positions contribute to the religious ideology that supports this false consciousness characteristic of the Western world. Theological justification for the interrelated dualisms of spirit/body, male/female, and man/nature reaches its ultimate expression in the symbol of God.

The Symbol of God

In the dominant Christian tradition, God is imaged as a spiritual, male, transcendent deity; a "white 'king' on a throne in heaven."[152] This God, "made in the image of the body-alienated 'male Ego,'"[153] is an independent Being who stands over and against nature, including "feminine" humanity as the sphere to be dominated and subjugated.[154]

The exclusively male God--a projection of the dominant group--is not only "an ideological bias that reflects the sociology of patriarchal societies."[155] This image of God also provides one of the major supports for relations and structures of patriarchal rule. In Ruether's words:

> Traditional theological images of
> God . . . have been the sanctifica-
> tion of sexism and hierarchicalism
> precisely by defining this rela-
> tionship of God as father to humanity
> in a domination-subordination model
> and by allowing ruling-class males
> to identify themselves with this
> divine fatherhood in such a way as
> to establish themselves in the same
> kind of hierarchical relationship to
> women and lower classes.[156]

Niebuhr's God is both transcendent to and intimately involved in time and history.[157] First of all, God
is the Eternal one who completely transcends the limitations of finiteness and history. His freedom and self-
sufficiency are absolute.[158] God is the apex of the
cosmological pyramid, and from the height of his transcendence God has the capacity to comprehend history
totally as an objective unity.[159] But God is not only
transcendent--mere discontinuity would result in complete unintelligibility; he is also immanent. God
enters into a meaningful and intimate relation with
human beings and history, without becoming identified
with them.

God's threefold relationship to the world is
revealed "at the edge of human consciousness."[160] As
Niebuhr explains:

> The general revelation of personal
> human experience, the sense of
> being confronted with a "wholly
> other" at the edge of human con-
> sciousness, contains three
> elements. . . . The first is the
> sense of reverence for a majesty
> and a dependence upon an ultimate
> source of being. The second is
> the sense of moral obligation laid
> upon one from beyond oneself and
> of moral unworthiness before a
> judge. The third . . . is the
> longing for forgiveness.[161]

God becomes specifically understood as Creator, Judge
and Redeemer.

All three of these roles are those of domination.
God stands over (and, as Judge, over against) His
creation and sinners. In all three types of relations,
God's subordinates are weak, finite, and dependent; and
"the real evil in the human situation lies in man's
unwillingness to recognize and acknowledge his position."[162] The primary sin for Niebuhr is "the unwillingness of man to acknowledge his creatureliness and
dependence upon God and his efforts to make his own
life independent and secure."[163] Hierarchicalism and
the domination-subordination model permeate Niebuhr's
understanding and discussions of God.

Niebuhr's claim that this notion of God is

"intuited in the deepest consciousness of human beings and intimated in their experience" is a partial truth. The weakness of this claim lies in Niebuhr's failure to critically analyze the social context which, in fact, shapes this "deepest consciousness" and directs personal human experience. There are no "depths of consciousness in each individual self-conscious" which are not in some way social.[164] There is no "free play of the imagination" which reveals "the 'supra-scientific' truth of the human situation before a Hidden God."[165] Rather, Niebuhr's God is made in man's own image. As Ruether argues, possibly with Niebuhr in mind and in a way that is applicable to his position:

> The exclusively male God who creates
> out of nothing, who is bodiless,
> transcendent to nature and history,
> wholly other from the natural world,
> upon whose domineering wrath and
> grace man hangs as a miserable,
> crestfallen sinner, is the theolog-
> ical self-image[166]

of the dominant male ego which has the power to project and perpetuate such a notion of God. This symbolic representation of God "illumines" our experience and is in turn validated by it, as Niebuhr contends,[167] but as a way of legitimating, sustaining and enforcing an unjust, alienating, and humanly created social system.

In this part of the chapter, I have described the religious symbols which reflect and ratify alienated consciousness. In each of these dualisms a pattern of domination and subordination has been identified. One element in the dualism (spirit, male, man) has been defined as more valuable or higher than the other (body, female, nature), and therefore destined to control the inferior element. I have also shown, by re-examining Niebuhr's writings, how his theological anthropology contributes to the religious ideology which supports a hierarchical model of society and reality.

The dualistic consciousness, which Ruether so aptly describes and which Niebuhr exemplifies, represents a world in which human beings are alienated from the earth, from each other both structurally and inter-personally, and from themselves in the very depth of their psyches. Within this world-view, essential sociality is denied and essentially social beings are dehumanized in and through relationships of domination and exploitation.

This dominant form of dualistic consciousness may appear to be the only one. As Gray writes: "Metaphors of dualism and hierarchy [have] etched the ontological skies for so long that they seem embedded in truth itself."[168] This makes it difficult, Ruether writes,

> for people dominated by such a dualistic image of reality to imagine a society where men and women can relate without this model of subordination or to recognize that fellow humanity itself is fundamentally vitiated at its heart by this inequality.[169]

But, as I have previously noted,[170] there is a different vision of the world which is based on relationships of mutuality and interdependence, and reflects essential sociality. The alternative vision, which Ruether suggests, defines interaction not in terms of "the conquest of an alien object,"[171] but in terms of communication between two equivalent and mutually supportive persons. Within this world-view, "the other" is not "that other form of life, or that other unique community [which] is the limit beyond which [one's] ambitions must not run and the boundary beyond which [one's] life must not expand,"[172] as Niebuhr contends. Rather, "the other" is, in fact, a part of oneself; he or she is the completion of oneself and one's own unrealized potential as a member of the human-species. The other is also a partner--acknowledged and equal--in bringing the future into being. "Intimations of this have reached us," writes Griffin, "that we are inseparable from all other beings in the universe."[173]

Such an alternative vision often tends to meet with the charge of "utopianism." Even those "practiced in criticism of the status quo resist a vision . . . which foresees an end to male privilege and a changed relationship between the sexes,"[174] as well as changed relationships among all human beings--and among all beings. In the final pages of this chapter, Ruether's alternative vision, which is based on the recognition of essential sociality, is presented in order to further clarify her interpretation of this notion.

From Domination and Dualisms
to Dynamic Unity

Ruether discerns rudimentary elements of an alternative consciousness in patriarchal myth--an alternative consciousness "based on dialectical interplay of the polarities of existence rather than hierarchical dualisms."[175] Ruether does not accept an either/or or a both/and dichotomy as a resolution, but "move[s] beyond both poles to a new synthesis--a dynamic unity--that [can] include them both."[176] This process involves going into one side of the apparent dualism in order to discover the other side within it. For Ruether, this process is a "conversion to relationality . . . in which the dialectics of human existence are converted from 'opposites' into mutual interdependence."[177] Feminist writers stress that this process does not imply a loss of diversity. Differences are not combined into a "holy indifference." Rather, there is a synthesis between the elements which is at once processual and conflictual.[178]

Using a dialectical approach, Ruether suggests the following interpretations for the dualisms that have been considered. First, there is not a separation between matter/spirit or body/soul. The body is not "objectified as an alien, dangerous force that must be crushed into submission,"[179] or defined as the inferior element of one's being. Instead, the body and soul are integrally related to form the human person. For Ruether, "the mind and the five senses are the organs of thinking and feeling in total organic existence."[180] Humans are not "clothed" in their bodies; they do not "dwell" in them; they are not unjustly "imprisoned" in them. Humans are their bodies; they are body-selves who experience all the pleasure and enjoyment, pain and suffering that body-life brings.[181] Within this worldview, body, flesh, carnality, sensuality and mortality are all recognized, accepted and celebrated as one's own, as inseparable dimensions of oneself.

Second, the dualism of male/female and the accompanying dualism of masculine/feminine are inadequate constructs for describing the traits which characterize human beings. For Ruether, there is a need for "a reconstruction which . . . give[s] each person the fullness of their being stolen from them by false polarizations."[182] New words or models are needed to adequately reflect the fact that "both males and females contain the total human psychic essence."[183]

125

As Ruether insists: "Men are just as capable of being receptive and intuitive as women; women are just as capable of being thinkers and decisive actors as men."[184] This view is not an anti-biological one as some critics would claim. Rather "it is a correction to the false biology"[185] presupposed by the dualisms of male/female and masculine/feminine, and a critique of the dualistic social roles that maintain and perpetuate these dualisms.[186]

The relationship between men and women is not seen as one of subject/object or I/it; nor is it the relation of half-selves which the ideology of complementarity suggests.[187] Rather, an authentic relationship between men and women, and between all human beings is a relation "between whole persons, when suppression and projection cease to distort the encounter."[188] It is a relation of interdependence "which is not competitive or hierarchical but mutually enhancing."[189] Each person participates in the relationship from a position of autonomy, self-esteem, and from an equality which is not confined by sex, race, and class. Such participation allows for authentic receptivity--a receptivity no longer equated with powerlessness and dependency,[190] but with the mutual recognition and acceptance of the essential part others have in creating who one is and what one's destiny is to be. What humans are and what they struggle to be together is recognized and celebrated (or at times lamented) as one's own.[191]

This change in sexual relationships and symbolism challenges all relationships which have been modeled on a sexual dualism, including the third form of dualism considered above--man and nature. As Ruether writes: "The liberation of all human relations from the false polarities of masculinity and femininity must also shape a new relationship of humanity to nature."[192]

The relationship between humanity and nature is not one of separation and opposition. Nature is not outside of human life and something to be mastered and controlled, dominated and exploited. Rather, there is an essential relationship between human beings and the world system in which they live and move and have their being.[193] Humans "are rooted in the earth and sensually in dialogue with it."[194] Thus, for Ruether, the relationship between humans and nature is one of cooperation and reciprocity, based on the model which nature itself provides. As Ruether writes:

126

> The human sociosphere must dupli-
> cate and interrelate with the natural
> ecosystems, on the model by which
> nature itself achieves this balance,
> by having each life system comple-
> ment and feed into the other in the
> cycles of soil, plants, air and
> water, and the interrelation of
> different animal communities.[195]

Nature is a "partner in the creation of that new world
where all things can be 'very good.'"[196] By recogniz-
ing nature as a part of human life, people not only
"redeem [their] sister earth from her bondage to
destruction,"[197] they also save themselves (if not too
late) from ecological disaster.

In the preceding pages I have described how
Ruether attempts to break down the category of what, in
patriarchal society, has been symbolized as the Other--
body, woman, nature. The reality which Ruether portrays is a complex and dynamic synthesis which simply
includes those interdependent elements which previously
were defined as polar opposites.

The alternative consciousness which Ruether
suggests is a partial one however, which is continually
clarified as oppressed peoples and those in solidarity
with them struggle to subvert the patriarchal system.[198]
A fundamental reconstruction of the basic model of
interrelationships presumes a radical reconstruction of
social structures and institutionalized patterns of
relating. As I have stated, and as Ruether herself
stresses: the "forms that condition our psychology are
objectively embodied in our socio-economic system."[199]
If our model of relationships is to become one of
mutuality--"a cooperative model of fellowship of life
systems"[200]--then the social patterns of domination and
subordination must be replaced by

> a living pattern of mutuality between
> men and women, between parents and
> children, among people in their
> social, economic and political rela-
> tionships and, finally, between
> [humankind] and the organic harmonies
> of nature.[201]

Within such a socio-historical context, alienation and
alienated consciousness which separate humans from each

other and mask their essential sociality would be, it is hoped, overcome.[202]

In the next chapter, I develop an ethical system which is based on Ruether's understanding of essential sociality. As part of this ethical system, I consider Ruether's approach to social change which is directed towards a radical reconstruction of society.

Notes

[1]Rosemary Radford Ruether, New Woman/New Earth: Sexist Ideologies and Human Liberation (New York: The Seabury Press, A Crossroad Book, 1975), pp. xii-xiii, hereafter cited as NWNE.

[2]Rosemary Radford Ruether, Liberation Theology: Human Hope Confronts Christian History and American Power (New York, Paramus, Toronto: Paulist Press, 1972), p. 124, hereafter cited as LT.

[3]NWNE, p. xiii.

[4]LT, p. 124. Feminist and social activist Sheila Collins also argues that "like most of the other liberation theologies and in contrast to most orthodox, neo-orthodox and fundamentalist Christian doctrine and practice, feminist theology understands human beings as social animals--the product of particular and collective experiences that have shaped their values, their self-concepts, and the ways in which they understand God and the world" ("Feminist Theology at the Crossroads," Christianity and Crisis 41 [December 14, 1981]: 344).

[5]Rosemary Radford Ruether, To Change the World: Christology and Cultural Criticism (New York: Crossroad, 1981), p. 67, hereafter cited as TCW. One of Ruether's analogies for this essentially social view of reality is that of "the connecting links of a dance in which each part is equally vital to the whole" (ibid.).

[6]Ibid. For example, "plants are not 'lower' than humans because they don't think or move. Rather their photosynthesis is the vital process which underlies the very existence of the animal and human world. We could not exist without them, whereas they could exist very well without us. Who then," asks Ruether, "is more important" (ibid.). See also Rosemary Radford Ruether, "Sexism and God-Talk: Toward a Feminist Theology."

Boston: Beacon Press, 1983. (Galley.), chapter 3, n.p.

[7]TCW, p. 67.

[8]See Ruether, "Sexism and God-Talk," chapter 3, n.p.

[9]This understanding of the integration of nature and humanity is a theme in many feminist works. For example, Susan Griffin writes: "We say our lives are part of nature. We say in every particle every act lives. The body of the tree reveals the past. That the waves from the stone falling into the water were frozen in the winter ice. That stars pull at the bodies of crabs and oysters know the phases of the moon" (Woman and Nature: The Roaring Inside Her [New York: Harper and Row, Publishers, Harper Colophon Books, 1980], p. 173). Gray expresses the notion of relationality in these terms: "When I now say that 'We are interconnected,' . . . I do not mean just that there exist certain relationships between discrete entities, which bridge otherwise empty space. On the contrary, what I am meaning to convey when I am speaking of connections is the sense of a continuous reality so much of one piece as to make the whole notion of empty space and solid objects totally inappropriate" (Green Paradise Lost, p. 62).

[10]Rosemary Radford Ruether, "The Biblical Vision of the Ecological Crisis," The Christian Century 95 (November 22, 1978):1131.

[11]Rosemary Radford Ruether, "Disputed Questions: On Being a Christian," 1981. (Galley.), p. 17. This expansion of the notion of essential sociality to include nature is one of Ruether's contributions to the conflict tradition. By rejecting a subject/object, superordinate/subordinate relationship between humans and nature, Ruether corrects the error of "metaphysical one-upmanship," such as is found in such thinkers as Marx. (See, for example, "Economic and Philosophical Manuscripts," in Karl Marx: Early Writings, pp. 349-50; Capital, vol. 1, cited in McLellan, The Thought of Karl Marx, p. 138; and Plamenatz, Karl Marx's Philosophy of Man, pp. 82, 115). Unger goes so far as to claim that "perhaps the main vice in the Hegelian-Marxist theory of work was its uncritical acceptance of the narcissism of the subject as an adequate solution to the problem of self and nature" (Knowledge and Politics, pp. 212-13).

[12]Rosemary Radford Ruether, "Paradoxes of Human Hope: The Messianic Horizon of Church and Society," Theological Studies 33 (June 1972):241.

[13]Ibid.

[14]Ruether, "Black Theology," p. 686.

[15]Rosemary Radford Ruether, "Male Clericalism and the Dread of Women," The Ecumenist 11 (July-August 1973):69.

[16]LT, p. 133, emphasis added.

[17]Rosemary Radford Ruether, "Home and Work: Women's Roles and the Transformation of Values," Theological Studies 36 (December 1975):659.

[18]Rosemary Ruether, "The Search for Soul Power in the White Community," Christianity and Crisis 30 (April 27, 1970):85. For a further discussion of community consciousness, see Rosemary Radford Ruether, "A Feminist Perspective on Religion and Science: Comments on Bishop Gregorios' Paper 'Science and Faith: Complementary or Contradictory?'," paper presented at the Conference on Faith, Science, and the Future, Cambridge, Massachusetts, July 1979. Implicit in this notion of community consciousness are the two stages of individuation described above: differentiation and integration (p. 82). Consciousness, according to Ruether, should not, in the end, be something to "separate male from female, advantaged from disadvantaged--or even humans from plants, animals, earth, air and water"; but rather, "should bind us together." For Ruether, human consciousness should be "the consciousness of earth, the consciousness of matter, [and] be used to refine, enhance and renew the great harmonies that bind animals and inanimate together in our ecology" (ibid., p. 4).

[19]Rosemary Ruether, "Crisis in Sex and Race: Black Theology vs. Feminist Theology," Christianity and Crisis 34 (April 15, 1974):72.

[20]Ibid.

[21]Ruether, "Sexism and God-Talk," Chapter 3, n.p.

[22]TCW, p. 2.

[23]Rosemary Ruether, "Ruether on Ruether,"

<u>Christianity and Crisis</u> 39 (May 14, 1979):126.

[24]Rosemary Radford Ruether, "Rich Nations/Poor Nations and the Exploitation of the Earth," <u>Dialog</u> 13 (Summer 1974):207.

[25]<u>LT</u>, p. 95.

[26]Ruether names three types of structures that specifically contribute to female subordination and inferiorization: (1) male puberty rites "which uproot the male from the female context"; (2) those that establish the domination of women's labor, including economic production and domestic production and reproduction, by men; and (3) those that reduce women to silence while promoting a male monopoly on cultural definition" (See "Sexism and God-Talk," Chapter 3, n.p.).

[27]Ruether, "Rich Nations/Poor Nations," p. 207. See also Collins, <u>A Different Heaven and Earth</u>, pp. 66-67.

[28]Ruether, "Disputed Questions," p. 55.

[29]Ruether, "Black Theology," pp. 684-85. As Ruether points out: "The pictures of the 'lower' groups projected by the dominant groups tend to be similar. The 'lower' group is always pictured as passive, dependent, unstable, emotional, potentially vicious, subject to unrestrained passion, lacking true intelligence or reasoning power" (ibid.)--that is, lacking full humanity.

[30]Ruether, "Crisis in Sex and Race," p. 72.

[31]See <u>LT</u>, p. 106.

[32]As Gray maintains: In a "hierarchical order of being . . . the lower orders--whether female or child or animal or plant--can be treated, mistreated, violated, sold, sacrificed or killed at the convenience of the higher states of spiritual beings found in males and in God" (<u>Green Paradise Lost</u>, p. 6).

[33]Hartmann, "The Unhappy Marriage Between Feminism and Marxism," p. 15. And, within the pecking order, "all men whatever their rank in the patriarchy, are bought off by being able to control at least some women" (ibid.). See also Ruether, "Sexism and

God-Talk," Chapter 6, n.p.

[34]NWNE, p. 117.

[35]Collins holds a view similar to Ruether's. She writes: "Racism and sexism--as predispositions to treat the Other as an alien and disvalued object-- predate the rise of capitalism, but these tendencies take a particularly virulent and intractable form within a capitalist economic system; indeed, they are the oil which keeps the engine of capitalism running smoothly. One could say that without the preexistence of racism and sexism, capitalism would have had to invent them" ("Sexism, Racism and the Church: A Socio- logical Analysis," paper presented at St. John's University, Jamaica, New York, Summer, 1978," p. 2).

[36]And, one might add, other "isms" as well--e.g., imperialism, ageism, heterosexism.

[37]Ruether, "Crisis in Sex and Race," p. 67.

[38]LT, pp. 8-9.

[39]Ruether, "Ruether on Ruether," p. 126.

[40]Ruether, "Male Clericalism," p. 66.

[41]Ruether is one of "a number of feminists [who] have observed that Western culture throughout its history has been pervaded by a series of mutually exclusive dualisms or dichotomies . . . [A]ll these dichotomies have exhibited a pattern of dominance and subordination. One member of each pair has been seen as more 'real,' more valuable, or more important than the other and therefore as inherently or ideally in control of its 'inferior' opposite" (Saiving, "Androgy- nous Life," p. 18). For Ruether's discussion of the relationship between dominant and subordinate social roles; linear, dichotomized thinking and spatial, rela- tional-thinking; and left-brain and right-brain special- ization and socialization, see "Sexism and God-Talk," Chapter 3, n.p. and Chapter 4, pp. 19-22.

[42]Collins gives the following relationships as examples: "Husband and wife, parent and child, boss and employee, priest and parishioner, president and people, white and black, brown, yellow, or red, American or foreigner" (A Different Heaven and Earth, p. 67).

[43]LT, p. 19.

[44]NWNE, p. 3.

[45]LT, pp. 16-17. To cite Ruether's own words, these three levels include: "(1) alienation from one-self; one's own body; (2) alienation from one's fellow person in the 'alien' community; (3) alienation from the 'world'; from the visible earth and sky" (ibid.).

[46]NWNE, p. 14.

[47]TCW, p. 60.

[48]Rosemary Radford Ruether, "Male Chauvinist Theology and the Anger of Women," Cross Currents 21 (Spring 1971):181.

[49]See Rosemary Ruether, "Sexism and Liberation: The Historical Experience," in From Machismo to Mutuality: Essays on Sexism and Woman-Man Liberation, ed. Eugene C. Bianchi and Rosemary Ruether (New York/ Paramus, N.J./Toronto: Paulist Press, 1976), p. 15; Rosemary Radford Ruether, "Women, Ecology and the Domination of Nature," The Ecumenist 14 (November-December, 1975):2; and TCW, p. 60.

[50]See Gray, Green Paradise Lost, pp. 61-62, for her discussion of the contributions of scientist Sir Isaac Newton and philosopher Rene Descartes to a dual-ist interpretation of the self.

[51]Ibid., p. 62.

[52]TCW, p. 60.

[53]NWNE, p. 181; see also Ruether, "Male Chauvinist Theology," p. 181.

[54]Ruether, "Sexism and Liberation," p. 15. In classical philosophy "this identification of women with the lower half of the body-soul dualism is especially developed in Aristotle, who divided humanity along the lines of this dualism into 'head-people' and the 'body-people'; the dominators and the dominated." Aristotle, as with others, "extend[s] this dualism along the lines of class and race, defining slaves and non-Greeks as servile persons. The free Greek male was the natural aristocracy of humankind" (ibid.).

133

[55]NWNE, p. 74. See also Ruether, "Sexism and God-Talk," Chapter 4, pp. 1-2, 20-21.

[56]Rosemary Ruether, "Mother Earth and the Mega-machine," Christianity and Crisis 31 (December 13, 1971):267.

[57]NWNE, p. 4. For a careful and extensive analysis of the male-female dualism as it relates to racism and classism, see Sheila Collins, "The Familial Economy of God," paper presented at the Second Women's Ordination Conference, Baltimore, Maryland, November 10, 1978. See also Susan Griffin's chapter "The Sacrificial Lamb" in Pornography and Silence: Culture's Revolt Against Nature (New York: Harper and Row, Harper Colophon Books, 1982), pp. 156-99.

[58]Lynda Glennon points out that "the precedent of pairing the 'feminine' or women in general with larger cultural entities stretches far back in social thought" (Women and Dualism: A Sociology of Knowledge Analysis [New York and London: Longman, 1979], p. 87). For example, Tonnies, a classical sociological theorist "offered a thorough-going parallel between women and Gemeinschaft" (ibid.).

[59]NWNE, p. 76.

[60]TCW, p. 52, emphasis added. See also Ruether, "Disputed Questions," pp. 105-106; Ruether, "Sexism and God-Talk," Chapter 4, pp. 12-14; and Elizabeth Janeway, Man's World, Woman's Place: A Study of Social Mythology (New York: Morrow and Company, Inc., 1971), pp. 11-26 for discussions of the rise of the cult of domesticity. For the importance of the rise of capitalism for the redefinition of the feminine, see Roberta Hamilton, The Liberation of Women: A Study of Patriarchy and Capitalism, Controversies in Sociology, no. 6 (London: George Allen & Unwin, 1978), especially pp. 23-49.

[61]Ruether, "Mother Earth," p. 268.

[62]See Ruether, "Male Clericalism," p. 67; also NWNE, p. 22; and Ruether, "Women, Ecology," p. 4.

[63]Rosemary R. Ruether, "Why Socialism Needs Feminism, and Vice Versa," Christianity and Crisis 40 (April 28, 1980):105.

[64]NWNE, p. 76.

[65]Ibid.

[66]Ruether, "Disputed Questions," p. 105.

[67]Ibid.

[68]Ruether, "Why Socialism Needs Feminism," p. 105.

[69]See Rosemary Radford Ruether, "The Cult of True Womanhood," Commonweal 99 (November 9, 1973):129-30; Ruether, "Home and Work," p. 652; and NWNE, p. 22. Feminist Adrienne Rich also portrays this polarization between home and work in her book On Lies, Secrets and Silence: Selected Prose from 1966-1978: "Fundamental to women's oppression is the assumption that [they] as a group belong to the 'private' sphere of the home, the hearth, the family, the sexual, the emotional, out of which men emerge as adults to act in the 'public' arena of power, the 'real' world, and to which they return for mothering, for access to female forms of intimacy, affection, and solace unavailable in the realm of male struggle and competition" ([New York: W. W. Norton & Company, 1979], p. 215).

[70]It is important to stress again, however, that "this whole concept of femininity [as developed in the nineteenth century] is . . . a middle class ideology. . . . Poor and working class women [fall] below the ideology of the 'lady' and are not accorded its respect or protection" (Ruether, "Disputed Questions," p. 105). See also Hamilton, The Liberation of Women, pp. 46-49.

[71]Ibid.

[72]Ruether, "Home and Work," p. 652.

[73]Ruether, "Disputed Questions," p. 106.

[74]Ruether, "Mother Earth," p. 268; also Ruether, "Disputed Questions," pp. 104-105.

[75]For example, the Moral Majority and the new Right, as well as the Roman Catholic hierarchy and Protestant fundamentalists advocate positions based on this ideology. See Ruether, "Male Clericalism," p. 67.

[76]Ruether, "Why Socialism Needs Feminism," p. 106.

[77]TCW, p. 55.

[78]Ruether, "Sexism and Liberation," p. 20.

[79]Sheila Collins expresses this third aspect of alienation in slightly different terms. She writes that "Westerners, conditioned by the Judeo-Christian tradition, are alienated from that part of themselves which belongs to the earth" ("Toward a Feminist Theology," The Christian Century 89 [August 2, 1972]: 798). This form of alienation is a major theme of Susan Griffin's Pornography and Silence. She argues throughout her book that "the pornographic mind" (or synonymously, "the chauvinist mind") is so terrified of woman and nature, and the force of eros, [it] must separate itself from what it fears" (p. 13).

[80]LT, p. 18; see also Rosemary Ruether, "Critic's Corner: An Unexpected Tribute to the Theologian," Theology Today 27 (October 1970):333-35.

[81]Ruether, "Women, Ecology," p. 1.

[82]TCW, p. 61. Similarly Gray writes: "Rebelling against any dependence upon 'Mother Nature,' he [i.e., the male] must of necessity put 'her' down into the dominated, submissive compliant-wife and sexual-woman role" (Green Paradise Lost, p. 48). For further discussion of the identification of women and nature in patriarchy, see Griffin, Woman and Nature; Dorothy Dinnerstein, The Mermaid and the Minotaur (New York: Harper & Row, 1976); and Ruether, "Sexism and God-Talk," Chapter 3.

[83]Although men and women alike have been affected by the Western Christian tradition, "'man's' domination of nature has never meant humans in general, but ruling class males" (TCW, p. 60). For a further criticism of the notion of responsible stewardship, see Gray, Green Paradise Lost, pp. 1-6, 138-40.

[84]Ruether, "Feminist Perspective on Religion and Science," p. 3. For Ruether, "the romantic project of the return to nature . . . fails to grapple with the interconnections of social and natural domination. So it does not envision a real transformation of the dominant system itself into a new relationship of humans with humans, humans with nature" ("Sexism and God-Talk," Chapter 3, n.p.).

[85]TCW, p. 61.

[86]Ruether, "Mother Earth," p. 269; see also LT, p. 119; and Ruether, "Sexism and God-Talk," Chapter 2, n.p. Ruether believes that "sexist and class polarizations did not immediately reshape the religious worldview" of ancient civilization. During these earliest times, "religious culture continued to reflect the more holistic view of society of the neolithic village, where the individual and the community, nature and society, male and female, earth goddess and sky god were seen in a total perspective of world renewal" (ibid.).

[87]LT, p. 6.

[88]Ruether, "A Feminist Perspective on Religion and Science," pp. 1-2. Although, in many ways, the Hebrew people clung with particular tenacity to their tribal beliefs and rituals, male monotheism and Yahwism repressed the feminine divine role. See Ruether, "Mother Earth," p. 270; Rosemary Radford Ruether, "The Female Nature of God: A Problem in Contemporary Religious Life," in Concilium: Religion in the Eighties, vol. 143: God as Father?, ed. Johannes-Baptist Metz and Edward Schillebeeckx (Edinburgh: T. & T. Clark LTD. and New York: The Seabury Press, 1981), pp. 62-64; and Ruether, "Sexism and God-Talk," Chapter 2.

[89]Rosemary Radford Ruether, "Misogynism and Virginal Feminism in the Fathers of the Church," in Religion and Sexism: Images of Woman in the Jewish and Christian Traditions, ed. Rosemary Radford Ruether (New York: Simon and Schuster, 1974), p. 153.

[90]Rosemary Ruether, "The Ethic of Celibacy," Commonweal 97 (February 2, 1973):393.

[91]See NWNE, p. 92; and Eleanor Commo McLaughlin, "Equality of Souls, Inequality of Sexes: Women in Medieval Theology," in Religion and Sexism, pp. 213-266.

[92]Niebuhr, for one, makes this claim. By "anti-asceticism" Niebuhr means "the opposition to the effort to establish goodness by the suppression of physical desires, particularly sexual ones" (SDH, p. 107).

[93]NWNE, p. 92. See also McLaughlin, "Equality of Souls, Inequality of Sexes," pp. 254-55.

[94]See NDM, 1:4-12; and SDH, pp. 75-84.

[95]REE, p. 198.

[96]NDM, 1:12. Niebuhr may be numbered among the contemporary Christians "embarrassed by classical Christian asceticism," who are, according to Ruether, "want to stress the naturalism of the Old Testament and to condemn body-soul dualism as Hellenistic and unbiblical" ("Misogynism and Virginal Feminism," p. 150). See, for example, NDM, 1:7, 13; and SDH, pp. 75ff. "But this thesis is misleading as a historical account of the development of that dualism in antiquity that became the cultural mold within which Christianity was formed. The fact is that every religion in antiquity--Babylonian, Canaanite, Persian, Greek and Jewish--passed from a naturalistic to an other-worldly religious hope in the period from approximately the sixth to the second centuries, B.C. . . . . Christianity, born in Jewish apocalypticism and nurtured in the world of Hellenistic syncretism, drew together all the streams of religious consciousness from antiquity, Greek, Jewish and Oriental but precisely in their alienated, anticosmic, stage of development" ("Misogynism and Virginal Feminism," p. 150).

[97]NDM, 1:270, emphasis added.

[98]According to the doctrine of the hierarchical order of being, "all of creation is ordered into a hierarchical pattern of relationships, which may be schematized by a ladder with God on the top rung followed by Angels, Jesus, Men, Women, Children on down to the lowliest creatures at the bottom" (Collins, A Different Heaven and Earth, p. 64). Ruether describes this order as a "chain of being" and "chain of command" ("Sexism and God-Talk," Chapter 3, n.p.).

[99]Gilkey, "Theology of History," p. 364.

[100]Ruether, "The Ethic of Celibacy," p. 393.

[101]See p. 146.

[102]Ruether, "Misogynism and Virginal Feminism," p. 157.

[103]Ruether, "A Feminist Perspective on Religion and Science," p. 2.

[104]Ruether, "Misogynism and Virginal Feminism," p. 157. Let us recall that other groups besides women

are "feminized" and are therefore also considered inferior and dangerous to men. See p. 108.

[105]Ruether, "Sexism and God-Talk," Chapter 4, p. 4.

[106]Simone de Beauvoir, The Second Sex, trans. and
ed. H. M. Parshley (New York: Alfred A. Knopf, 1952;
Vintage Books, 1974), p. 693.

[107]Ruether, "The Cult of True Womanhood," p. 128.

[108]Ibid.

[109]In fact, Niebuhr criticizes the Reformation for
failing (1) to exploit the conception of human wholeness to its full extent, and (2) to adequately "rethink
the whole Christian attitude toward man's sexual
problems" (SDH, pp. 107-108).

[110]NDM, 1:236.

[111]Ibid. For Niebuhr, "sex is the most obvious
occasion for the expression of [the sin of] sensuality
and the most vivid expression of it" (ibid., p. 239,
emphasis added). Niebuhr's treatment of the use of sex
for expressions of pride and the will-to-power is
sorely limited. For discussions of the forms of sexism
implicit in Niebuhr's treatment of sin, see Valerie
Saiving Goldstein, "The Human Situation: A Feminist
Viewpoint," Journal of Religion 40 (April 1960):100-112;
and Judith Plaskow, Sex, Sin and Grace: Women's
Experience and the Theologies of Reinhold Niebuhr and
Paul Tillich (Lanham, MD: University Press of America,
Inc., 1980).

[112]See pp. 49-50.

[113]NDM, 1:282.

[114]Ibid., emphasis added.

[115]CPP, pp. 62-63.

[116]SNE, p. 40.

[117]Ibid., p. 33. By his statements on the dominion
of the father, Niebuhr avoids what he considers to be
Aristotle's error of "regarding the dominion of the
father as primordial" (MNHC, p. 34, emphasis added),
while he affirms and sanctions paternal authority.

Although Niebuhr mentions the "struggle between the original matriarchal and emerging patriarchal forms of family authority" (ibid.), it is not a theme he develops in any detail--an interesting omission for a theologian who identifies the will-to-power as the original sin.

[118]Ruether, "A Feminist Perspective on Religion and Science," p. 2.

[119]TCW, p. 52; see also Ruether, "Sexism and God-Talk," Chapter 4, p. 14.

[120]NWNE, p. 76.

[121]Ruether, "The Cult of True Womanhood," p. 129.

[122]Ibid. As Ruether writes: "Women were to be, above all, religious, to nurture faith in a religion in which men no longer believed but wished to believe that they still believed" (ibid.).

[123]NWNE, p. 76.

[124]Ibid., p. 199.

[125]See ibid., pp. 76, 199.

[126]Ruether, "The Cult of True Womanhood," p. 131.

[127]NWNE, p. 199.

[128]Ibid.

[129]Ibid.

[130]See pp. 25-26.

[131]Reinhold Niebuhr, "Some Things I Have Learned," Saturday Review, November 6, 1965, p. 22, emphasis added.

[132]LJ, p. 11, emphasis added.

[133]Reinhold Niebuhr, "Radicalism and Religion," The World Tomorrow 14 (October 1931):327. Women are so associated with the private sphere and ignored by Niebuhr that in 1958 he could write that "in a culture that prided itself on its openness and social mobility, the Negro alone was reduced to the status of the

medieval serf. . . . [and] prevented by law or by custom from participating in the process" (PSA, p. 78, emphasis added). Thus Niebuhr makes invisible the suffrage movement in women's history and women's struggle to participate actively in the public sphere.

[134]See Ruether, "The Cult of True Womanhood," p. 131.

[135]See Ruether, "Home and Work," p. 652. In Ruether's words, the female is defined as: (1) "the devil's gateway, font of sin, and unsealer of the forbidden fruit"; as well as, in later years (2) "'too pure,' too noble to descend into the base world of work and politics" (ibid.).

[136]Ruether has written extensively on the use of these two symbols to perpetuate patriarchalism. See, for example, "Misogynism and Virginal Feminism," pp. 156-79 passim; NWNE; "The Meaning of Mariology," pp. 36-62; Mary--The Feminine Face of the Church (Philadelphia: The Westminister Press, 1977), pp. 53-75; and "Sexism and God-Talk," Chapter 6, n.p.

[137]Ruether, "Why Socialism Needs Feminism," p. 105.

[138]Ibid. As Ruether critically observes: "The white lady of Mariology always lands woman on her knees before her 'divine Son' as the sublimated, and sexually alienated servant of the male ego" ("Crisis in Sex and Race," p. 73). De Beauvoir also writes of this stress placed on obedience: "The passivity enforced upon women is sanctified. Telling her beads by the fire, she knows she is nearer heaven than her husband, gadding about at political meetings. There is no need to do anything to save her soul, it is enough to live in obedience" (The Second Sex, p. 693).

[139]Ruether, "Why Socialism Needs Feminism," p. 105.

[140]NWNE, p. 20.

[141]See p. 113.

[142]Ruether, "The Ethic of Celibacy," p. 391; and "Disputed Questions," pp. 49-51.

[143]Ruether explains the transition in this way: "During the period from the Maccabees to the Jewish

141

wars (200 B.C. to 100 A.D.), a change took place in the messianic tradition in Judaism. Under the pressure of repeated experience of imperial conquest and the frustration of all hopes of liberation as an autonomous nation, messianic hope became more and more radicalized and cut off from continuity with finite creation and social life" (Ruether, "The Ethic of Celibacy," p. 391).

[144]Ruether, "Disputed Questions," p. 18.

[145]CPP, p. 294.

[146]Edward Farley, The Transcendence of God (Philadelphia: The Westminister Press, 1958), p. 64.

[147]REE, p. 294.

[148]MMIS, p. 81.

[149]Ibid.

[150]NDM, 2:287.

[151]FH, p. 235.

[152]Rosemary Ruether, "Individual Repentance is Not Enough," Explor 2 (Spring 1976):50. See also NWNE, p. 13.

[153]Ruether, "Male Clericalism," p. 66.

[154]NWNE, p. 56. This symbolism of God has its counterparts in Christology, ecclesiology and ministry. The same patriarchal hierarchy of male over female can be found--e.g., Christ as the male head of the body and Lord over the female Church; the minister as ruling male over a feminized laity (ibid.). See also Ruether's "Male Clericalism," p. 66; "The Ordination of Women in the Roman Catholic Church: What is the Problem?," speech given at the Women's Ordination Conference, Detroit, Michigan, November 1975; and NWNE, p. 75.

[155]Ruether, "The Female Nature of God," p. 61.

[156]NWNE, p. 65. Gregory Bateson issues a similar warning: "If you put God outside and set him vis-a-vis his creation and if you have an idea that you are created in his image, you will logically and naturally see yourself as outside and against the things around you" (Steps to an Ecology of Mind [New York:

Ballentine Books, 1972], p. 463, cited in Green Paradise Lost, p. 154).

[157]See NDM, 1:133; and Niebuhr, "The Truth in Myths," p. 121.

[158]See NDM, 1:169; and Farley, The Transcendence of God, pp. 69-70.

[159]The transcendence of God is explained by way of analogy: "Even as man through his freedom of transcendence partially comprehends unities and coherences in history, so God through his unqualified freedom of transcendence comprehends history as a complete unity and totality" (Minnema, Social Ethics, p. 41; see also NDM, 2:9-10).

[160]NDM, 1:131.

[161]Ibid.

[162]NDM, Ibid., p. 137.

[163]Ibid., pp. 137-38.

[164]See REE, p. 92. What is disputed here is Niebuhr's assertion that "in all great religions the individual finally faces the eternal mystery of life alone; and the very heart of that mystery is the reality of self-consciousness, seemingly dwarfed and yet not dwarfed by a world of physical immensity" (ibid.).

[165]See McCann, Christian Realism, pp. 37-38 for this interpretation of Niebuhr's position.

[166]Ruether, "Male Chauvinist Theology," p. 181.

[167]See NDM, 2:63.

[168]Gray, Green Paradise Lost, p. 54.

[169]Ruether, "Male Chauvinist Theology," p. 182.

[170]See Chapter 1, pp. 7-8; and Chapter 4, pp. 80-83.

[171]Ruether, "Women, Ecology," p. 5.

[172]Niebuhr, On Politics, p. 120.

[173]Griffin, Pornography and Silence, p. 260.

[174]Rich, On Lies, Secrets, and Silence, p. 153.

[175]NWNE, p. 157.

[176]See Rosemary Ruether, "Beginnings: An Intellectual Biography," in Journeys: The Impact of Personal
Experience on Religious Thought, ed. Gregory Baum (New
York, N.Y./Paramus, N.J.: Paulist Press, 1975), p. 44;
and LT, p. 7.

[177]Ruether, "Sexism and God-Talk," Chapter 7, n.p.

[178]See, for example, Daly, Gyn/Ecology, p. 388;
and Robin Morgan, Going Too Far: The Personal Chronical
of a Feminist (New York: Vintage Books, 1978), pp. 15,
248, and 294.

[179]Rosemary Ruether, "The Personalization of
Sexuality," in From Machismo to Mutuality, p. 73.

[180]Ibid., p. 83.

[181]This interconnectedness can be demonstrated in
numerous ways. For example, the human spirit's "loft-
iest dreams and most grand abstractions, as well as the
most exquisite and intimate ecstasies of personhood--all
are products of nerve endings, atoms and energy" (Gray,
Green Paradise Lost, p. 92). The soul expresses
itself in and through body-language: e.g., in tears
and laughter, in song and dance, in writing and paint-
ing.

[182]NWNE, p. 26. See also Griffin, Woman and
Nature, p. xvi.

[183]Ruether, "The Personalization of Sexuality," p.
84. At one time the term "androgyny" was used by
feminists to express this integrity and wholeness, but
as Ruether points out, "this word itself is formed out
of dualistic origins" (NWNE, p. 26, also p. 57), and
"retains all too closely [these] origins" ("The
Personalization of Sexuality," p. 84). See also
Ruether, "Sexism and God-Talk," Chapter 4, pp. 19-20.
Mary Daly also critically reflects on the use and
misuse of this term in Gyn/Ecology, pp. 387-88. For
Ruether's treatment of a related issue, see her
appraisal of the Jungian tradition and its concept of
femininity in NWNE, pp. 151-59.

[184]Ruether, "The Personalization of Sexuality," p. 84.

[185]Ibid.

[186]See Ruether, "Sexism and God-Talk," Chapter 4, p. 21.

[187]Rosemary Ruether, "Sexism and the Liberation of Women," in From Machismo to Mutuality, p. 104.

[188]NWNE, p. 26.

[189]Ibid.

[190]See NWNE, p. 57.

[191]As Jean Miller writes: "One can, and ultimately must, place one's faith in others, in the context of being a social being, related to other human beings, in their hands as well as one's own" (Toward a New Psychology of Women [Boston: Beacon Press, 1976], p. 87).

[192]NWNE, p. 83.

[193]See ibid., p. 83.

[194]Gray, Green Paradise Lost, p. 93.

[195]Ruether, "Rich Nations/Poor Nations," p. 207.

[196]NWNE, p. 83.

[197]Ibid.

[198]See NWNE, pp. 157-58.

[199]Ibid., p. 24.

[200]Ibid., p. 31.

[201]LT, p. 125.

[202]See LT, p. 149. As Avineri expresses this hope: "In such a society the need for the other human being, which is at the root of human existence, rises to consciousness" (Social and Political Thought, p. 88).

CHAPTER VI

COMMUNAL SOCIAL ETHICS
AND SOCIAL CHANGE

Rosemary Ruether expresses a need for "a new communal social ethic"[1]--an ethic grounded on a notion of the human person as <u>essentially</u> social--to guide activity in the world. In the first part of this chapter, I have created a communal social ethic based on Ruether's interpretation of sociality. Though this ethical system is my construction, it is compatible with, and indeed based on, Ruether's writings as a whole.[2] For the purpose of comparison, it is divided into similar components to the ones found in Niebuhr's system: (1) sin, (2) the ethical agent, and (3) ethical norms. In this section, I also describe Ruether's interpretation of certain religious symbols that relate to and help to explicate the three aspects of her communal social ethics. In the second part of the chapter I discuss Ruether's approach to social change within the context of the general ethical system previously developed. The discussion in this chapter serves as preparation for the comparison of Niebuhr's and Ruether's ethics in the concluding chapter.

The Ethical System

Alienation as Social Sin

One of the fundamental assumptions from which Christian ethics proceeds is that the human condition is marked by a fall from grace, or sin. In Ruether's words:

> The reality of the Fall . . .
> mean[s] that God's original creation
> has become obscured and overlaid
> with a denatured world man, not God,
> has created. This denatured world
> springs from a relationship between
> man, nature and society defined by
> exploitative relationships, aliena-
> tion and domination, rather than
> communion.[3]

The Christian tradition suggests that the original and eschatological condition is one of wholeness and equality.[4] However, when human history is reviewed, we see that alienation and oppression prevail. This social condition is, for Ruether, the meaning of sin.[5]

Sin is relational; it "exists precisely in the distortion of relationality."[6] It is also structural or systemic. Relationships of alienation and domination that occur within the self, between the self and others, and between humans and the earth--relationships which limit our full humanity--become institutionalized in social structures. In Ruether's words, "sin means . . . also the structural evils of war, racism, sexism, and economic exploitation which allow some people to dehumanize others."[7] These sinful social structures of alienation and oppression, which are both a result and cause of sinful relations, make up "a social and cosmic anti-creation,"[8] or a sinful world.

These two dimensions of sin--the relational and the structural--are integrally related to the third dimension: a person's alienation from God. Sin occurs not only "in the world"; it also exists within the person. Ruether expresses this dimension of sin as the brokenness of the human heart.[9] Because of the understanding of God, which I only mention here and develop in greater depth later, this dimension of sin is both personal and profoundly social.

God symbolizes the fullness of social relations. The God who is within humans is, at the same time, the totality of reality. Thus persons contain within themselves the fullness of social relations, or this totality of reality. Thus to sin against God is to separate oneself from others and from the fullness of humanity which is possible as a person-in-relation. To sin against others, both in direct relationships and as participants in structural evil, is to sin against God and oneself. The three dimensions of sin--the relational, structural, and personal--are interpenetrating; they mutually condition each other.

Sin is perpetuated throughout history. As Ruether writes: "Social sin continues across generations."[10] Individuals are born into a sinful social context and "are socialized into roles of domination and oppression and taught that these are normal and right."[11] Sin is inherited, not through biology, but through society. "It is historically inherited."[12] A sinful social context is the starting point for any consideration of human beings as ethical agents.

148

The Person-in-Relation
as Ethical Agent

By birth, human beings fall victim to a false
world, "a world . . . which biases [their] opportuni-
ties, either as oppressed people or privileged people,
even before [they] have been able to make personal
choices."[13] This means that persons do evil and profit
from evil simply because of their social context.
Individuals participate in sinful relations and contribute to sinful social structures as if these were
the only possible forms of activity.[14]

Moral responsibility arises when a person recognizes evil and experiences good; when a person sees
through the false world to the true world which is
obscured.[15] In religious terms, this is a graced
moment, an encounter with one's authentic self and with
God.[16] Ruether describes it as "a gratuitous mystery
of freedom that happens to us within our situation yet
beyond the capacities of the alienated situation."[17]
This graced moment or encounter with God and one's
authentic self occurs in and through interaction with
others, experienced either as a reality outside of oneself (e.g., in relations of sisterhood, in base
communities) or discerned as a reality within oneself
(e.g., through contemplation). Although the process by
which a person comes to understand the good differs,
the good experienced is fundamentally the same. It is
that of a renewed community.[18]

At this initial moment, and then repeatedly after-
wards, a person is able to recognize the discrepancy
between what is and what ought to be. At a particular
time or place in history, this discrepancy between the
is and the ought may actually be greater than at other
times and places. Also, a person's perceptions of this
discrepancy may be, at times, more or less clear,
ambiguous or complex. At any one time, however, a discrepancy between the false world of alienation and the
true world of communion exists and is capable of being
discovered. According to Ruether, "the discovery that
the social system of which [one is] a part is engaged
in chronic duplicity and contradiction comes as a shock
and an awakening."[19]

The recognition or discovery of "two worlds" presupposes the human capacity for freedom--the ability to
co-determine what reality becomes,[20] or the ability to
respond to the present in the light of future

possibilities. To remain unfree--that is, not to realize one's capacity for freedom, not to assume one's moral responsibility--is to continue to exist in a sinful, dehumanized and dehumanizing condition. It is to fail to become truly human.

To accept one's capacity for freedom and to assume responsibility is to become an ethical agent. This means, first of all, that persons disaffiliate themselves from the evils of their times. Ruether acknowledges that steps towards disaffiliation are necessarily limited since "the larger system still entraps its members and limits their choices."[21] But freedom and responsibility demand some form of dissent. They also entail creating a new way of being in relationship in the world. The multidimensional character of sin requires that an ethical agent engage in these two tasks of resistance and reconstruction in ways that will affect the relational, structural and personal spheres of human existence.

Given the conditions of finitude and tragedy, the basic human tendency toward evil as well as good, and the necessity of participating in sinful social reality even while one works to transform it, an ethical agent remains, to some degree, a sinner and irresponsible; and therefore, less than fully human.

In summary, the development of moral responsibility is a social phenomenon. A person becomes an ethical agent only in relationship with others. The awareness of the discrepancy between what is and what ought to be, of one's capacity for freedom, and of one's ability to respond, depends on others. The realization of freedom and responsibility occurs in the shared struggle to break down the barriers--relational, structural and personal--that separate persons from one another. The fullness of freedom and responsibility is found in communion and cooperation with others. In the next section, the ethical norms which guide the exercise of moral responsibility are considered.

Empowerment and Universal Community as Ethical Norms

Universal community is the ultimate ethical norm that guides the activity of ethical agents as they engage in the tasks of resistance and reconstruction. Universal community is the ethical expression of essential sociality. It is rooted in our common

150

humanity and our shared participation in and relationship to all reality.[22] This norm, derived from an
adequate notion of sociality, necessarily implies
participation, reciprocity, cooperation, and mutual
affirmation.[23]

Although the ethical norm of universal community
supports judgments and guides activities that cut
across space and time, it is not an abstract or formal
principle which is beyond history. Rather, universal
community is always and only manifested and developed
in concrete ways in history. Therefore, its meaning
must be discovered in and through particular, historic
forms of community--forms which vary immensely throughout history. But it is also important to note that the
meaning of universal community can never be fully
understood by human beings who are located at a specific time and place in history. This ultimate ideal can
never be reduced to a particular form or forms of
community that has or have been achieved. It encompasses the totality of social reality. Given the
limitations of finitude, all the implications of this
norm, for the present as well as the future, escape a
person's grasp.

Universal community and the qualities that characterize it--participation, reciprocity, cooperation, and
mutual affirmation--imply shared power. Therefore, in
a social context marked by domination and subordination,
universal community requires, first of all, a redistribution of power so that all members have the ability to
interact freely. The empowerment of those who are
powerless is a necessary condition for authentic
community and, as such, is a proximate norm. After
describing the proximate norm of empowerment, further
consideration is given to the ultimate norm of universal
community.

Empowerment

For Christians, the empowerment demanded by universal community and essential sociality is the meaning
and message of Jesus' life and death. As Ruether notes,
"in Jesus, God has 'emptied himself' and become a servant. (See Phil. 2:5-11). God, too, refuses to be seen
as a lordly King,"[24] or all-powerful Being.

Jesus' message during his lifetime is one of empowerment. In Ruether's words, Jesus preached

151

a new era of God's justice and peace
coming about when all the systems
of domination of money, rank and
religious hierarchy are overthrown,
when those who wish to be first are
willing to be last and servant of
all, and in which those who are
nothing in this present system are
lifted up. This is not simply a
reversal of domination, but the
overcoming of the whole structure
that sets people in oppressive relationships to one another.[25]

Jesus denounces the social order which keeps people
poor and powerless and announces the Kingdom of God--an
alternative world of love with justice and harmony.
Jesus' commitment to the struggle for empowerment and
the coming of the Kingdom costs him his life. He
suffers and is killed for the sake of justice. Jesus'
death becomes a "rallying point" for new energy and
life in the struggle for empowerment and community.
The response to this directive for empowerment is
determined by a person's position in the relationships
and structures of which he or she is a part.

The moral responsibility for those who are powerless and assigned to subordinate positions in society
is to reclaim the power that is rightfully theirs by
virtue of being human. It is to demand the power to
define themselves in relationship to others and to co-
determine what reality becomes. The failure by the
powerless to assume this responsibility results in such
actions as the passive acceptance of, conformity,
deferrence, submission or surrender to the definition
of the self, expected roles, and life-conditions
imposed by those in power.

One of the factors which make acts of defiance
against the established system difficult for those in
positions of subordination is the dominant moral and
religious ideology that identifies love as the ultimate
norm, and then defines it as charity, meekness, humility, self-abnegation, sacrifice, and service.[26] With
this understanding of love, Collins points out, "one
gives up one's autonomy, one's restless drive for life
and self-actualization, and becomes obedient to an
image of God which demands constant self-denial."[27]
The proof of love is that one is "willing" to be
destroyed by and/or for the one that is loved.[28]

Self-sacrifice and service, without power, is destructive to the self and, given essential sociality, to others.

This scapegoat mentality, fostered by a theology of victimization with its "suffering servant" typology, must be rejected as an oppressive device developed by those in power and imposed on subordinates to keep them powerless. Though the rejection of this ideology is often difficult,[29] it is essential to the process of empowerment. Ruether notes that "no . . . group that seeks liberation from historic oppression is into the suffering servant myth."[30] Rather, for empowerment to occur, anger and pride are frequently the needed qualities. As Ruether explains:

> Anger and pride, two qualities viewed negatively in traditional spirituality, are the vital "virtues" in the salvation of the oppressed community. . . . Anger, here, is felt as the power to revolt against and judge a system to which one was formerly a powerless and buried victim. Pride is experienced as the recovery of that authentic humanity and good created nature "upon which God looked in the beginning and, behold, it was very good."[31]

The development of these qualities often is a response, on the part of the powerless, to the ethical imperative of universal community with its proximate norm of empowerment. Anger and pride provide force and impetus for overcoming relationships and structures of oppression.

The moral response to the directive of empowerment differs both in degree and kind for those who are in power. The degree of responsibility is greater for those who already have power and can, through their decisions and actions, voluntarily keep others in subordinate positions and use force to oppose the efforts of those seeking to claim power.[32]

The kind of moral responsibility for those who occupy positions of domination requires the relinquishment of their power over others and of the privileges associated with excessive power. It prescribes letting go of unjust power and giving it back to the powerless,

153

so that together all may share in the exercise of power. This relinquishment is not a matter of benevolence but of giving back to others what has been taken from them and is, in fact, rightfully theirs.[33] The failure of those in power to assume this responsibility results in such continued actions as the isolation, marginalization, repression, exploitation, rejection, or even extermination of the powerless.

It is important to note that due particularly to the interstructuring of the forms of oppression, most people occupy, at least in some ways, positions of both domination and subordination. Ruether makes a point of emphasizing that humans need "to deal with [them]selves, not as simply oppressed or oppressors, but as people who are sometimes one and sometimes the other in different contexts."[34] This realization of being both oppressed and oppressor serves three important functions: (1) it produces "a more mature and chastened analysis of the capacities of human beings for good and evil"; (2) it tempers "the flood gates of righteous anger . . . by critical self-knowledge";[35] and (3) it prevents the projection of all evil upon an "alien community" and the total polarization between "God's people" and "God's enemy," between saints and sinners.[36] At the same time, however, this realization cannot distract from the responsibility for empowerment especially in those contexts where relative superfluity and absolute poverty exist; where conditions of abundance and destitution threaten the very physical survival of human beings, which is the most basic requirement for actualizing human potential. Rebellion against and transformation of these relationships and structures of domination take priority in the process of empowerment for the realization of universal community.[37]

Empowerment is preparation for community. It is the establishment of relationships of shared power which allows for the discovery and affirmation of one's own humanity and the humanity of others. It is, in Ruether's words, "a breaking of silence . . . and the initiation of true communication for the first time"[38] between autonomous but related persons who share a common human existence and a common social reality. Beyond empowerment remains universal community.

Universal Community

Community depends, first of all, on participation

and cooperation, but community requires more than just the interaction of its members. It also demands a reciprocity in the relationships among members which entails the exercise of <u>shared</u> power leading to the autonomy and actualization of all.[39] Reciprocity, based on the mutual recognition and affirmation of each one's unique contribution and relationship to the whole, precludes the domination of others or the surrender of oneself--i.e., of one's capacity for free and conscious activity.

Love emerges, in Ruether's thought, as the animating spirit of universal community. This spirit of community--the spirit of what ought to be--which exists within human beings as their authentic selves, can only be expressed in concrete forms in history. To respond to the spirit--that is, to love--is to create community; it is to struggle to form relationships and structures marked by participation, cooperation, reciprocity and mutual affirmation. In Ruether's words, "love . . . become[s] the functional solidarity of men and women struggling for a new and different future."[40] As such, love appears both harsh and tender depending upon the social context and one's position in it. Love involves both anger and compassion, self-assertion and self-sacrifice.[41] Finally, love risks the suffering which "is endured in acting to overcome an oppressive situation [but not] that which accompanies abject submission to such a situation."[42] What remains constant in love is the commitment to the struggle in solidarity with others for empowerment and community.

In the preceding pages universal community has been identified as the ultimate norm that directs ethical activity, and empowerment as a necessary condition for achieving it. Salvation and God/ess are two of Ruether's religious symbols which serve as expressions of this ultimate norm. In the next section, these two symbols are briefly examined in order to further clarify the meaning of universal community.

Salvation and God/ess: Religious
Symbols of Universal Community

Salvation, as a religious symbol of universal community, is understood both holistically and historically. Salvation is holistic insofar as it includes personal conversion and restored relations between dimensions of oneself, between individuals, between groups, and between humans and nature. As Ruether

155

writes, using the New Testament language of the kingdom, salvation does "not split the human community from the cosmos, but look[s] forward to a total transformation of men and nature in the Kingdom of God."[43]

This holistic understanding has important implications for the interpretation of individual salvation. The meaning of eternal life "must be sought somehow in solidarity with the race, with the earth, and with the matrix that binds us together."[44] By the fact that we _are_ participants in the universal community, we are saved. To the _extent_ that universal community is achieved at _particular_ moments throughout history, so too is salvation realized.

The salvation of the single cosmic community is one, with all participants responsible, according to their capacities, for bringing it about. To the extent that humans _fail_ to assume responsibility, they limit salvation and deprive universal community of what it ought to be.[45]

Salvation is, second of all, a historical project. In contradistinction to a notion of salvation that is "other-worldly" or **beyond** history, salvation is the renewal of this present universe _within_ history, in accordance with God/ess' original intent for creational community.[46] As Ruether argues: "Ultimate redemption cannot be divorced from historical redemption."[47] It is located in concrete historical forms.

Salvation takes its _meaning_ from the historical conditions in which people live and need to be saved or liberated.[48] To witness the transformation of sinful relations and structures which keep people in bondage into those of mutuality and shared power is to witness, in New Testament language, the coming of the Kingdom.[49] It is to witness "an inbreaking of grace."[50] To participate in this transformation is to engage in salvific activity; it is to respond to grace.[51] In this interpretation of salvation, the historical enterprise comes into its own as the locus of fulfillment.

Salvation is fulfilled in concrete historical forms of community, but only partially. Since the universality of salvation applies to the totality of reality, including the "massive repentance of all humanity,"[52] it cannot be incarnated completely in any one particular social system.[53] But, Ruether warns, "this does not reduce all social systems and situations to the same

level."[54]   Rather, it is possible, even in the midst of
the limits, transitoriness and sinfulness of human
existence, "to make societies which are more liberating
and less oppressive,"[55] and hence more salvific.
Ruether cites this example:

> In our present world, when we see a
> society where a few rich families
> own almost all the land, where they
> suppress all protest with guns and
> tanks, where they manipulate religion
> and education to justify this exploi-
> tation, there we are far from the
> Kingdom. But when we see the vast
> majority rising up against these
> evils, overthrowing the police state,
> beginning to create a new society
> where the hungry are fed, and the
> poor are able to participate in the
> decisions that govern their lives,
> there the Kingdom has come "close."[56]

Because salvation is partially but never completely
realized in any one historical moment, human beings
live in a dialectic of unfulfillment and fulfillment,
experiencing "a tension and contradiction between the
is and the ought of life."[57]   Ethical agents respond to
both sides of this contradiction. They denounce and
struggle against the false world of alienation which is
demonic, even while they announce and celebrate the
salvation that is already present--the community that
exists in their midst.

The understanding of salvation presented here is a
dynamic one but, Ruether suggests, this process is not
directed toward a "final salvific end-point of
history."[58]   Rather, salvation is an ongoing process of
conversion and the recovery of authentic creational
life which cannot be done once and for all. It is,
instead, "a historical project that has to be undertaken again and again in changing circumstances."[59]
Each generation contributes to salvation in its own
time and place. Through essential sociality, everyone
shares in the salvation that is achieved for all times
and in all places.

The ethical norm of universal community is also
expressed by the ultimate religious symbol of God or
Goddess.[60] Consistent with the notions of both essential sociality and universal community, God/ess is

understood as social and communal. These qualities of God/ess have several dimensions.

Since to be is to be interrelated, God/ess who is the perfection of such being, must be related to other persons. For Christians, this reality has been expressed in the symbol of the Trinity.[61] God/ess, who is subsistent relation, exists as community. As such, God/ess is what ought to be. This divine or universal community serves as the "Empowering Matrix"[62] within which all things "both come to be and are renewed."[63] This is one dimension of God/ess.

The characteristics of universal community provide insight into the second dimension of divine sociality. As the model of what ought to be--universal community-- God/ess necessarily shares power and interacts with all existents according to the capabilities of their species. Universal community is not just composed of divine persons-in-relation, but encompasses the relations of all entities in the cosmos. God/ess is what was, is and will be--the totality of reality. As this being unfolds, God/ess too is shaped and formed.[64]

These two dimensions of God/ess are interpenetrating and mutually transforming. God/ess is, inseparably, (1) a community which serves as the matrix for the interrelations of all other entities, and (2) the interrelation of these entities. Bracken's definition of God/ess as "a society of societies"[65] is an accurate one.[66]

The spirit of God/ess is within each person--this is a tenet of faith based on Jesus' word. This means that human beings contain within themselves the two dimensions of divine sociality: (1) universal community, or what ought to be, and (2) the totality of reality, or what is. The tension between these two dimensions of the is and the ought, which is in reality, in God/ess and in each person, is expressed in the anguish and groaning of the spirit referred to in New Testament writings. It is communicated in human longing which, even if it remains unrecognized or unnamed, is longing "for a reconciled world that God and humanity have yet to create out of their sufferings and hopes."[67]

Insofar as persons respond to the spirit and cooperate with God/ess in the renewal of the world, they share in the activity of God/ess, or more precisely, they share activity with God/ess. As Ruether states, "a real co-creatorship [exists] between God/ess and humanity."[68] By the refusal to cooperate with God/ess, persons limit what reality becomes thus depriving God/ess, themselves, and others of the fullness of community or salvation--a fullness which is realized only through each one's own unique participation and cooperation.[69]

The religious symbols of salvation and God/ess, which help to clarify the ethical norm of universal community, also provide insight into the relationship between transcendence and immanence.[70] To be consistent with the interpretations described above, the transcendent cannot be understood as a heaven or an eternity unrelated to history, or as above and beyond creation. Rather, "the language of transcendence is essentially a language of oughtness."[71] As such, the transcendent stands in tension with relationships and structures that are less than what they ought to be, offering new possibilities for the future "imagined and projected on the basis of the present situation."[72] It "impinges on the present as an inextinguishable aspiration to a different heaven and earth."[73]

The transcendent exists, however, only within and through the immanent. History and creation are the time and place for the appearance of transcendence. As Ruether maintains: "Indeed, in a real sense, it has no being . . . until it . . . is incarnate in historical expression."[74] There are moments of transcendence when it is possible to say that what is is an expression of what ought to be.

According to Ruether, the transcendent and immanent are interpenetrating, but they are not identical. The transcendent cannot be completely incarnated in any one particular form or forms of immanence, since transcendence, or what ought to be, encompasses all of reality. The ability to incarnate the transcendent in its entirety is more than human capabilities allow.[75]

Persons can, however, participate in historical expressions of transcendence and experience some understanding of the renovation of the universe. In Ruether's words, participation in the transcendent fills human beings "with a proleptic experience of wholeness, but also an absence that keeps us ever searching and struggling, drawing us on to that 'still more' which is 'not yet.'"[76]

159

The transcendent, as the unique synthesis of being as it truly is, constantly changes as the ideal is made actual in concrete historical forms, and as future possibilities become reality. The transcendent, like the reality it encompasses, is not fixed but is in the process of becoming as new forms of community are created which expand the horizon of what ought to be. Thus, the transcendent and the immanent are mutually transforming.

In the preceding pages, the ethical norms of empowerment and universal community have been described. The symbols of salvation and God/ess, which serve as religious expressions of these norms, have been examined. The implications of these symbols for the notions of transcendence and immanence have been shown. The ethical dilemma which now must be addressed is how to seek social transformation in a way that is compatible with the ethical norms of empowerment and universal community.[77] In the second major section of this chapter, Ruether's approach to social change is presented.

The Liberation Process

Rosemary Ruether's approach to social change is described by focusing, first, on her understanding of revolutionary praxis; and second, on the development of a program of action. As with her ethical system, Ruether's interpretation of persons as essentially social permeates each dimension of the liberation process.

Revolutionary Praxis

Consciousness-Raising as the Starting Point

Social change, which Ruether also refers to as the process of liberation, begins with consciousness-raising or conscientization.[78] Rooted in personal experiences of domination and subordination, conscientization focuses on the hierarchical system of oppression of which these experiences are a part. Consciousness-raising is not, as some would describe it, a strictly psychological phenomenon related to change in an individual's consciousness and behavior. Such a description fails to take sufficient account of (1) the social structuring of individual consciousness, and (2) the related fact that what first appears as one person's

experience is discovered to be a number of people's
experience and a public issue.[79]

By conscientization is meant "learning to perceive
social, political and economic contradictions and to
take action against the oppressive elements of
reality."[80] As Ruether explains, conscientization is
the development of a revolutionary consciousness "which
breaks out beyond the present form of society, and the
false consciousness that it creates, and perceives its
ideological character."[81] It is the development of a
critical consciousness that enables people to analyze
social reality and act upon it for social transformation.[82]

In religious terms, conscientization means revelation. It

> is the liberating and redeeming
> insight that enables people to per-
> ceive the social conditions that
> control their lives and to transcend
> their spiritual bondage to enter
> into the process of liberation from
> dependency.[83]

This insight "breaks through the monolith of the
dominant consciousness to stand over against it; to
define oneself in opposition to it and to glimpse a new
possibility beyond it."[84]

Since "oppression creates a psychology in the
oppressed,"[85] part of the initial process of conscientization involves an angry assertion of selfhood and
solidarity as oppressed peoples move away from the

> self-hatred and self-destruction
> which have possessed them and
> [towards] the resurrection of
> autonomy and self-esteem, as well
> as the discovery of a new power
> and possibility of community with
> their own brothers and sisters in
> suffering.[86]

Ruether believes that "the leaders of the oppressed
community are not incorrect when they recognize that
they have, as their primary responsibility, the leading
of their own people through a process of self-exorcism
and renewed humanity."[87] "It is this rebirth which is

161

the foundation of the 'new man' who can create a new
society"[88] in solidarity with other groups seeking
social transformation.

Conscientization, as the definition implies, leads
to a deepening awareness of the capacity to transform
social reality. It leads to action directed toward
social change. And, in the ongoing struggle, further
conscientization and action become one dynamic process
of analysis, action and reflection--it becomes revolutionary praxis.[89]

Utopian Thought

A significant aspect of revolutionary praxis is
utopian thought or creative imagination. By utopian
thought is meant "a set of ideas and values that tends
to dominate the direction that social change should
take."[90] It is, as such, a vision of what ought to be
for a particular society; it is universal community
made specific.[91]

Utopian thought is characterized by a dynamic relationship to historical reality. It embodies, first of
all, an implicit criticism of the prevailing social
order. As Ruether writes: "The 'new' that is projected
takes off by way of critique of the status quo, and is
therefore shaped by it."[92] At the same time, utopian
thought reconstructs an alternative reality that relates
to the potential of existing material and socio-
economic conditions.[93] This alternative vision must
then be verified through political action for social
transformation. If utopian thought does not lead to
action, it is an illusion.[94]

As revolutionary praxis proceeds, latent incongrui-
ties are made manifest and new possibilities are dis-
closed. Ruether warns revolutionaries that they must
resist dogmatizing or eternalizing their historical
works and remain ready for "constant exoduses to new
possibilities."[95] The realization of each relative
utopia provides a glimpse of the absolute utopia of
universal community which is beyond the boundaries of
any one social system or historical era.

Solidarity with the Oppressed

Revolutionary praxis in the process of liberation
is to be shaped by the powerless. There are several
reasons for this. First, as Ruether argues, "one

162

cannot reflect correctly on our historical reality
without keeping clear that knowledge of the system from
the side of the oppressed."[96] Since false consciousness reflects the experience and interests of elite
groups, the experience of the oppressed is "a privileged
medium of truth."[97] The powerless are the "prophetic
community, for it is in the contradictions of their
condition that the contradictions of the whole society
are revealed."[98] Secondly, the suppression of elitism
and the claiming of control by the powerless over their
own change process meets the proximate norm of empowerment.

Thus, to participate authentically in revolutionary praxis is to be in solidarity with the oppressed,
particularly those whose struggle for full humanity is
thwarted at the basic level of survival by conditions
of poverty. It is to see and experience reality from
the perspective of the powerless and to work with them
for social change.

Women as Revolutionary Leaders

According to radical social thought, social change
is as transformative as those who carry it out--that is,
the more subordinate the group that leads the revolution, the more radical is the social change.[99] Consistent with this principle, Ruether argues that in a
patriarchal world system, defined by racism, classism
and sexism, it is women especially poor, working women
of color who occupy the most subordinate positions in
the hierarchy.[100] Therefore, these women are the legitimate leaders of revolutionary praxis for radical
social change. They have the least to gain from
preserving the present system, and are the ones most
capable of seeing through distorted reality to a revolutionary consciousness and way of being human.[101]

As a part of revolutionary praxis, a program for
political action is drawn up, including particular
strategies and tactics to achieve social change.
Although Ruether recognizes that political activity can
be fully determined only in relationship to specific
circumstances, she does suggest some general guidelines.

A Program of Action as
a Part of Praxis

The analysis of present reality indicates that
whole groups of human beings exist today in societies

marked by conditions which violate personhood. The
very structures of these societies produce an
inordinate amount of deprivation, suffering and destruction for the majority of people.[102] Violence is
already present in the world, supported and perpetuated
by an ideological dehumanization characteristic of
war.[103] It is within this context that those committed
to radical social change engage in political activity,
denouncing the existing order and announcing what is
not yet, but will be; rejecting the present power
system and struggling to create a new one of shared
power.

Denunciation, Empowerment and Armed Resistance

Denunciation and rejection of the present system
of domination by those who are powerless requires a
militant stance toward oppressive powers. Besieged
peoples must fight back to claim power and free themselves. The defense of one's own life and livelihood,
and the refusal to be victimized takes many forms.
Regardless of the specific strategies and tactics
(e.g., confronting, acting against, separating from,
or using the system), a plan of political action
involves eventually breaking the silence between
oppressor and oppressed, "rejecting a false 'law and
order' which is really systemized disorder,"[104] and
demanding the recognition of the authentic personhood
of all. In situations where violence is the dominant
reality, where even the physical survival of the powerless is at stake, militant participation in the liberation process justifiably turns to armed resistance.

Denunciation and rejection of the present system
by those who have power requires "breaking with anything and everything that hinders real and effective
solidarity with those who are suffering from a situation of injustice and spoliation."[105] The relinquishment of unjust power and the commitment to share in the
struggle to empower the powerless may be strategically
acted out in different ways.

For example, some people may serve in a supportive
role in the initial conscientization process, enabling
the powerless to organize themselves and gain some
control over oppressive structures. Others may contribute types of supportive expertise. Still others
may focus on the education and conscientization of
members of the dominant society. A variety of means

164

may be used to raise the dominant society's awareness of structural oppression and create new political consciousness: e.g., lectures, articles, workshops, media statements. Direct actions, such as socio-dramas, demonstrations, sit-ins, or other media events, may also be employed. To be an effective means of education for social change as well as a statement of symbolic opposition to the status quo, the meaning of these actions needs to be communicated to the broader public, and linked to political organization for further action.[106]

Finally, some may participate to a degree in the dominant society, using their power within the established system (1) to open up access to power for members of oppressed groups; (2) to serve as a mediator between those in power and the powerless, translating the protest and demands of the powerless into words that those in power are able to understand; or (3) to influence those in power to support the revolt of the oppressed, or at least "to back off the counter-revolutionary attack."[107] This type of activity rests on the assumption that a shift in the power structure and radical change in a society can be achieved through some type of democratic process.[108]

Whether one considers societies which have some form of democratic structures, or societies which have none, experience teaches that those at the top do not willingly share power.[109] In Ruether's words, there is a "massive unwillingness of those in power--even those who claim to be 'open'--to make an even partially adequate response."[110] Rather, as claims to power are made, the use of coercion and repressive measures by those in power are increased in order to maintain the status quo.[111] Repeatedly in history, armed resistance becomes a "last resort" for those defending themselves against the violence of the system.[112] According to Ruether,

> this is not a question of violence
> or nonviolence on the part of those
> who struggle. Non-violent struggle
> is no protection against unjust
> violence in a system which is main-
> tained by unjust violence.[113]

Armed resistance is a response. It is the refusal by a group of people to be dehumanized to the point of death. It is, in Ruether's words,

165

> a grim holding out in the face of
> evil, stupidity and blindness to
> elementary justice, [and] an effort
> to carve out some small spaces of
> humanization within which to keep
> one's sanity and soul[114]

and, one might add, life.[115] The decision as to
whether or not armed resistance becomes a necessity for
the powerless lies with those who hold the power.

Given the customary strength of domestic military
and police forces, and the interventionist policies of
the major world powers, careful preparation and planning
must surround armed resistance so that those claiming
power are not completely destroyed. Material factors,
as well as knowledge, skill, political organization,
coalition building and popular support are needed.[116]

In a situation of total violence where armed
resistance is being used, a number of options for
action exist for those who are in solidarity with the
powerless. One possible position is to take up arms
and fight alongside the oppressed. Another is to
engage in various kinds of support activities that are
needed in the struggle, such as the following: supply-
ing food and shelter for those who are armed; caring
for those who are left homeless; raising money for
weapons and supplies; providing medical and legal assistance; pressuring those in positions of authority to
cease their repressive measures; or, when intervention
by outside forces is a factor, creating a national con-
sensus against this kind of international role. There
are many responsible ways "to accompany the people"[117]
in their fight for freedom. To remain "neutral" in
violent revolutionary struggles is irresponsible action.
It is, in fact, to act in favor of the status quo, or
to side with those in power positions who instigate,
maintain, and perpetuate structural violence, repression, and counter-revolution.

Annunciation, Universal
Community and Nonviolence

Revolutionary praxis and political action include
not only denunciation but annunciation as well. In the
struggle against the present system, a new way of
being-in-relationship is imagined, announced and
created. "Through rebellion," writes Ruether, "the
true values of a common human life which have been

buried underneath a distorted system"[118] are
uncovered.[119] In the struggle against a dehumanized
and alienated existence, a glimpse of what true humanity
and a community of shared power might mean emerges.

A group committed to social transformation
announces a new vision of community by their words and
actions directed toward the larger society, as well as
by their own interaction as a group.[120] This fact has
several important implications for a group's (1) program
of action, (2) selection of strategies and tactics, (3)
process of decision-making, and (4) expressions of
solidarity.

First, a group's program of action must be built
on the realization that one can reject the inhumanity,
but not the humanity, of the oppressor.[121] As Ruether
writes:

> The rejection of inauthentic society
> can never be construed as the rejec-
> tion of the humanity of those people.
> Rather, it is a rejection of the
> false, demonic powers that possess
> them, but in the name of a community
> that lies buried beneath that
> alienating power.[122]

In fact, given essential sociality, "the liberation of
the oppressed must also be the liberation of the
oppressors as well, and the creation of a new possibility for everyone,"[123] or no one is free. "There is no
liberation from the enemy that is not liberation of the
enemy."[124]

This position prevents the liberation process from
becoming merely an exchange of roles of oppressor and
oppressed. It also prevents "the revolt . . . if
successful, [from] rush[ing] forward to murder and self-
aggrandizement" so that "the last state is worse than
the first."[125]

Second, a group must choose strategies and tactics
which are nonviolent, whenever possible. Armed resistance, as stated above, may prove necessary for survival
and empowerment. But as the revolutionary process
moves toward the realization of a new political
community, "means which stand for the rejection and
ultimately the murder of the person of [the]
adversary"[126] are no longer appropriate.[127] Rather,

167

strategies and tactics must be selected that reflect
revolutionary goals--beginning with life-sustenance for
all.[128] To attempt to create community "through murder
is to destroy the common nature upon which the rebellion
itself must take its stand."[129]

Third, a group's process of decision-making must
reflect the norms of empowerment and universal community. Since a collective process and non-hierarchical
distribution of power is part of the vision of a revolutionary society, so too must these conditions characterize the movement. This means that power in the
group is no longer defined as power-over but rather as
power to co-create.[130] The diversity of the members is
recognized and each one's unique contribution to the
group and to the struggle is valued.[131] Any relationships or structures of oppression within the group must
be continually challenged.

Fourth, the members--both those who belong to
oppressed groups and those who are acting in solidarity
with them--must commit themselves "to an untiring
effort for unity among the oppressed in order to
achieve liberation."[132] This is in contrast to the
devisiveness among oppressed groups which is fostered
by those in power to preserve the system of oppression.[133] A group's expressions of solidarity must be
critiqued in the light of empowerment and universal
community. Solidarity needs to be continually extended
to a greater number of oppressed groups in order to
gain an ever deepening awareness of the interstructuring of the forms of oppression which together make up
the one world system that is to be transformed.[134]

To the extent that a group is able to incorporate
these conditions of community into its own actions and
organization, it becomes a witness to what conversion
and social transformation mean. At the same time, the
group serves as a base of support for those who dissent
from the dominant society, and provides an alternative
community for the emergence of an alternative consciousness of reality.[135]

In the preceding pages, revolutionary praxis has
been described as a dynamic process of social analysis,
political action and reflection which is directed
towards liberation and social transformation. We have
seen that social change requires both the denunciation
of the existing system of domination and alienation,
and the annunciation of a new political community of

shared power. Social change is a process marked by
both militancy and an ever-widening solidarity, and by
both armed resistance to systemic violence and an
option for nonviolence.

The relationship between these dimensions of
social change is a dialectical one. In order to move
toward a community of shared power and the institution-
alization of nonviolence,[136] the powerless must defend
themselves against a violent system and claim their
power, even at times to the point of armed resistance.
As Ruether maintains, "we must recognize that the movement of revolt against false and oppressive worlds
. . . is integral to the renewal of the world."[137]
Negation is necessary for the projection of an alternative.[138]

The conflict involved in relating these contrasting dimensions of the one liberation process is mani-
fold. This conflict cannot be resolved, however, by
choosing to engage in one type of activity to the
exclusion of the other. Empowerment and community,
denunciation and annunciation, militancy and solidarity
are equally important aspects of social change. To opt
for community without empowerment is simply to preserve
the status quo. Community "that is rooted in subordination rather than autonomy is merely a guise for
continued domination."[139] To opt for empowerment
without community is to deny the basis on which persons
become truly human and truly free.[140]

The struggle for liberation entails a constant
search for the unity of these two dimensions--that is,
shared power in community--but, in different contexts,
one dimension may necessarily be emphasized over the
other to meet the needs of a particular situation.
Part of revolutionary praxis is making the difficult
choice as to which aspect or dimension is to be
emphasized at any given moment.[141] Given the immensity
of the global system and the complexity of social
structures, as well as human limitations and the
capacity for evil, these decisions are always ambiguous,
conflictual, and in need of continual reflection and
assessment.[142]

The process of social change which has been
described in this chapter provides a pattern for revolutionary activity. But the movement from domination
to shared power, from alienation to universal community,
and from illusion to a liberated consciousness is given

specific content in "each cultural area and [by] each
people striving to realize this revolutionary possibility in the context of its own identity and integrity as
historical people."[143] It is in and through the
numerous social revolutions in history that aim to
establish communities of shared power--and in the link-
ages among these revolutions--that "the revolution" and
social transformation is given its fullest meaning.

Conclusion

In the second part of this chapter I have been
concerned with Ruether's approach to social change as
it relates to her ethical system. In accordance with
Ruether's ethics, each aspect of the liberation process
reflects the fundamental assumption that persons are
essentially social. Revolutionary praxis--an ongoing
process of analysis, action and reflection--occurs in
and through interaction with others. As a part of
praxis, persons-in-relation develop a program of action
which is constantly verified and revised through the
test of their political activity.

Ruether's ethical system and approach to social
change, which is based on an adequate notion of sociality, overcomes the limitations in Niebuhr's position
which result from his interpretation of the individual
as ultimately discontinuous with and above society. In
Chapter VI, I point out the ways in which Ruether's
work overcomes these limitations.

Notes

[1]LT, p. 124.

[2]Ruether has not, as yet, systematized her
writings in the area of ethics to the same degree that
Niebuhr has. Thus, in this chapter, it is necessary to
construct an ethical system based on her works. This
systematizing of Ruether's writings and the construction of a feminist ethical system is one of the contributions of this study to social ethics.

[3]Ruether, "Critic's Corner," p. 338.

[4]See Ruether, "Sexism and Liberation," p. 14.

[5]In one of her recent articles, Sheila Collins
argues that feminist theology must develop another
approach to the question of sin than that of alienation.

For Collins, this term, rooted in the disciplines of psychology and political science, reveals a middle-class bias ("Feminist Theology at the Crossroads," Christianity and Crisis 41 [December 14, 1982]:346). But alienation, let us recall from Chapter IV, transcends any one discipline or disciplines. It is a social reality that permeates the multiple relations that are a part of the human condition--not just self with self, but also the self with others, and with the earth. It is also important to note that Ruether attributes her understanding of sin as alienation and broken community to Black theology and her interaction with the Black community. See LT, p. 132.

⁶Ruether, "Sexism and God-Talk," Chapter 7, n.p.

⁷TCW, p. 19.

⁸LT, p. 8.

⁹Rosemary Ruether, The Church Against Itself (London and Melbourne: Sheed and Ward, 1967), p. 10, hereafter cited as CAI; and Rosemary Radford Ruether, "Outlines for a Theology of Liberation," Dialog 11 (Autumn 1972):253.

¹⁰Rosemary Radford Ruether, "What Is Shaping My Theology," Commonwealth 108 (January 30, 1981):46.

¹¹Ibid.

¹²Ibid. Ruether also offers this "new understanding of the Christian doctrine of inherited sin" in "Disputed Questions," p. 78; and Ruether, "Sexism and God-Talk," Chapter 7, n.p.

¹³Ruether, "Disputed Questions," p. 78.

¹⁴As Ruether points out, "justification [for these activities] is lodged with 'nature' or God which serve as ultimate sanctions of the culture" ("Disputed Questions," p. 103).

¹⁵The initial stages described by William E. Cross, Jr. in "Negro-to-Black Conversion" (in The Death of White Sociology) are useful here. Cross calls the stage in which a person is programed to think and act in the world according to the dominant ideology as the pre-encounter stage. The encounter stage occurs when "some experience manages to slip by or even shatter" a

person's interpretation of the world. For Cross, "the encounter entails two steps: first, experiencing the encounter, and; second, beginning to reinterpret the world as a consequence of the encounter" (see pp. 270-73).

[16]Ruether, "Sexism and God-Talk," Chapter 7, n.p.

[17]Ruether, "Theology of Liberation," p. 253; see also CAI, p. 119.

[18]Ruether, "Sexism and God-Talk," Chapter 7, n.p.

[19]Ruether, "What Is Shaping My Theology," p. 46. Denis Goulet makes an important distinction between responsibility and guilt which is applicable here: "Responsibility concerns the present and the future; it presupposes freedom--that is, the possibility of responding to an exigency which is perceived and accepted. . . . Guilt, on the contrary, is the negative burden of past fault or injustice. Guilt is passive and recriminating, not active and creative" (The Cruel Choice, p. 135).

[20]See Chapter IV, p. 83. In Ruether's words, humans have "the ability to choose good rather than evil and hence [the] capacity for responsibility" ("Sexism and God-Talk," Chapter 7, n.p.).

[21]Ruether, "Sexism and God-Talk," Chapter 7, n.p.

[22]As stated in Chapter IV, and as Goulet also emphasizes, "all reality" means both planetary and cosmic reality. See The Cruel Choice, p. 139; and TCW, p. 59. What I am calling universal community, Collins refers to as wholeness, and suggests some specific examples of where its meaning can be discovered. "It is found in myth, in literature, in art, in song, in movements such as the medieval peasant revolts, in utopian thought, and yes, even in the dreams of Marxism." It is an ideal that "run[s] like translucent thread throughout the garment of patriarchy" (A Different Heaven and Earth, p. 176).

[23]Given this description of universal community, it is clear that community and society are not synonymous. There are societies, at many different levels of human existence, that do not possess the qualities of community. This is true even for some societies that have been traditionally considered communities, but

172

which in fact, fail to take the unique identity of each
individual member into account. For example, sociologist Ferdinand Tonnies uses the family as the prototype
of Gemeinschaft or community (see Nisbet, The Sociological Tradition, p. 75). But insofar as families are
characterized by relationships of domination rather
than reciprocity, cooperation, and mutual affirmation,
they do not fulfill the norm of community. To the
extent that a society realizes these qualities, it
becomes a community.

[24]Ruether, Mary, p. 84.

[25]TCW, p. 17.

[26]This ideology particularly works against women
because, as is stated in Chapter V, religion and
morality are identified with the private sphere and the
home, or "women's place" (see pp. 116-17).
Chesler observes that it is "women [who] are impaled on
the cross of self-sacrifice" (Women and Madness, p. 31).
See also Daly, Gyn/Ecology, p. 75. This criticism of
self-sacrifice is found repeatedly in feminist writings
and is taken up again in the concluding chapter.

[27]Collins, A Different Heaven and Earth, p. 204.
As Ruether writes: "women become 'Christlike' by having
no self of their own" ("Sexism and God-Talk," Chapter 7,
n.p.).

[28]See Andrea Dworkin, Our Blood: Prophecies and
Discourses on Sexual Politics (New York: Harper & Row,
Publishers, 1976), p. 105. Referring specifically to
women, Chesler writes: "Psychologically, self-preservation is precisely what patriarchal society forbids
women. Traditionally, the ideal female is trained to
'lose' and the ideal male to 'win' (i.e., psychologically, females are trained to die, males to survive).
And women are trained to mount the sacrificial altar
willingly" (Women and Madness, pp. 293-94).

[29]In Women and Madness, Chesler maintains that
such a shift to an ego-focus "grates and screeches
against the grain of 'feminine' nerves and feelings, and
implies grave retribution. Some women go 'mad' when
they make such a shift in focus or when it occurs
within them" (p. 300).

[30]Rosemary Radford Ruether, "The Suffering Servant
Myth," Worldview 17 (March 1974):45.

[31]LT, p. 12; see also Ruether, "Male Chauvinist Theology," p. 182; and Rosemary Ruether, "On Women's Lib," Dialog 11 (Summer 1972):226.

[32]Ruether, "Sexism and God-Talk," Chapter 7, n.p.; see also Gustavo Gutierrez, A Theology of Liberation: History, Politics and Salvation, trans. and ed. Sister Caridad Inda and John Eagleson (Maryknoll, N.Y.: Orbis Books, 1973), p. 274. Ironically, but not surprisingly, being in a position of power often makes it more difficult to recognize alienating and dehumanizing conditions, and to respond. See Lee Cormie, "Hermeneutical Privilege of the Oppressed: Liberation Theologies, Biblical Faith and Marxist Sociology of Knowledge," in the Catholic Theological Society of America, Proceedings of the Thirty-Third Annual Convention, ed. Luke Salm, F.S.C. (Milwaukee, Wisconsin: n.p., 1978), p. 177.

[33]Describing the possession of superfluous wealth and power as a form of thievery is an age-old doctrine. As Goulet points out, "the early Fathers of the Church, notably Basil the Great and John Chrysostom . . . minced no words accusing the wealthy of having 'stolen' whatever goods they possessed over and above their own needs. Centuries later Ghandi also declared that . . . 'Whenever I live in a situation where others are in need, . . . whether or not I am responsible for it, I have become a thief'" (The Cruel Choice, p. 133).

[34]NWNE, p. 132.

[35]Ibid.

[36]LT, p. 11; and Ruether, "Ruether on Ruether," p. 126.

[37]The position that responsibility for empowerment in some areas takes priority over others is influenced by Denis Goulet's principle of "priority needs" discussed in The Cruel Choice, pp. 128-38.

[38]Ruether, "Black Theology," p. 684.

[39]See NWNE, pp. 57-58; and Ruether, Mary, p. 80.

[40]LT, p. 142.

[41]While an ethic which identifies love totally with self-giving is rejected, sacrificial acts can be

legitimate. As Daly writes: "The 'sacrifice' that is required is not mutilation by men, but the discipline needed for acting/creating on a planet which is under the Reign of Terror, the reign of the fathers and sons" (Gyn/Ecology, p. 40). Those who are in subordinate positions need to determine among themselves and "for themselves those situations in which they would willingly sacrifice their own interests to benefit others" (Barbara Hilkert Andolsen, "Agape in Feminist Ethics," Journal of Religious Studies 9 [Spring 1981]:76), which, given essential sociality, would also benefit themselves.

[42]Mary Daly, Beyond God the Father (Boston: Beacon Press, 1973), p. 110.

[43]Ruether, "Paradoxes of Human Hope," p. 235.

[44]Ruether, "Beginnings," p. 39; see also Ruether, "Sexism and God-Talk," Chapter 10.

[45]Expanding on this understanding of salvation, Ruether writes: "We must learn that a redeemed future does not mean a divinized human, endlessly approximating the Infinite, but a converted person, who learns again what it means to be a creature; a finite created being who is authentically related to God by accepting particularly, spacio-temporal limits and relations to others in mutuality" ("Rich Nations/Poor Nations," p. 7). Ruether admits that this understanding contrasts starkly with "religious visions of angelic souls flying off to heaven" ("Beginnings," p. 39), but if to be is to be in relationship, a social understanding of salvation is necessary.

[46]See Ruether's "Critic's Corner," p. 337; "Paradoxes of Human Hope," p. 239; and "Disputed Questions," p. 18.

[47]Rosemary Radford Ruether, "Sexism and the Theology of Liberation," The Christian Century 90 (Spring 1973):1228.

[48]For a thorough discussion of and argument for the historical conception of salvation, see J. Dean Brackley, S.J., "Salvation and the Social Good in the Thought of Jacques Maritain and Gustavo Gutierrez" (Ph.D. dissertation, University of Chicago, 1980), Chapter 6.

[49]See Ruether, "Disputed Questions," p. 75.

[50]TCW, p. 22.

[51]According to Gustavo Gutierrez, who is a leader among liberation theologians: "To place oneself in the perspective of the Kingdom means to participate in the struggle for the liberation of those oppressed by others" (Theology of Liberation, pp. 203-205).

[52]Ruether, "Sexism and God-Talk," Chapter 7, n.p.

[53]See Rosemary Radford Ruether, The Radical Kingdom: The Western Experience of Messianic Hope (New York, Paramus, Toronto: Paulist Press, 1970), p. 193, hereafter cited as RK. McCann's claim that there is no "eschatological priviso" in liberation theology, of which Ruether's writings are a part, is just one example of his serious misreading of this body of literature. See Christian Realism, pp. 171, 174-75.

[54]Ruether, "Disputed Questions," p. 74.

[55]Ibid., p. 75.

[56]Ruether, "Disputed Questions," p. 74. Ruether also uses "sisterhood" as an example of a salvific structure. She writes: "Sisterhood represents redemption and revelatory co-humanity in many ways" ("Sexism," p. 1228).

[57]Ruether, "Paradoxes of Human Hope," p. 238.

[58]TCW, p. 68. See Ruether, "Sexism and God-Talk," Chapter 10, for a further critique of a "final salvific end-point" based on a linear view of history.

[59]TCW, p. 69.

[60]Although I am using God/ess to indicate a more inclusive understanding of God than that of patriarchal male, warrior, king, judge, or male superordinate Ego (see Ruether, "Ordination of Women," p. 1; and Ruether, "Male Clericalism," p. 69), this term is still inadequate. In Ruether's words: "God/ess must be seen as beyond maleness and femaleness. . . . The God/ess who is both male and female, and neither male or female, points us to unrealized new humanity. In this expanding image of God/ess we glimpse our own expanding human potential, as selves and as social beings, that have

176

remained truncated and confined in patriarchal, hierarchical relationships. We begin to give new content to the vision of the messianic humanity that is neither 'Jew nor Greek, that is neither slave nor free, that is neither male nor female' (Gal. 3:28) in which God/ess has 'broken down the dividing wall of hostility' (Eph. 2:14)"(Ruether, "The Female Nature of God," p. 66; in this quote, God(ess) is replaced by God/ess, the symbol Ruether uses in her most recent book). As people participate in transformative activity to challenge oppressive relationships and structures, new patterns of relating will arise which will be reflected in new images of the diety.

[61]The Trinity serves as an example of the sociality of God/ess, but this symbol, as it has been developed in traditional, patriarchal theology, is limited. As Daly warns: "The unwholeness of the Christian Trinitarian symbol is evident in the one-sidedness of the images of the Father and Son. . . . Language about the Holy Spirit is used in a privitized and often hypocritical way and is not generally perceived as the spirit of love that confronts loveless institutions. The qualities attributed to the Holy Spirit in traditional theology are stereotypically 'feminine,' but 'he' is referred to by the masculine pronoun" (Beyond God the Father, p. 214). Ruether similarly writes that "it is doubtful that we should settle for a concept of the Trinity that consists of two males and one female 'persons.' Such a concept of God falls easily into an androcentric or male-dominant perspective. The female side becomes a subordinant (sic) principle underneath the dominant image of male divine sovereignty" ("Sexism and God-Talk," Chapter 2, n.p.).

[62]Ruether, "Disputed Questions," p. 10. Ruether also refers to God/ess in other similar terms throughout her writings: e.g., Divine Matrix, Ground of Being, Mother Power, Primal Matrix. For a history of the understanding of God/ess as Primal Matrix, see "Sexism and God-Talk," Chapter 2, n.p.

[63]Ruether, "Male Clericalism," p. 69.

[64]Rosemary Radford Ruether, "God-Talk After the End of Christendom," Commonweal 105 (June 16, 1978):370.

[65]Bracken, "God and World Reconsidered," p. 8.

[66]In the traditional language of Being and

Becoming, God/ess can also be described as a "unity of Being as Becoming through which Being comes to be" (Ruether, "God-Talk," p. 270).

[67]Ruether, "God-Talk," p. 375.

[68]Ruether, "Sexism and God-Talk," Chapter 6, n.p.

[69]This image of God/ess as limited and impotent because of the refusal of human beings to share power purposely differs from the concept of God as an "omnipotent sovereign." The latter God is "modeled after the powers of domination . . . who reduce others to dependency" (Ruether, "Disputed Questions," p. 83). See also Daniel C. Maguire, "The Feminization of God and Ethics," Christianity and Crisis 42 (March 15, 1981):66.

[70]Because the understanding of transcendence is one of the major differences between the ethical system presented in this chapter and Niebuhr's, it is important to briefly describe the relationship between transcendence and immanence here.

[71]Rosemary Ruether, "Mediating Between the 'Is' and 'Ought' of History: A Radical-Liberal in the Streets of Washington," Christianity and Crisis 31 (July 12, 1971):144.

[72]Ibid.

[73]Ibid., p. 146.

[74]CAI, p. 235.

[75]The extent to which humans can experience and participate in the transcendent is, at present, an "unknown border that we cannot define because we do not know the limits of man's potential" (Ruether, "Paradoxes of Human Hope," p. 245).

[76]Rosemary R. Ruether, "Christian Origins and the Counter Culture," Dialog 10 (Summer 1971):199.

[77]Using Goulet's terminology, empowerment and universal community are the "strategic principles," i.e., the normative judgments as to how goals ought to be achieved. See The Cruel Choice, p. 123.

[78]In Ruether's words: "Liberation begins as a

terrifying explosion of consciousness . . . a self-and-world-transcending conversion experience. Conscious-ness-raising parallels what blacks mean by black con-sciousness and what Latin Americans mean by conscienti-zation" ("Sexism and the Liberation of Women," in From Machismo to Mutuality, p. 108).

[79]For an argument against psychologizing the notion of consciousness-raising see Collins, "The Familial Economy of God," p. 1; and Collins, A Different Heaven and Earth, pp. 159-61.

[80]Paulo Friere, Pedagogy of the Oppressed, trans. Myra Bergman Ramos (New York: Seabury Press, 1974), p. 19; also cited in LT, p. 178. Friere's work and writings on conscientization have been significant for the development of this concept in liberation theology.

[81]LT, p. 179; see also Ruether, "Christian Origins," p. 197.

[82]LT, p. 179.

[83]Rosemary Ruether, "Monks and Marxists: A Look at the Catholic Left," Christianity and Crisis 33 (April 30, 1973):78. As I have stated earlier in this chapter, this insight is a gift of grace mediated through our experiences. See pp. 149-50.

[84]Ruether, "Mediating Between the 'Is' and 'Ought' of History," p. 146.

[85]Kate Millett, Sexual Politics (New York: Ballantine Books, 1969, 1970), pp. 490, 496. Ruether writes of "the internalization of negative images by the oppressed" in LT, pp. 11-12, 129-30.

[86]LT, p. 12.

[87]Ibid., p. 12. Rowbotham similarly maintains that "in order to discover its own identity as distinct from that of the oppressor, it [i.e., an oppressed group] has to become visible to itself" (Woman's Con-sciousness, Man's World, p. 27).

[88]LT, p. 179.

[89]For Christians, Scripture is used as part of the reflective process, and new dimensions of biblical meaning are discovered through praxis, and vice versa.

179

[90]Fals-Borda, Subversion and Social Change, pp. 12-13. Fals-Borda draws primarily upon Karl Mannheim's Ideology and Utopia for his conception of utopia. Gutierrez similarly defines utopia as "a historical plan for a qualitatively different society and . . . [an] express[ion of] the aspiration to establish new social relations" (Theology of Liberation, p. 232).

[91]Visions of what ought to be for a specific society at a particular time in history are, according to Mannheim and Fals-Borda "relative utopias." Fals-Borda writes: "The absolute utopian statements concerning new social goals are affected by the environmental reality and produce relative utopias with their own portion of ideology" (Subversion and Social Change, p. 12). Ruether's conception of "an absolute set of polarities [i.e., final salvation and final annihilation] . . . and a relative set of polarities, set within the absolute polarities" ("The Radical and the Mediator: Their Roles in Social Change," America 121 [November 29, 1969]:522) is similar to the distinction between utopias.

[92]LT, pp. 166-67.

[93]See Fals-Borda, Subversion and Social Change, pp. 162-63. Gutierrez emphasizes that "utopia is deceiving when it is not concretely related to the possibilities offered to each era" (Theology of Liberation, p. 234).

[94]As Gutierrez writes: "Authentic utopian thought postulates, enriches, and supplies new goals for political action, while at the same time it is verified by this action. Its fruitfulness depends upon this relationship" (Theology of Liberation, p. 234).

[95]LT, p. 190.

[96]Ruether, "What Is Shaping My Own Theology?," p. 47. Ruether considers the civil rights and peace struggles as her own "peak experiences" that awakened this awareness in her. "Here, for the first time," she writes, "I learned to look at America from the Black side; to see safety in the Black community and danger in nightriding whites or white officers of the law" (ibid.). See also Ruether, "Christian Origins," p. 197.

[97]Cormie, "The Hermeneutical Privilege of the Oppressed," p. 168. Ideologies as the reflection of

the experiences and interests of elite groups, and the hermeneutical privilege of the oppressed are two sides of the same issue of ideology. But, as Cormie points out, a great deal of attention has been paid to the former, while the latter has received very little.

[98]LT, p. 178.

[99]For example, Marx argues that "the proletariat, the lowest stratum of our present society, cannot stir, cannot raise itself up, without the whole superincumbent strata of official society being exploded into the air" (as cited in McLellan, The Thought of Karl Marx, p. 198).

[100]In Ruether's words: "Women of the oppressed classes and social groups represent the poorest of the poor, the most despised of society" ("Sexism and God-Talk," Chapter 6, n.p.; see also Chapter 5, n.p.).

[101]See Ruether, "Sexism and God-Talk," Chapter 6, n.p.; Sandra Harding, "What is the Real Material Base of Patriarchy and Capital?" in Women and Revolution, pp. 140-41; Morgan, Going Too Far, pp. 61, 123; and Sheila Rowbotham, Women, Resistance and Revolution: A History of Women and Revolution in the Modern World (London: The Penguin Press, 1972; New York: Vintage Books, 1974), p. 206.

[102]See Goulet, The Cruel Choice, p. 317.

[103]Ruether writes: "Before one is prepared to kill another man, one first predicates this upon an inner turn of heart which strips that man of his community of being and nature with ourselves. . . . The enemy is . . . always given some kind of name which marks him off as being fundamentally 'other' than our-selves. . . . In this naming of the enemy one places him beyond the pale of a humanity continuous with our own, and the basis for his annihilation is laid" ("'Love Your Enemies' as Rebellion: A New Testament Basis for Nonviolence," Fellowship 36 [July 1970]:8). As stated above in the discussion of false consciousness, human beings who occupy subordinate positions in society are defined as less than human. See pp. 105-106.

[104]Ruether, "'Love Your Enemies,'" p. 23; see also LT, p. 130.

[105]Gustavo Gutierrez, "Liberation Praxis and

Christian Faith," in Frontiers of Theology in Latin America, ed. Rosino Gibellini, trans. John Drury (Maryknoll, New York: Orbis Books, 1979), p. 9. Solidarity, a political expression of our essential sociality and universal community, implies shared activity, value-commitments, and feelings. As I immediately show, solidarity takes many different forms. One obvious and important measure of solidarity is, however, the extent to which it is recognized by the powerless themselves.

[106]Ruether argues against "the idea that direct action is an alternative to political organizing and communication" ("Letter to Catholic Radicals: After the 'Actions,' What Next?," National Catholic Reporter 2 [October 1970]:14, emphasis added). Rhetoric and ingenious activities fail if they don't make "contact with concrete needs and any real strategy that might relate to those needs" ("The White Left in the Mother Country," Commonweal 93 [November 6, 1970]:143).

[107]LT, pp. 141, 159.

[108]For a brief discussion of the possibility of achieving radical change through a democratic process, see Arthur McGovern, Marxism: An American Christian Perspective (Maryknoll, New York: Orbis Books, 1980), pp. 287-88. Also, those who remain in the present structures always risk accepting "present presuppositions tacitly if not actively, and so . . . giv[ing] a new lease on life to the inauthentic society which they represent, instead of bringing this inauthentic life of man to an end so something quite different can be born" (Rosemary Ruether, "The Messianic Code," Commonweal 91 [January 16, 1970]:424).

[109]The election of Salvador Allende in Chile, in 1970, is one of the few examples where radical change was initiated through some type of democratic process; but in this case, the elites in Chile, with the support of the United States government and corporate elites who occupy the top positions in the world order, subverted the revolution through armed force. See McGovern, Marxism, pp. 217-21, 288.

[110]LT, p. 168. Denis Goulet similarly maintains that "there is scant reason to hope that beneficiaries of extant privileged social systems will meet the demands of poorer claimants in time to obviate serious conflict. Available evidence suggests, on the contrary,

that power elites will adamantly refuse to alter the rules of the game, except insofar as they can 'domesticate' change to their advantage" (The Cruel Choice, pp. 106-107).

[111]Ruether writes: "As one struggles against evil, one also risks suffering and becomes vulnerable to retaliation and violence by those who are intent on keeping the present system intact" ("Disputed Questions," pp. 81-82).

[112]Ruether cites El Salvador as one example of a country in which "there is no way to protest or struggle without evoking violence" (TCW, p. 29). The decision that armed resistance is a "last resort" is a political and ethical judgment that must be made in praxis.

[113]Ruether, "Disputed Questions," p. 82.

[114]Ruether, "Monks and Marxists," p. 79.

[115]Many moral theologians and ethicists attempt to use the just war theory to support armed resistance. In The Cruel Choice, Denis Goulet argues against this use of the just war theory and demonstrates, by raising a number of significant questions, how it "fails to come to grips with the psychological and political realities of revolutionary situations" (p. 312; see pp. 309-14).

[116]See Marx and Engels, The German Ideology, pp. 59, 61.

[117]This phrase was frequently used by the archbishop of San Salvador, Oscar Arnulfo Romero, before his assassination. It was his expression for solidarity with oppressed peoples in their liberation process.

[118]Rosemary Ruether, "A New Political Consciousness," Ecumenist 8 (May-June 1970):63.

[119]Without the dimension of annunciation, "the revolution degenerates to counterrevolution because, lacking a creative alternative, the new order can only ape the old" (Millett, Sexual Politics, p. 492).

[120]See Sève, Man in Marxist Theory, p. 376.

[121]See LT, p. 136. Ruether writes: "Although he

rejects the oppressor as a master, he may not reject
him as a man. While rejecting the oppressor as an
oppressor, he must equally claim him as a brother"
("'Love Your Enemies,'" p. 23).

[122]LT, pp. 136-37.

[123]Ruether, "A New Political Consciousness," p.
64.

[124]Ruether, "Male Chauvinist Theology," p. 183.

[125]LT, p. 13.

[126]Ruether, "'Love Your Enemies,'" p. 23.

[127]See Avineri, Social and Political Thought, pp.
92-93.

[128]See Goulet, The Cruel Choice, p. 113.

[129]Ruether, "Critic's Corner," p. 339.

[130]See LT, p. 133. As Ruether writes: "The mores
of political exploitation are countered by a community
which struggles with authentic democracy as self-
representation in the primary forum of the local group"
("Christian Origins," p. 198). See also Goulet, The
Cruel Choice, p. 123.

[131]See Ruether, "Search for Soul Power," pp. 83-84.

[132]Friere, Pedagogy of the Oppressed, pp. 172-73.

[133]See p. 140 above. Speaking of the workers'
revolution, Marx warns that the absence of solidarity
and a feeling of mutual independence can be the main
cause of a revolution's failure (see Avineri, Social
and Political Thought, pp. 92-93).

[134]See LT, p. 175.

[135]Ruether, "Disputed Questions," p. 103. Ruether
points out that "the old consciousness is held in place
by the old practice which incarnates and perpetuates it
so that even those in revolt are bound to it because it
is the social reality which dominates their lives.
Before the hold of the old consciousness can be broken,
those in revolt need to find out what it is like to
live in a new kind of society, one based on different

presuppositions" ("New Wine, Maybe New Wineskins for
the Church," The Christian Century 86 [April 2, 1969]:
449). A revolutionary group serves as this "new kind
of society." It becomes "an alternative base upon
which [to] stand to wage a cultural and social struggle
against . . . counter reality" ("Sexism and God-Talk,"
Chapter 7, n.p.).

[136]Beverly Woodward describes the institutionaliza-
tion of nonviolence as the creation of "institutions
that [are] truly universal and which in some measure
both require and make possible responsible supportive
behavior by each . . . towards all other members of the
human community" ("Violence, Non-Violence and Human
Struggle," Study Encounter 12 [1976]:25).

[137]LT, p. 10.

[138]RK, p. 282.

[139]Ferguson, Self, Society, and Womankind, pp.
108-109.

[140]As Ruether writes: "The community of the
oppressed against the oppressors, while it is a
necessary part of the process of liberation, cannot
represent the community of reconciliation. That can be
represented only by a community which brings together
oppressor and oppressed in a new relationship that
liberates both from their previous pathologies in relation to each other" ("Sexism," p. 1228).

[141]The revolutionary activity in Nicaragua gives
evidence of this selection of a particular dimension
for emphasis in relationship to the socio-historical
context. The option of the FSLN is for nonviolence,
but the reality of the situation under Anastasio Somoza
Dubayle "obligated them to a defense of the innocent
and of the right of the people to life and livelihood."
However, after the Nicaraguan people's victory and the
establishment of the Provisional Government, the death
penalty was abolished. Followers of Somoza and members
of the National Guard were not executed in spite of the
atrocities they committed against the people. In fact,
compassion towards the National Guard was a part of the
revolution from the start. As Peter Hinde reports:
"The tactics of the Sandinistas when they had the
National Guard bottled up and surrounded in their
garrisons, were to persuade them to lay down their arms,
to join the people and not fight them. They repeatedly

gave the National Guard an opening to escape . . . and
those Guardsmen who were recent recruits forced into
the service and who had not committed atrocities--they
invited into their ranks" ("Look! A New Thing in the
Americas!," ed. William R. Callahan, S.J. with the
communities of Tabor House and the Quixote Center
[Hyattsville, M.D.: Quixote Center, Inc., 1981], p.
20).

[142]Unger, whose position is similar to the one
presented here, summarizes this dialectical process in
these words: "The progressive diminishment of domination makes community possible; the advance of community
helps us understand and thereby erase domination. At
different moments, the two aspects of this process
demand varying degrees of attention. At first, the
obstacles of domination are paramount, and community
appears as the indeterminate ideal that guides political practice from afar. . . . As the harsher forms of
domination are abolished, the issues of community gain
the upper hand.
All . . . should work toward the day when the
priority of the fight against domination to the
development of community will be reversed" (Knowledge
and Politics, p. 253).

[143]LT, p. 189.

CHAPTER VII

TWO ETHICS: A CRITICAL APPRAISAL

This study has suggested a way to critically evaluate approaches to social change, as well as the ethical systems of which they are a part. Since an acceptable ethical system must be based on an adequate anthropology, it is at this level--the level of fundamental assumptions--that the evaluation of Reinhold Niebuhr's and Rosemary Ruether's ethics has occurred.

Among anthropological presuppositions, sociality or the social dimension of being human, has been the focus of this work. I have argued that an adequate notion of sociality is one that defines humans as essentially social. This notion of sociality, which has served as the criterion of adequacy, has been developed from radical social thought, and in particular from the conflict tradition in the social sciences and from feminist writings. In the preceding pages I have demonstrated, in accordance with my thesis, that Rosemary Ruether's interpretation of sociality conforms to what has been judged as the adequate notion, while Reinhold Niebuhr's does not. Thus, in the search for an ethical system, including an approach to social change, Ruether's position is to be preferred.

In this final chapter, Niebuhr's and Ruether's positions are compared in order to show how Ruether's ethical system and approach to social change overcome the limitations in Niebuhr's ethics. In the first part, a number of significant differences in the two ethical systems, due to differing interpretations of sociality, are pointed out. In the second part, Niebuhr's and Ruether's approaches to social change are compared, and what I claim are the advantages of Ruether's approach are indicated.

The Ethical Systems Compared

The differences in Niebuhr's and Ruether's ethical systems are summarized by recalling four areas: (1) the ethical agent; (2) ethical norms; (3) the failure to achieve ethical norms or, in religious language, sin; and (4) the realization of ethical norms, or salvation. Following a consideration of these four areas, two general differences that characterize the ethical systems as a whole are mentioned.

Differences Related to
the Ethical Agent

Although Niebuhr does not completely dismiss the influence of society on ethical decision-making, he maintains an interior view of morality.[1] Human beings are free and autonomous individuals, capable of transcending their social contexts in order to make choices concerning their own motivations and actions. These choices are judged in the light of the eternal and infinite--the absolute ideal of love. From Niebuhr's perspective, a person's motive of goodwill or ill-will is critical in determining the intrinsic morality or immorality of his or her actions.

In contrast to Niebuhr's position is the assertion that individuals become ethical agents, just as they become human, in relationship to others. Born and socialized into a world marked by alienation and false consciousness, persons discover the discrepancy between what is and what ought to be, and realize their responsibility (i.e., their ability to respond) only in and through interaction. Even motives for behavior are shaped by a particular social context, and are learned and developed relationally.

A second major difference in this area of the ethical agent relates to Niebuhr's distinction between the individual and society as two types of ethical agent, and the corresponding distinction between individual and social morality, and personal and social ethics. For Niebuhr, when persons enter into relationship and form groups or societies, the possibilities for ethical action become limited. Because societies lack a capacity for self-transcendence that is similar to humans, they are bound, for the most part, to their own self-preservation and interests. It is the individual above society who alone can challenge the group to act from motives other than self-interest.

In an ethical system based on Ruether's interpretation of sociality, there is no such distinction between types of ethical agents, moralities, and ethics. Rather, the only type of ethical agent is the person-in-relation. The only ethics are social ethics since the autonomous individual acting above or apart from others does not exist. Persons-in-relation form society. As stated in Chapter IV,[2] the interaction among social individuals constitutes the complex of relationships and network of institutions that make up society; but a society exists and is expressed only in and through social individuals. This is not to deny that "society"--i.e., groups of individuals who make up part of a society--can be challenged by others, but those who pose the challenge are social individuals: ethical agents acting out of a specific social context at the same time they are seeking to transform it. The differences in these two descriptions of the ethical agent result in contrasting interpretations of the private and public spheres where ethical activity occurs.

For Niebuhr, the private sphere, and specifically the home, is where personal ethics guide activity and individual morality is binding. This sphere is a place of retreat from the power struggles that characterize the political arena. Thus the interpersonal relations that make up the private dimension of one's life more easily conform to the ideal of love. Private, altruistic morality, though not directly appropriate for the public sphere, provides a critical perspective and judgment on political activity. An individual ethic serves as "a 'dispositional ethic' for politicians and social activists."[3]

For Ruether, the private sphere cannot be dissociated from the public sphere. Rather, the two levels are interpenetrating. One example of this interrelationship is the constant adaptation of the meaning and structure of the family according to the needs of capitalism.[4] What may appear as personal experiences are, in fact, affected by the external reality of which they are a part.[5] All social relations that make up human existence are political problems; thus one and the same social ethic guides activity on the relational and structural levels.

Differences Related to Ethical Norms

In this area of ethical norms, the first major difference between the two positions is the ethical norms themselves. Niebuhr identifies love and justice as the norms that guide activity; universal community and empowerment emerge as the norms in Ruether's writings. Although Niebuhr, at times, describes love as "perfect harmony," or "the harmony of life with life," and justice as "the balance of power," these two sets of norms--love and justice, and universal community and empowerment--remain significantly different.

189

As we have seen in Chapter III,[6] the ultimate norm
for Niebuhr is divine love which is revealed in history
as sacrificial, suffering, and self-giving. It requires
perfect disinterestedness and a disavowal of power. A
person becomes aware of this absolute ideal in a moment
of transcendence and contemplation of the infinite.
Given the nature of historical existence, sacrificial
love is a rare occurrence. Mutual love, which is marked
by conditionality, reciprocity and some degree of self-
interest, is the highest good of history.

Justice, which is a level below mutual love and
the proper norm for society, presupposes the power
realities of society and "demands rational calculation
and cautions adjustments to reconcile conflicting
interests."[7] Niebuhr defines justice primarily in terms
of principles and structures of social organization.
The regulative principles of justice include liberty,
equality and order. The purpose of justice is to allow
the maximum use of creative power (liberty) for the
greatest number of individuals (equality) within an
atmosphere of unity, stability, harmony and peace
(order). In applying these principles, allowances must
be made for the factors of natural inequalities, social
heritages and the differences of need or social function. Justice requires a social organization characterized by the balance of power, and it is the role of
government to ensure this equilibrium.

In the ethical system based on Ruether's writings,
love, which is the animating spirit of universal
community, implies participation, reciprocity, cooperation and mutual affirmation. Unlike Niebuhr's conception of sacrificial love, in this system the ultimate
ideal requires the integration of self-concern and concern for others, as well as the sharing of power.
Self-concern and concern for others are not mutually
exclusive, but rather, given essential sociality, are
two necessary dimensions of the same reality.[8] Since
love exists only through concrete historical expressions, a person becomes aware of the absolute ideal
through participation in history. Transcendence and
contemplation of the infinite do not take a person out
of history, but rather immerse him or her deeper in
history through an ever-widening experience and awareness of solidarity.[9]

The purpose of empowerment, the norm which
accompanies universal community, is to establish relationships and structures which allow for the sharing of

190

power. Empowerment requires claiming or relinquishing power depending on one's position in the social order. Unlike Niebuhr's understanding of justice which flows out of an ultimately individualistic interpretation of human nature, empowerment represents the essential sociality of human beings. Empowerment is for the sake of community in which all humans in relationship with others freely co-create themselves and history. In this system, the balance of power is not considered primarily a means for protecting the individual rights of liberty and equality,[10] or for preventing tyranny and anarchy, but is considered a necessary condition for the shared fulfillment of members of a society. The state, in a system of domination, creates the illusion of liberty, equality and order among its citizens. As human beings reclaim their political power--which is, in fact their own power and not the economic power of a minority--the state is transformed and able to perform its proper function of coordinating the activities of various groups according to the principle of shared power.[11]

The second major difference in the area of ethical norms is the understanding of the relationship between the norms. Niebuhr describes the relationship between love and justice as a paradoxical or dialectical one. The concern of some critics over Niebuhr's use of dialectic has already been noted.[12] Of greater importance for our purposes here is the fact that, for Niebuhr, this relationship between love and justice is a vertical one. Love is higher than justice; love is the fulfillment and the negation of justice. And justice is the approximation and contradiction of love. Since the pursuit of justice necessarily involves self-interest and the use of power and coercion, justice is always found lacking. Love ultimately fulfills justice, but outside of history.

For Ruether, the relationship between the norms of universal community and empowerment is a horizontal one. Empowerment is a necessary condition for community. Without empowerment, which results in the sharing of power, universal community is impossible. This relationship may also be understood as a dialectical one. As domination and submission are negated through empowerment, a universal community of shared power is realized. In history, this process of claiming and relinquishing power in order to create community is ongoing, and aimed at realizing an ever-widening solidarity.

191

In this section on ethical norms, two major differences have been described: (1) the identification of the norms, and (2) the relationship between norms. In the next section, the differences in the two positions concerning sin, or the failure to achieve these ethical norms are pointed out.

Differences Related to the
Understanding of Sin

Both systems start with the assumption that there are natural capacities for good and evil in human beings. However, there are fundamental differences concerning the nature and types of sin. For Niebuhr, sin is predominantly an individual phenomenon. It results from a person's refusal to accept the human condition of finitude and freedom. Sin is, first of all, an offense against God, although it does have social consequences.

A person's full awareness of sin arises only when the self is confronted with the absolute ideal of love which comes from beyond history. In this encounter, individuals realize the inevitability of sin because, living in history, they always fall short of achieving the absolute ethical norm. This knowledge can lead to despair, or to repentance, humility, and trust in God for forgiveness. Sin is ultimately resolved at the trans-historical level of existence.

The understanding of sin found in Ruether's writings is different in relation to each of these points. Sin is a profoundly social phenomenon. It is the socio-historical condition of alienation which leads to dehumanization, destruction, and the denial of essential sociality. Sin is, at one and the same time, an offense against the self and others, and an offense against God/ess.

Persons-in-relation are socialized to participate in a sinful society. A person's awareness of sin arises in historical moments of transcendence when, through interaction with others, he or she experiences community and solidarity, and realizes the discrepancy between the "is" and the "ought" of existence. The recognition of one's own contribution to the sinful situation unfolds through conscientization. In this process, one continually chooses to act to perpetuate present reality or to subvert it. It is in the struggle for liberation and social transformation that sin is forgiven and ultimately resolved.

Not only do the two systems differ as to the
nature of sin, but also to the types of sin. The two
types of sin for Niebuhr are: (1) pride, which is
expressed in the will-to-power; and (2) sensuality,
which is the attempt to escape from the possibilities
of freedom. Of the two, Niebuhr considers pride as the
most important--it is the "original sin"--and focuses
most of his attention on it in his writings.

All relationships are effected to some degree by
pride and the will-to-power, but when relationships
become more complex and the size of the group grows
larger, collective self-interest (that is, the culmina-
tion of the self-interest of individual members
increased by the spirit of group loyalty) and the pursuit of power increase as well. Given the unchange-
ableness in the basic structure of human beings--the
paradoxical relation of nature and spirit--individual
and collective sin is inevitable in history.

In the ethical system based on essential sociality,
sin, or the failure to transform conditions of alienation into those of communion, is of two types: the
refusal to relinquish power and the refusal to claim
power. These two types of sin are inseparable as long
as relationships and systems of domination and submission exist. One type requires the other and thus,
unlike Niebuhr's position, one type of sin is not more
prevalent or important than the other. Both the
failure to relinquish power and the failure to claim
power perpetuate a false consciousness which experiences
the self as either separate from others or as a mere
appendage of others. Both types of sin prevent acting
in solidarity within a community of shared power.

Sin is relational, structural and personal. These
dimensions of sin, though conceptually distinguishable,
are part of a single complex phenomenon. Sinful relationships cannot be separated from the systemic evil of
which they are a part; nor can sinful social structures
be separated from the sinful relationships of which
they consist. As alienation is overcome and a new way
of being human and living together is won, sin is overcome and salvation realized. Next, the differences in
the two positions regarding salvation, or the realization of ethical norms, are described.

193

Differences Related to the
Understanding of Salvation

Salvation, for Niebuhr, is a trans-historical phenomenon which occurs at the end of time. Salvific moments, which are an individual's experience of repentance, forgiveness and redemption, all point to perfection and fulfillment beyond history. It is only in the transcendent God that a spirit is saved from guilt and sin, and thus able to meet other spirits in perfect harmony and selfless love. Until the tensions of the human condition and historical existence are resolved by a God who exists outside of spacio-temporal creation, salvation exists in principle but not in fact. [13]

In contrast to this view, Ruether's view of salvation or the realization of universal community, is achieved in history. Salvific moments are those in which alienation and oppression are overcome, and relationships of mutuality and shared power are formed. It is in and through cooperation with others that repentance, forgiveness and redemption occur. Although no one salvific moment is identifiable with the whole of salvation, each realization of community at a particular point in history is, in fact, a part of the universal salvation, which everyone and everything shares through essential sociality. Finally, salvation is an ongoing process. It is the continual transformation or conversion of what is into what ought to be. Thus the tension of being and becoming, experienced as part of the human condition, does not end as long as God/ess, who encompasses this process and is changed by it, exists.

Two additional and crucial differences become apparent when considering these systems as a whole. First, Niebuhr's ethical system, like his anthropology, is an expression of false consciousness which supports the very system he wants to change. The vertical and horizontal dimensions, the two moralities, the two norms, the notions of sin and salvation all foster an awareness of individuals as separate and apart from others, and deny the power and responsibility that persons-in-relation have for creating a new humanity and a fundamentally different society in history. In contrast, the ethical system based on an understanding of sociality found in Ruether's writings is an

194

expression of a more adequate consciousness which, as society is transformed, will continue to be clarified.

Second, among the facts that have become apparent through the comparison of the two systems is the invisibility of women, or at least their subordinate positions, in the process of social change in Niebuhr's writings. Niebuhr's perspective inhibits the efforts of women to develop a critical awareness of the essentially oppressive nature of their society, and to respond, angrily and creatively, to change it. It is only when we turn to Ruether's writings that women (as women) find themselves as active participants in the revolutionary process and leaders in the struggle.

In these pages, a number of major differences between Reinhold Niebuhr's and Rosemary Ruether's ethical systems have been described. To conclude this chapter and the work, the implications and what I claim are the advantages of Ruether's ethics for an approach to social change are pointed out. At the same time, the ways in which an ethical system based on essential sociality overcomes the limitations in Niebuhr's position on social change are demonstrated.

An Adequate Approach
to Social Change

Before presenting the ways in which Ruether's approach to social change overcomes the limitations found in Niebuhr's position, it is important to recognize certain areas of agreement between the two ethicist-theologians. Both Niebuhr and Ruether agree on the following points:

- dominant social systems are marked by injustice and violence;

- there is an unwillingness of those in privileged positions in society to relinquish power;

- coercion is necessary to effect a redistribution of power;

- the use of democratic structures and non-violent means to bring about social change has a moral priority;

195

- the use of repressive measures by those who occupy the dominant positions in society increases as pressure for a redistribution of power continues;

- a norm or a goal beyond that of a redistribution of power (or empowerment) directs political activity;

- an ongoing consideration of the social situation (i.e., social analysis) is an important component of any decision concerning strategies and tactics;

- social analysis should focus on the existing injustices to the oppressed and powerless;

- although nonviolence is preferable, both morally and pragmatically, in some circumstances the selection of violent means is a legitimate choice;

- practical conditions which make violence a viable option must also exist for it to be justified;

- regardless of the means that are chosen, love still influences the way revolutionary activity is carried out;

- a program of action must be continually reassessed in the light of changing circumstances;

- strategies and tactics for social change are always ambiguous and pose an ethical dilemma.

However, given their contrasting notions of sociality, there are also significant differences between the two approaches. Ruether's approach to social change, derived from communal social ethics based on essential sociality, overcomes the limitations in Niebuhr's approach in a number of major ways related to his understanding of the ethical agent, ethical norms, sin, and salvation.

First, a recognition of the social conditioning of ethical agents suggests that all ethical decisions concerning social change be made in solidarity with others engaged in revolutionary praxis. Through this process, ethical agents become continually aware of the false consciousness that influences their own decision-making. Even a person's motives are understood to be a social product and subject to critique.

Second, the elimination of the distinction between the individual and society as ethical agents implies that persons-in-relation, who make up and create society, are morally responsible for both interpersonal and social life. Individual morality cannot be a substitute for social morality; nor can the notion of "immoral society" be used to justify a conservative stance toward social change or a limited utopian vision.

Third, by eliminating the distinction between the public sphere of morality and the private sphere of religion, and by no longer identifying women with the private sphere, all persons are recognized as ethical agents and active participants in social transformation. At the same time, the prophetic function of religion is restored to social life.

Fourth, the identification of empowerment as a norm necessary for and integral to universal community provides guidance for both oppressors and oppressed in the process of social change. It also enables those who are engaged in claiming power--as well as those who are relinquishing or "sacrificing" power--to recognize their activity as moral and, in religious terms, salvific.

Fifth, given the dialectical relationship between empowerment and universal community, the spirit of love permeates all ethical activity directed towards a universal community of shared power. However, because the meaning of love can only be discovered within a specific socio-historical context, no one meaning (e.g., self-sacrifice) can be given moral precedence in the abstract. Rather, authentic expressions of love must be sought in the concrete struggle for empowerment and community. This awareness also strengthens the powerless to resist the pressures by those in power for reconciliation and community before the process of empowerment has been undertaken.

Sixth, by having the norms of universal community and empowerment guide all ethical activity, a person-in-relation cannot ignore the injustices and violence which often mar interpersonal or domestic relationships. All relationships of domination and subordination--

whether between two people or within a system comprised of many people—need to be overcome. Nor can one allow a group's heroic love in the power struggle for community to go unnoticed or be falsely identified as the activity of isolated, individual selves.

Seventh, the definition of sin as predominantly pride and the will-to-power undermines the very moral virtues and partial motives that are needed by those in subordinate positions to claim their power. The definition of sin as the refusal to claim or relinquish power restores the human ability to act in relationship with others in order to co-determine what reality becomes (i.e., power) to its rightful place in the process of humanization and social transformation.

Eighth, the interpenetration of the relational, structural and personal dimensions of sin requires that those who are committed to social change give careful attention to all of these areas. Liberation from sin involves, at one and the same time, (1) the development of mutually affirming relationships; (2) the transformation of unjust social structures and systems; and (3) reconciliation with God/ess. One and the same process of conversion necessarily requires struggling against systemic evil which conditions personal choices and limits social relationships.

Finally, the fact that salvation is historical and shared gives impetus and a sense of urgency to the task of creating a form of universal community in which people are able to realize their human potential to the greatest degree in and through relationships and structures of mutuality and shared power. Given the sinful relations in the world and the entrenchment of oppressive systems, such an understanding of universal salvation could lead to despair if those committed to radical social change did not believe that God/ess is with them in the struggle. In salvific moments of solidarity and community, this hope is renewed.

Notes

[1] See Chapter III, p. 38.

[2] See pp. 84-85.

[3] McCann, Christian Realism, p. 80.

[4] See Ruether, "The Cult of True Womanhood"; and

198

Ruether, "Why Socialism Needs Feminism," p. 105.
Rowbotham maintains that "amidst all the sanctimony of
respect for personal life and the need to conserve the
family, the capitalist organization of work, whose
criterion is the profitable production of commodities
for the market proceeds to penetrate the private world
of the family, making a mockery of its own protesta-
tions" (Woman's Consciousness, Man's World, p. 52).

[5]See ibid., p. 55. As is cited from Charlotte
Bunch's Personal Politics: "There is no private domain
of a person's life that is not political and there is
no political issue that is not personal" (Lydia Sargent,
"New Left Women and Men: The Honeymoon is Over," in
Women and Revolution, p. xix). This theme is found
repeatedly in feminist writings.

[6]See pp. 40-42.

[7]Veldhuis, Realism Versus Utopianism?, p. 113.

[8]Self-concern and concern for others are related
to the two aspects of individuation--differentiation
and integration--described in Chapter IV, pp. 112-13.
For a further discussion of the integration of self-
concern and concern for others, see Larry Blum, Marcia
Homiak, Judy Housman, Naomi Scheman, "Altruism and
Women's Oppression," in Women and Philosophy, pp. 222-
24; and Gregory Vlastos, "What Is Love?," Christendom 1
(October 1935):127-28. This position is compatible
with a Whiteheadian perspective in which "a rhythmic
alternation between giving and receiving, between the
appropriation of others for the enrichment of oneself
and the yielding up of oneself for the enrichment of
others" is required for the process of being (Saiving,
"Androgynous Life," p. 26). Marx maintains that the
apparent antagonism between egoism and self-sacrifice
disappears of itself when the material basis engender-
ing it, is transformed. See Marx and Engels, The
German Ideology, pp. 104-105. For Ruether, social
structures and systems can facilitate the process of
integrating self-concern and concern for others, but
conflict and tension remain between these two dimensions for as long as reality exists.

[9]This is one of Muelder's criticisms of Niebuhr:
his "scant recognition, in fact none at all, that
mutuality and communitarian solidarity may be normal
forms of self-transcendence" ("Reinhold Niebuhr's
Conception of Man," The Personalist [1945]:288).

[10]See Minnema, _Social Ethics_, pp. 28-29. Marx's reaction to "the rights of man," described by McLellan, is applicable to Niebuhr's principles of justice. McLellan writes: "Liberty, 'the right to do and perform what does not harm others,' was, according to Marx, 'not based on the union of man from man. It is the right to this separation, the right of the limited individual who is limited to himself.' . . . Equality was no more than the equal right to the liberty described above, and security [i.e., for Niebuhr, order] was the guarantee of egoism" (_Karl Marx_, p. 83. See also McGovern, _Marxism_, p. 20).

[11]See McGovern, _Marxism_, pp. 157-62; McLellan, _The Thought of Karl Marx_, p. 182; and Unger, _Knowledge and Politics_, pp. 281-84.

[12]See Chapter II, pp. 26-27.

[13]_NDM_, 2:49.

BIBLIOGRAPHY

Works by Reinhold Niebuhr

Beyond Tragedy. New York: Charles Scribner's Sons, 1937.

The Children of Light and the Children of Darkness. New York: Charles Scribner's Sons, 1944.

"Christ and Our Political Decisions." Christianity and Crisis 1 (August 11, 1941):1-2.

"Christian Faith and Natural Law." Theology 40 (February 1940):86-94.

"A Christian Philosophy of Compromise." The Christian Century 50 (June 7, 1933):746-48.

Christian Realism and Political Problems. New York: Charles Scribner's Sons, 1953; reprint ed., Fairfield: Augustus M. Kelley, Publishers, 1977.

Christianity and Power Politics. New York: Charles Scribner's Sons, 1940.

"Coercion, Self-Interest, and Love." In The Organizational Revolution, by Kenneth E. Boulding. New York: Harper & Brothers, Publishers, 1953. Pp. 228-44.

"The Confession of a Tired Radical." The Christian Century 45 (August 30, 1928):1046-47.

"A Critique of Pacifism." Atlantic Monthly, May 1927, pp. 637-41.

Does Civilization Need Religion? New York: The Macmillan Company, 1927.

"The Ethic of Jesus and the Social Problem." Religion in Life 1 (Spring 1932):198-202.

Faith and History. New York: Charles Scribner's Sons, 1949.

Faith and Politics. Edited by Ronald H. Stone. New York: George Braziller, 1968.

"Idealists as Cynics." Nation 150 (January 20, 1940): 72-74.

"Ideology and Pretense." Nation 149 (December 9, 1939):645-46.

"The Individual and the Social Dimension of our Existence." Episcopal Churchnews 120 (October 16, 1955):9.

An Interpretation of Christian Ethics. New York: Harper & Brothers, 1935; reprint ed., New York: Meridian Books, 1956.

The Irony of American History. New York: Charles Scribner's Sons, 1952.

"Is Peace or Justice the Goal?" The World Tomorrow 15 (September 21, 1932):275-77.

Justice and Mercy. Edited by Ursula M. Niebuhr. New York: Harper & Row, Publishers, 1974.

Love and Justice. Edited by D. B. Robertson. Gloucester, Mass.: Peter Smith, 1976.

"Making Radicalism Effective." The World Tomorrow 16 (December 21, 1933):682-84.

Man's Nature and His Communities. New York: Charles Scribner's Sons, 1965.

"Marx, Barth and Israel's Prophets." The Christian Century 52 (January 30, 1935):138-40.

Moral Man and Immoral Society. New York: Charles Scribner's Sons, 1932.

"Moralists and Politics." The Christian Century 49 (July 6, 1932):857-59.

"Morality." In The Search for America. Edited by Huston Smith. Englewood Cliffs, N.J.: Prentice-Hall, Inc., 1959. Pp. 147-53.

"The Nation's Crime Against the Individual." Atlantic Monthly, November 1916, pp. 609-14.

The Nature and Destiny of Man. 2 vols. New York: Charles Scribner's Sons, 1941 and 1943.

"A New Strategy for Socialists." The World Tomorrow 16
     (August 31, 1933):490-92.

Pious and Secular America. New York: Charles
     Scribner's Sons, 1958.

"Political Action and Social Change." The World
     Tomorrow 12 (December 1929):491-93.

"Politics and the Christian Ethic." Christianity and
     Society 5 (Spring 1940):24-28.

"The Problem of a Protestant Political Ethic." The
     Christian Century 77 (September 21, 1960):1085-87.

"The Problem of a Protestant Social Ethic." Union
     Seminary Quarterly Review 15 (November 1959):1-11.

"The Quality of Our Lives." The Christian Century 77
     (May 11, 1960):568-72.

"Radicalism and Religion." The World Tomorrow 14
     (October 1961):324-27.

Reflections on the End of an Era. New York, London:
     Charles Scribner's Sons, 1934.

Reinhold Niebuhr on Politics. Edited by Harry R. Davis
     and Robert C. Good. New York: Charles Scribner's
     Sons, 1960.

"A Reorientation of Radicalism." The World Tomorrow 16
     (July 1933):443-44.

"Revolution in an Open Society." The New Leader 46
     (May 27, 1963):7-8.

"The Scylla and Charybdis of Society." Christianity
     and Crisis 1 (November 17, 1941):2.

The Self and the Dramas of History. New York: Charles
     Scribner's Sons, 1955.

"Socialism and Christianity." The Christian Century 48
     (August 19, 1931):1038-40.

"Some Things I have Learned." Saturday Review,
     November 6, 1965, pp. 21-24, 63-64.

The Structure of Nations and Empires. New York:
    Charles Scribner's Sons, 1959; reprint ed.,
    Fairfield: Augustus M. Kelley, Publishers, 1977.

"Ten Years that Shook My World." The Christian Century
    56 (April 26, 1939):542-46.

"Theology and Political Thought in the Western World."
    The Ecumenical Review 9 (April 1957):253-61.

"The Truth in Myths." In The Nature of Religious
    Experience: Essays in Honor of Douglas Clyde
    Macintosh. Edited by J. S. Bixler, R. L. Calhoun
    and H. R. Niebuhr. New York & London: Harper &
    Brothers, Publishers, 1937. Pp. 117-35.

"The Way of Non-Violent Resistance." Christianity and
    Society 21 (Spring 1956):3.

"What Chance Has Ghandi?" The Christian Century 41
    (October 14, 1931):1274-76.

"What the War Did to My Mind." The Christian Century
    45 (September 27, 1928):1161-63.

Coe, George A., and Niebuhr, Reinhold. "Two Communica-
    tions." The Christian Century 50 (March 15, 1933):
    362-63.

Dun, Angus, and Niebuhr, Reinhold. "God Wills Both
    Justice and Peace." Christianity and Crisis 15
    (June 13, 1955):75-78.

Works by Rosemary Radford Ruether

"Beginnings: An Intellectual Autobiography." In
    Journeys: The Impact of Personal Experience on
    Religious Thought. Edited by Gregory Baum. New
    York, N.Y./Paramus, N.J.: Paulist Press, 1975.
    Pp. 34-56.

"Beyond Confrontation: The Therapeutic Task." In The
    Berrigans. Edited by William VanEtten Casey, S.J.
    and Philip Nobile. New York: Avon, 1970. Pp.
    113-21.

"The Bible and Social Justice." Ecumenist 14 (January-
    February 1976):24-27.

"The Biblical Vision of the Ecological Crisis." The
    Christianity Century 95 (November 22, 1978):1129-
    32.

"Black Theology and Black Church." America 120 (June
    14, 1969):684-87.

"Christian Origins and the Counter Culture." Dialog 10
    (Summer 1971):193-200.

The Church Against Itself. London and Melbourne:
    Sheed and Ward, 1967.

"Confrontation and Communication." The Christian
    Century 86 (September 10, 1969):1163-65.

"Crisis in Sex and Race: Black Theology vs. Feminist
    Theology." Christianity and Crisis 34 (April 15,
    1974):67-73.

"Critic's Corner: An Unexpected Tribute to the
    Theologian." Theology Today 27 (October 1970):
    332-39.

"The Cult of True Womanhood." Commonweal 99 (November
    9, 1973):127-32.

"Disputed Questions: On Being a Christian." 1981.
    (Galley.)

"Education in Tandem: White Liberal, Black Militant."
    America 122 (May 30, 1970):582-84.

"The Ethic of Celibacy." Commonweal 97 (February 2,
    1973):390-94.

Faith and Fratricide: The Theological Roots of Anti-
    Semitism. New York: The Seabury Press, A
    Crossroad Book, 1979.

"The Female Nature of God: A Problem in Contemporary
    Religious Life." In Concilium: Religion in the
    Eighties. Vol. 143: God as Father? Edited by
    Johannes-Baptise Metz and Edward Schillebeeckx.
    Edinburgh: T. & T. Clark LTD. and New York: The
    Seabury Press, 1981. Pp. 61-66.

"A Feminist Perspective on Religion and Science:
    Comments on Bishop Gregorios' Paper 'Science and
    Faith: Complementary or Contradictory?.'" Paper

presented at the Conference on Faith, Science, and the Future, Cambridge, Massachusetts, July 1979.

"Goddesses and Witches: Liberation and Countercultural Feminism." The Christian Century 97 (September 10-17, 1980):842-47.

"God-Talk After the End of Christendom." Commonweal 105 (June 16, 1978):369-75.

"Home and Work: Women's Roles and the Transformation of Values." Theological Studies 36 (December 1975):647-59.

"Individual Repentance Is Not Enough." Explor 2 (Spring 1976):47-52.

"Letter to Catholic Radicals: After the 'Actions,' What Next?" National Catholic Reporter, October 2, 1970, p. 14.

Liberation Theology: Human Hope Confronts Christian History and American Power. New York, Paramus, Toronto: Paulist Press, 1972.

"Libertarianism and Neocolonialism: The Two Faces of America." Christianity and Crisis 36 (August 16, 1976):180-83.

"'Love Your Enemies' as Rebellion: A New Testament Basis for Nonviolence." Fellowship 36 (July 1970):7-8, 23, 30.

"Male Chauvinist Theology and the Anger of Women." Cross Currents 21 (Spring 1971):172-85.

"Male Clericalism and the Dread of Women." Ecumenist 11 (July-August 1973):65-69.

Mary--The Feminine Face of the Church. Philadelphia: The Westminister Press, 1977.

"Mediating Between the 'Is' and 'Ought' of History: A Radical Liberal in the Streets of Washington." Christianity and Crisis 31 (July 12, 1971):144-47.

"The Messianic Code." Commonweal 91 (January 16, 1970):423-25.

"Monks and Marxists: A Look at the Catholic Left."
Christianity and Crisis 33 (April 30, 1973):75-79.

"Mother Earth and the Megamachine." Christianity and
Crisis 31 (December 13, 1971):262-72.

"A New Political Consciousness." Ecumenist 8 (May-June
1970):61-64.

"New Wine, Maybe New Wineskins, for the Church." The
Christian Century 86 (April 2, 1969):445-49.

New Woman/New Earth: Sexist Ideologies and Human
Liberation. New York: The Seabury Press, 1975.

"On Solving the Liberal-Radical Dilemma." National
Catholic Reporter, August 27, 1969, p. 6.

"On Women's Lib." Dialog 11 (Summer 1972):225-26.

"The Ordination of Women in the Roman Catholic Church:
What is the Problem?" Speech given at the Women's
Ordination Conference, Detroit, Michigan,
November 1975.

"Outlines for a Theology of Liberation." Dialog 11
(Autumn 1972):252-57.

"Paradoxes of Human Hope: The Messianic Horizon of
Church and Society." Theological Studies 33 (June
1972):235-52.

"The Persecution of Witches: A Case of Sexism and
Ageism?" Christianity and Crisis 34 (December 23,
1974):291-95.

"The Radical and the Mediator: Their Roles in Social
Change." America 121 (November 29, 1969):521-23.

The Radical Kingdom: The Western Experience of
Messianic Hope. New York, Paramus, Toronto:
Paulist Press, 1970.

Religion and Sexism: Images of Women in the Jewish and
Christian Traditions. Edited by Rosemary Radford
Ruether. New York: Simon and Schuster, 1974.

"Rich Nations/Poor Nations and the Exploitation of the
Earth." Dialog 13 (Summer 1974):201-7.

"Ruether on Ruether." Christianity and Crisis 39 (May
    14, 1979):126.

"The Search for Soul Power in the White Community."
    Christianity and Crisis 30 (April 27, 1970):83-85.

"Sexism and God-Talk: Toward a Feminist Theology."
    Boston: Beacon Press, 1983. (Galley.)

"Sexism and the Theology of Liberation." The Christian
    Century 90 (Spring 1973):1224-29.

"The Suffering Servant Myth." Worldview 17 (March
    1974):45-46.

"The Task of the Church in Contemporary America."
    Dialog 12 (August 1973):284-88.

To Change the World: Christology and Cultural
    Criticism. New York: Crossroad, 1981.

"Toward New Solutions: Working Women and the Male
    Workday." Christianity and Crisis 37 (February 7,
    1977):3-8.

"What is Shaping My Own Theology?" Commonweal 108
    (January 30, 1981):46-48.

"The White Left in the Mother Country." Commonweal 93
    (November 6, 1970):142-45.

"Why Socialism Needs Feminism, and Vice Versa."
    Christianity and Crisis 40 (April 28, 1980):103-8.

"Women, Ecology and the Domination of Nature."
    Ecumenist 14 (November-December 1975):1-5.

Bianchi, Eugene C., and Ruether, Rosemary Radford.
    From Machismo to Mutuality: Essays on Sexism and
    Woman-Man Liberation. New York/Paramus, N.J./
    Toronto: Paulist Press, 1976.

Other Works

Andolsen, Barbara Hilkert. "Agape in Feminist Ethics."
    Journal of Religious Ethics 9 (Spring 1981):69-83.

Asian and Pacific Center for Women and Development.
    Report on the International Workshop on Feminist
    Ideology and Structures in the First Half of the

<u>Decade for Women</u>. Bangkok, Thailand: Erawan Printing Lp., 1979.

Avineri, Shlomo. <u>The Social and Political Thought of Karl Marx</u>. Cambridge: Cambridge University Press, 1968.

Bartky, Sandra Lee. "Toward a Phenomenology of Feminist Consciousness." <u>Social Theory and Practice</u> 3 (Fall 1975):425-39.

Baum, Gregory. <u>Religion and Alienation</u>. New York/ Paramus/Toronto: Paulist Press, 1975.

Bennett, John C. <u>The Radical Imperative</u>. Philadelphia: The Westminister Press, 1975.

Bingham, June. <u>Courage to Change</u>. New York: Charles Scribner's Sons, 1961.

Bracken, Joseph A., S.J. "God and World Reconsidered: Principles for a New Synthesis." Marquette University, Milwaukee, Wisconsin, 1981.

Brackley, J. Dean, S.J. "Salvation and the Social Good in the Thought of Jacques Maritain and Gustavo Gutierrez." Ph.D. dissertation, University of Chicago, 1980.

Brown, Robert McAfee. <u>Religion and Violence</u>. Philadelphia: The Westminister Press, 1973.

Camara, Dom Helder. <u>Spiral of Violence</u>. Translated by Della Couling. London and Sydney: Sheed and Ward, 1971.

Carr, Anne, B.V.M. "Theological Anthropology and the Experience of Women." <u>Chicago Studies</u> 19 (Summer 1980):113-28.

Carnell, Edward John. <u>The Theology of Reinhold Niebuhr</u>. Grand Rapids, Michigan: Wm. B. Eerdmans Publishing Company, 1950.

Cassidy, Richard J. <u>Jesus, Politics, and Society</u>. Maryknoll, New York: Orbis Books, 1978.

Chesler, Phyllis. <u>Women and Madness</u>. New York: Avon Books, 1972.

209

Childress, James F. "Reinhold Niebuhr's Critique of
    Pacifism." The Review of Politics 36 (October
    1974):467-91.

Church and Society Committee of the World Council of
    Churches. "Violence, Nonviolence and the Struggle
    for Social Justice." The Ecumenical Review 25
    (October 1973):430-46.

Collins, Randall and Makowsky, Michael. The Discovery
    of Society. New York: Random House, 1972.

Collins, Sheila D. A Different Heaven and Earth.
    Valley Forge: Judson Press, 1974.

_____. "The Familial Economy of God." Paper presented
    at the Second Women's Ordination Conference,
    Baltimore, Maryland, November 10, 1978.

_____. "Feminist Theology at the Crossroads."
    Christianity and Crisis 41 (December 14, 1981):
    342-47.

_____. "Sexism, Racism and the Church: A Sociological
    Analysis." Paper presented at St. John's
    University, Jamaica, New York, Summer 1978.

_____. "Toward a Feminist Theology." The Christian
    Century 89 (August 2, 1972):796-99.

Cormie, Lee. "Hermeneutical Privilege of the Oppressed:
    Liberation Theologies, Biblical Faith and Marxist
    Sociology of Knowledge." In Catholic Theological
    Society of America: Proceedings of the Thirty-
    Third Annual Convention. Edited by Luke Salm,
    F.S.C. Milwaukee, Wisconsin: n.p., 1978. Pp.
    155-81.

_____. "Society, History and Meaning: Perspectives
    from the Social Sciences." (Mimeographed.)

Cowan, Wayne H., ed. "Christian Realism: Retrospect
    and Prospect." Christianity and Crisis 28 (August
    5, 1968):175-90.

Daly, Mary. Beyond God the Father: Toward a Philosophy
    of Women's Liberation. Boston: Beacon Press,
    1973.

_____. Gyn/Ecology: The Metaethics of Radical
Feminism. Boston: Beacon Press, 1978.

Davaney, Sheila Greeve, ed. Feminism and Process
Thought: The Harvard Divinity School/Claremont
Center for Process Studies Symposium Papers.
Symposium Series, no. 6. New York and Toronto:
The Edwin Mellen Press, 1981.

Davies, D. R. Reinhold Niebuhr: Prophet from America.
5 Wardrobe Place, Carter Lane, London, E. C. 4:
James Clarke & Co., LTD., 1945.

Davis, Harry Rex. "The Political Philosophy of
Reinhold Niebuhr." Ph.D. dissertation, University
of Chicago, 1951.

Dawe, Alan. "Theories of Social Action." In A History
of Sociological Analysis. Edited by Tom Bottomore
and Robert Nisbet. New York: Basic Books, Inc.,
Publishers, 1978. Pp. 362-417.

de Beauvoir, Simone. The Second Sex. Translated and
edited by H. M. Parshley. New York: Alfred A.
Knopf, 1952; Vintage Books, 1974.

Dworkin, Andrea. Our Blood: Prophecies and Discourses
on Sexual Politics. New York: Harper & Row,
Publishers, 1976.

Elshtain, Jean Bethke. Public Man, Private Woman:
Women in Social and Political Thought. Princeton,
New Jersey: Princeton University Press, 1981.

Fals Borda, Orlando. Subversion and Social Change in
Colombia. Translated by Jacqueline D. Skiles.
New York and London: Columbia University Press,
1969.

Farley, Edward. The Transcendence of God.
Philadelphia: The Westminister Press, 1958.

Fay, Brian. Social Theory and Political Practice.
Controversies in Sociology, no. 1. New York:
Holmes and Meier Publishers, 1975.

Ferguson, Kathy E. Self, Society and Womankind: The
Dialectic of Liberation. Contributions in Women's
Studies, no. 17. Westport, Connecticut; London,
England: Greenwood Press, 1980.

Fierro, Alfredo. The Militant Gospel: A Critical
    Introduction to Political Theologies. Edited by
    John Drury. Maryknoll, New York: Orbis Books,
    1977.

Friedrichs, Robert W. "Dialectical Sociology: Toward
    a Resolution of the Current 'Crisis' in Western
    Sociology." British Journal of Sociology 23
    (September 1972):263-74.

_____. A Sociology of Sociology. New York: The Free
    Press, 1970.

Friere, Paulo. Pedagogy of the Oppressed. Translated
    by Myra Bergman Ramos. New York: Seabury Press,
    1974.

Geertz, Clifford. The Interpretation of Cultures. New
    York: Basic Books, Inc., Publishers, 1973.

Gibellini, Rosino, ed. Frontiers of Theology in Latin
    America. Translated by John Drury. Maryknoll,
    New York: Orbis Books, 1979.

Giddens, Anthony. "Classical Social Theory and the
    Origins of Modern Sociology." American Journal of
    Sociology 81 (January 1976):703-729.

_____. Studies in Social and Political Theory. New
    York: Basic Books, Inc., Publishers, 1977.

Gilkey, Langdon. "Reinhold Niebuhr's Theology of
    History." Journal of Religion 54 (October 1974):
    360-86.

Gill, David M. "Power, Violence, Nonviolence and
    Social Change." Study Encounter 6 (1970):66-72.

Glennon, Lynda M. Women and Dualism: A Sociology of
    Knowledge Analysis. New York and London:
    Longman, 1979.

Goldstein, Valerie Saiving. "The Human Situation: A
    Feminine Viewpoint." Journal of Religion 40
    (April 1960):100-112.

Gould, Carol C. Marx's Social Ontology: Individuality
    and Community in Marx's Theory of Social Reality.
    Cambridge, Massachusetts, and London, England:
    The MIT Press, 1978.

Gould, Carol C., and Wartofsky, Marx, eds. Women and Philosophy: Toward a Theory of Liberation. New York: G. P. Putnam's Sons, Capricorn Books, 1976.

Gouldner, Alvin W. The Coming Crisis of Western Sociology. New York: Equinox Books, 1970.

Goulet, Denis. The Cruel Choice. New York: Atheneum, 1971.

_____. The New Moral Order: Studies in Development Ethics and Liberation Theology. Foreward by Paulo Friere. Maryknoll, N.Y.: Orbis Books, 1974.

_____. "The Troubled Conscience of the Revolutionary." The Center Magazine, May 1969, pp. 43-50.

Gray, Elizabeth Dodson. Green Paradise Lost. Wellesley, Massachusetts: Roundtable Press, 1979.

Griffin, David. "Whitehead and Niebuhr on God, Man, and the World." Journal of Religion 53 (April 1973):149-75.

Griffin, Susan. Pornography and Silence: Culture's Revolt Against Nature. New York: Harper & Row, Harper Colophon Books, 1982.

_____. Woman and Nature: The Roaring Inside Her. New York: Harper & Row, Publishers, Harper Colophon Books, 1980.

Gunti, Frederick W. "Conflict and Reconciliation in the Thought of Reinhold Neibuhr." The American Ecclesiastical Review 168 (April 1974):219-35.

Guthrie, Dr. Shirley Caperton, Jr. The Theological Character of Reinhold Niebuhr's Social Ethic. Winterthur: Verlag P. G. Keller, 1959.

Gutierrez, Gustavo. A Theology of Liberation: History, Politics and Salvation. Translated and edited by Sister Caridad Inda and John Eagleson. Maryknoll, N.Y.: Orbis Books, 1973.

Hamilton, Roberta. The Liberation of Women: A Study of Patriarchy and Capitalism. Controversies in Sociology, no. 6. London: George Allen & Unwin, 1978.

Hammer, George. Christian Realism in Contemporary American Theology. Uppsala: Appelbergs Boktryckeriaktiebolac, 1940.

Hansen, Donald. An Invitation to Critical Sociology. New York: The Free Press, 1976.

Harland, Gordon. The Thought of Reinhold Niebuhr. New York: Oxford University Press, 1960.

Heyward, Carter. "Ruether and Daly: Theologians/ Speaking and Sparking, Building and Burning." Christianity and Crisis 39 (April 2, 1979):66-72.

Hinde, Peter, O. Carm. "Look! A New Thing in the Americas!" Edited by William R. Callahan, S.J. with the Communities of Tabor House and Quixote Center. Hyattsville, MD: Quixote Center, 1981. (Tabloid.)

Homans, Peter. "The Meaning of Selfhood in the Thought of Reinhold Niebuhr and Sigmund Freud." Ph.D. dissertation, University of Chicago, 1964.

Hutchinson, John A. Christian Faith and Social Action. New York, London: Charles Scribner's Sons, 1953.

Janeway, Elizabeth. Between Myth and Morning: Women Awakening. New York: William Morrow & Company, Inc., 1974.

Jordan, Pat. "Illuminating Dark Times." The Catholic Worker, December 1980, pp. 6-7.

Kegley, Charles W., and Bretall, Robert W., eds. Reinhold Niebuhr: His Religious, Social and Political Thought. New York: The Macmillan Company, 1956.

Kuhn, Thomas S. The Structure of Scientific Revolutions. 2nd ed., enlarged. Chicago: The University of Chicago Press, 1970.

Ladner, Joyce A., ed. The Death of White Sociology. New York: Random House, 1973.

Landon, Harold R., ed. Reinhold Niebuhr: A Prophetic Voice in Our Time. Greenwich, Connecticut: Seabury Press, 1962.

Lassere, Jean. _War and the Gospel_. Scottdale, Pa.:
Herald Press, 1974.

Lochman, Jan Millic; Houser, George; Cone, James; and
Shinn, Roger. "Violence: The Just Revolution."
Christianity and Crisis 32 (July 10, 1972):163-68.

Lukes, Steven. _Individualism_. Key Concepts in the
Social Sciences, no. 3. Oxford: Basil Blackwell,
1973.

Maguire, Daniel C. "The Feminization of God and
Ethics." _Christianity and Crisis_ 42 (March 15,
1982):59-67.

Martindale, Don. _The Nature and Types of Sociological
Theory_. Boston: Houghton Mifflin Company, 1960.

_____. _Prominent Sociologists Since World War II_.
Columbus, Ohio: Charles E. Merrill Publishing
Company, 1975.

Marx, Karl. _Early Writings_. Translated by Rodney
Livingstone and Gregor Benton. Introduction by
Lucio Colletti. New York: Vintage Books, 1975.

_____. _Karl Marx: Early Writings_. Translated and
edited by T. B. Bottomore. Foreward by Erich
Fromm. New York: McGraw-Hill Books, 1964.

_____. _On Religion_. The Karl Marx Library, vol. 5.
Edited and translated by Saul K. Padover. New
York: McGraw-Hill Book Company, 1974.

Marx, Karl, and Engels, Frederick. _The German
Ideology_. With selections from parts 2 and 3 and
supplementary texts. Edited with an introduction
by C. J. Arthur. New York: International
Publishers, 1977.

McCann, Dennis P. _Christian Realism and Liberation
Theology_. Maryknoll, New York: Orbis Books, 1981.

_____. "Reinhold Niebuhr and Jacques Maritain on
Marxism: A Comparison of Two Traditional Models
of Practical Theology." _Journal of Religion_ 58
(April 1978):140-68.

McFaul, Thomas R. "Reinhold Niebuhr: An Alledged
'Individualist.'" _Religion in Life_ 42 (Summer

215

1973):194-205.

McGovern, Arthur. Marxism: An American Christian
    Perspective. Maryknoll, New York: Orbis Books,
    1980.

McLellan, David. Karl Marx: His Life and Thought.
    New York, Hagerstown, San Francisco, London:
    Harper & Row, Publishers, Harper Colophon Books,
    1977.

_____. The Thought of Karl Marx: An Introduction.
    New York, Evanston, San Francisco, London:
    Harper & Row, Publishers, Harper Torchbooks, 1974.

McMurty, John. The Structure of Marx's World-View.
    Princeton, New Jersey: Princeton University
    Press, 1978.

Merkley, Paul. Reinhold Niebuhr: A Political Account.
    Montreal and London: McGill-Queen's University
    Press, 1975.

Miller, Jean Baker. Toward a New Psychology of Women.
    Boston: Beacon Press, 1976.

Millett, Kate. Sexual Politics. New York: Ballantine
    Books, 1969, 1970.

Millman, Marcia, and Kanter, Rosabeth Moss, eds.
    Another Voice: Feminist Perspectives on Social
    Life and Social Science. Garden City, New York:
    Anchor Press/Doubleday, Anchor Books, 1975.

Mills, C. Wright. The Sociological Imagination. New
    York: Oxford University Press, 1959.

Minnema, Theodore. The Social Ethics of Reinhold
    Niebuhr. Grand Rapids, Michigan: Wm. B. Eerdmans
    Publishing Company, 1958.

Moraga, Cherríe, and Anzaldúa, Gloria, eds. This
    Bridge Called My Back: Writings by Radical Women
    of Color. Foreword by Toni Cade Bambara.
    Watertown, Massachusetts: Persephone Press, 1981.

Morgan, Robin. Going Too Far: The Personal Chronicle
    of a Feminist. New York: Vintage Books, 1978.

Muelder, Walter C. "Reinhold Niebuhr's Conception of Man." The Personalist 26 (Summer 1945):282-93.

Murray, Pauli. "Black, Feminist Theologies: Links, Parallels and Tensions." Christianity and Crisis 40 (April 14, 1980):86-95.

Nisbet, Robert. The Sociological Tradition. New York: Basic Books, Inc., Publishers, 1966.

Ollman, Bertell. Alienation: Marx's Conception of Man in Capitalist Society. 2nd ed. Cambridge: Cambridge University Press, 1976.

Outka, Gene. Agape: An Ethical Analysis. New Haven and London: Yale University Press, 1972.

Parsons, Talcott. The Social System. Glencoe, Ill.: Free Press, 1951.

Patterson, Bob E. Reinhold Niebuhr. Waco, Texas: Word Books, Publishers, 1977.

Payne, Ernest A. "Violence, Non-violence and Human Rights." The Ecumenical Review 23 (July 1971): 222-36.

Paynton, Clifford T., and Blackley, Robert, eds. Why Revolution? Theories and Analyses. Cambridge, Massachusetts and London, England: Shenkman Publishing Company, Inc., 1971.

Peardon, Thomas P. Introduction to Second Treatise of Government, by John Locke. Indianapolis: The Bobbs-Merrill Company, Inc., 1952.

Plamenatz, John. Karl Marx's Philosophy of Man. Oxford: Clarendon Press, 1975.

Plaskow, Judith. Sex, Sin and Grace: Women's Experience and the Theologies of Reinhold Niebuhr and Paul Tillich. Lanham, MD: University Press of America, Inc., 1980.

Proudfoot, Wayne. God and the Self. Cranbury, New Jersey: Associated University Presses, Inc., 1976.

Raines, John C. "Sin as Pride and Sin as Sloth." Christianity and Crisis 29 (February 3, 1969):4-8.

Rasmussen, David. "Between Autonomy and Sociality."
    Cultural Hermeneutics 1 (April 1973):3-45.

Rhoades, Dan. "The Prophetic Insight and Theoretical-
    Analytical Inadequacy of 'Christian Realism.'"
    Ethics 75 (October 1964):1-15.

Rich, Adrienne. On Lies, Secrets, and Silence:
    Selected Prose 1966-1978. New York: W. W. Norton
    & Company, 1979.

Ricoeur, Paul. History and Truth. Translated by
    Charles A. Kelbley. Evanston: Northwestern
    University Press, 1975.

Robb, Carol. "A Framework for Feminist Ethics."
    Journal of Religious Ethics 9 (Spring 1981):48-68.

Rowbotham, Sheila. Women, Resistance and Revolution:
    A History of Women and Revolution in the Modern
    World. London: The Penguin Press, 1972; New
    York: Vintage Books, 1974.

_____. Woman's Consciousness, Man's World. Baltimore,
    Maryland: Penguin Books, Inc., 1973.

Sabine, George H. A History of Political Theory.
    Revised by Thomas Landon Thorson. Hinsdale,
    Illinois: Dryden Press, 1973.

Sabrosky, Judith A. From Rationality to Liberation:
    The Evolution of Feminist Ideology. Contributions
    in Political Science, no. 32. Westport,
    Connecticut: Greenwood Press, 1979.

Sargent, Lydia, ed. Women and Revolution: A Discus-
    sion of the Unhappy Marriage of Marxism and
    Feminism. South End Press Political Controversies
    Series, no. 2. Boston: South End Press, 1981.

Schaef, Anne Wilson. Women's Reality: An Emerging
    Female System in the White Male Society.
    Minnesota: Winston Press, 1981.

Scheuner, Ulrich. "The Ecumenical Debate on Violence
    and Violent Social Change." The Ecumenical Review
    23 (July 1971):237-51.

Scott, Nathan A., Jr. The Legacy of Reinhold Niebuhr.
    Chicago and London: The University of Chicago

Press, 1974.

Segundo, Juan Luis, S.J. The Liberation of Theology.
    Translated by John Drury. Maryknoll, New York:
    Orbis Books, 1976.

Sève, Lucien. Man in Marxist Theory and the Psychology
    of Personality. Translated by John McGreal.
    Sussex: The Harvester Press and New Jersey:
    Humanities Press, 1978.

Shakur, Assata. From Somewhere in the World Assata
    Shakur Speaks--Message to the New Afrikan Nation.
    New York: New Afrikan Women's Organization, 1980.

Sherman, Howard J., and Wood, James L. Sociology:
    Traditional and Radical Perspectives. New York:
    Harper & Row, Publishers, 1979.

Stack, Carol B. All Our Kin: Strategies for Survival
    in a Black Community. New York, Evanston, San
    Francisco, London: Harper & Row, Publishers,
    1974.

Sternberg, David Joel. Radical Sociology: A Critical
    Introduction to American Behavioral Science.
    Hicksville, New York: Exposition Press, 1977.

Stone, Ronald H. Reinhold Niebuhr: Prophet to
    Politicians. Wash., University Press of America, 1981.

Tucker, Robert C., ed. The Marx-Engels Reader. New
    York: W. W. Norton & Company, Inc., 1972.

Unger, Roberto Mangabeira. Knowledge and Politics.
    New York: The Free Press, 1975.

Veldhuis, Ruurd. Realism Versus Utopianism? The
    Netherlands: Van Gorcum, Assen, 1975.

Vlastos, Gregory. "What is Love?" Christendom 1
    (October 1935):117-31.

Wells, Alan, ed. Contemporary Sociological Theories.
    Santa Monica, California: Goodyear Publishing
    Company, Inc., 1978.

Westkott, Marcia. "Feminist Criticism of the Social
    Sciences." Harvard Educational Review 49
    (November 1979):422-30.

Wiener, Philip P., and Fisher, John, eds. Violence and
Aggression in the History of Ideas. Introduction
by Philip P. Wiener. New Brunswick, New Jersey:
Rutgers University Press, 1974.

William, Daniel Day. The Spirit and the Forms of Love.
New York and Evanston: Harper & Row, Publishers,
1968.

Winter, Gibson. Elements for a Social Ethic. New York,
New York: The Macmillan Company, 1968.

_____. "Human Science and Ethics in a Reflective
Society." (Mimeographed.)

Woodward, Beverly. "Violence, Non-Violence and Human
Struggle." Study Encounter 12 (1976):19-35.

World Council of Churches. "Violence, Nonviolence and
the Struggle for Social Justice." Study Encounter
7 (1971):1-8.

Yoder, John. The Politics of Jesus. Grand Rapids,
Michigan: William B. Eerdmans Publishing Company,
1972.

Zaretsky, Eli. Capitalism, the Family, and Personal
Life. New York, Hagerstown, San Francisco,
London: Harper & Row, Publishers, Harper
Colophon Books, 1973.